Designing Search

D1467526

Designing Search

UX STRATEGIES FOR ECOMMERCE SUCCESS

GREG NUDELMAN

Wiley Publishing, Inc.

Designing Search: UX Strategies for eCommerce Success

Published by
Wiley Publishing, Inc
10475 Crosspoint Boulevard
Indianapolis, IN 46256
www.wiley.com

Copyright © 2011 by UXmatters

Published by Wiley Publishing, Inc., Indianapolis, Indiana

Published simultaneously in Canada

ISBN: 978-0-470-94223-9

ISBN: 978-1-118-10996-0 (ebk)

ISBN: 978-1-118-10995-3 (ebk)

ISBN: 978-1-118-10997-7 (ebk)

Manufactured in the United States of America

10 9 8 7 6 5 4 3 2 1

No part of this publication may be reproduced, stored in a retrieval system or transmitted in any form or by any means, electronic, mechanical, photocopying, recording, scanning or otherwise, except as permitted under Sections 107 or 108 of the 1976 United States Copyright Act, without either the prior written permission of the Publisher, or authorization through payment of the appropriate per-copy fee to the Copyright Clearance Center, 222 Rosewood Drive, Danvers, MA 01923, (978) 750-8400, fax (978) 646-8600. Requests to the Publisher for permission should be addressed to the Permissions Department, John Wiley & Sons, Inc., 111 River Street, Hoboken, NJ 07030, (201) 748-6011, fax (201) 748-6008, or online at http://www.wiley.com/go/permissions.

Limit of Liability/Disclaimer of Warranty: The publisher and the author make no representations or warranties with respect to the accuracy or completeness of the contents of this work and specifically disclaim all warranties, including without limitation warranties of fitness for a particular purpose. No warranty may be created or extended by sales or promotional materials. The advice and strategies contained herein may not be suitable for every situation. This work is sold with the understanding that the publisher is not engaged in rendering legal, accounting, or other professional services. If professional assistance is required, the services of a competent professional person should be sought. Neither the publisher nor the author shall be liable for damages arising herefrom. The fact that an organization or Web site is referred to in this work as a citation and/or a potential source of further information does not mean that the author or the publisher endorses the information the organization or website may provide or recommendations it may make. Further, readers should be aware that Internet websites listed in this work may have changed or disappeared between when this work was written and when it is read.

For general information on our other products and services please contact our Customer Care Department within the United States at (877) 762-2974, outside the United States at (317) 572-3993 or fax (317) 572-4002.

Wiley also publishes its books in a variety of electronic formats. Some content that appears in print may not be available in electronic books.

Library of Congress Control Number: 2011924908

Trademarks: Wiley and the Wiley logo are trademarks or registered trademarks of John Wiley & Sons, Inc. and/or its affiliates, in the United States and other countries, and may not be used without written permission. All other trademarks are the property of their respective owners. Wiley Publishing, Inc. is not associated with any product or vendor mentioned in this book.

To my parents, who taught me the value of human-centered design; to Shannon, who supported my endless hours of writing and put up with my occasional absent-mindedness; to Katie and Juliette, for giving me endless joy and teaching me not to take myself too seriously.

—GREG NUDELMAN

About the Author

GREG NUDELMAN is the founder of DesignCaffeine, Inc., a user experience design business consultancy specializing in search, social networking, business dashboards and process redesign for the mobile and Web platforms. Widely recognized as an experience design expert, Greg has published over 30 articles and speaks regularly to audiences around the world about how to design intuitive and elegant systems that improve the quality of people's lives while creating abundant ROI. He has led design projects for Fortune 500 companies (Cisco/WebEx, Wells Fargo Mobile, eBay, PayPal, CapitalOne) and creative startups (Groupon, Ketera, ThirstyPocket, Grockit, Traveltipz). Greg is a sought-after speaker and teacher and his presentations about mobile and Web UX design are consistently given top ratings at conferences and by clients alike. Greg lives in Pleasanton, CA with his wife and two children. He blogs at DesignCaffeine.com.

About the Technical Editor

PABINI GABRIEL-PETIT is the Founder, Publisher, and Editor in Chief of UXmatters, a preeminent Web magazine focusing on user experience (UX) strategy, design, and research. UXmatters brings insights and inspiration to the UX community worldwide. Pabini was also a Cofounder and Director of the Interaction Design Association (IxDA).

Over more than 16 years, at companies such as Google, Cisco, WebEx, and Apple, Pabini has set strategic direction for user experience, led UX design and user research, and designed Web, mobile, and desktop applications. Pabini has applied her expertise in UX design to the design of innovative applications for diverse product domains, encompassing both consumer and enterprise products.

Currently, Pabini is the Principal User Experience Architect at Spirit Softworks LLC, her Silicon Valley consultancy, which provides UX strategy and design services to leading technology corporations and startups. Clients have included Apple, Cisco, GetJar, Google, Tellme, TRIRIGA, and WebEx.

Previously, as VP of UX at scanR, Pabini led UX strategy and design for award-winning mobile and Web applications that let users scan digital photos of whiteboards and documents, then view and manage their scans.

Formerly, as UX Manager at WebEx, Pabini led UX strategy, design, and user research for online meeting and collaboration applications. She designed the award-winning Meeting Center and Training Center, setting the industry standard for online meeting software.

About the Contributors

PETE BELL is the co-founder of Endeca, a company with more than ten years of experience designing search & business intelligence solutions for more than 600 companies. Pete writes and speaks frequently about information science and user experience for audiences like User Interface Engineering, the Simmons Graduate School of Library and Information Science, the Dublin Core Metadata Initiative conference, and the Boston Museum of Science.

JOSH CLARK is a designer, developer, and author specializing in mobile design strategy and user experience. He's the author of the O'Reilly books *Tapworthy: Designing Great iPhone Apps* and *Best iPhone Apps: The Guide for Discriminating Downloaders*. Josh's outfit Global Moxie offers consulting services and workshops to help creative companies build tapworthy mobile apps and effective Web sites.

TRICIA CLEMENT is the Founder of jUXtworks Inc., the consulting firm devoted to humanizing digital environments. Through a combination of research and behavioral modeling she dives into the consumer mindset to uncover potential threats, identify market opportunities, and find dynamic ways for companies to create meaningful connections with consumers. Tricia thrives on helping clients trounce their competition while aligning their strategy with the mind of the market. Tricia received her Ph.D. in Experimental Psychology in 2002 and as an NRSA Postdoctoral Fellow at Stanford University she explored ways in which social situations control thinking, learning, and behavior. She has written extensively and published over 30 journal articles on how memory and learning strategies translate into real world behavior. Tricia has conducted user and market research exploring consumer behavior, cultural differences, and how that impacts digital interactions in over 10 markets and can be reached at www.jUXtworks.com.

CHRISTIAN CRUMLISH is a consumer experience evangelist for AOL, director of the Information Architecture Institute, and co-chair of the monthly BayCHI program. He is the author of *The Power of Many*, 2004 and co-author of *Designing Social Interfaces*, 2009 from O'Reilly Media and Yahoo! Press.

BRYNN EVANS is obsessed with the intersection of social networks and human behavior. At first she shunned social psychology, finding joy in neuroscience and dissecting brains. But after a 6-year stint as a neuropsychologist, she began studying how people interact with and use technology. Three years later, she completed the graduate program in the Cognitive Science at UC San Diego and moved on to more practical applications of user experience and interaction design. Since then, she's been a freelance consultant, social interaction designer, and gamestorming facilitator. Today, she's the Chief Experience Officer at a stealth tech startup in San Francisco. Brynn is an active speaker and writer, and is involved in community events such as hackathons, workshops, and conferences that bring together designers, developers, and entrepreneurs. She's also a board member of the Awesome Foundation in San Francisco, which gives out mini-grants to "awesome" local projects every month. Her Web site is brynnevans.com.

FRANK GUO has extensive industry and scientific research experience related to user experience management. With user research experience at major IT and financial companies and a PhD in cognitive psychology from UCLA, he set up and currently leads the Web research function for iShares, one of the largest asset management companies in the US, responsible for both Web surveys and qualitative user research. Prior to that, he led major user research initiatives such as advertising/merchandising research, seller tool research, and design guidelines research, and established eyetracking as a key research method at eBay. Frank also worked on design guidelines research and eyetracking methodology when conducting research on enterprise applications at Oracle.

DR. MARTI HEARST is a professor in the School of Information at the University of California, Berkeley. She received BA, MS, and PhD degrees in Computer Science from UC Berkeley and was a Member of the Research Staff at Xerox PARC from 1994 to 1997. A primary focus of Dr. Hearst's research is user interfaces for search. She has invented or participated in several well-known search interface projects, including Scatter/Gather clustering of search results, TileBars query term visualization, BioText search over the bioscience literature, and the Flamenco project that investigated and promoted the use of faceted metadata for collection navigation. She has published extensively on this and other topics. The Flamenco project has had a significant impact in industry and practice; interfaces similar in design to Flamenco are now the standard on ecommerce sites, image navigation sites, and library catalog sites, and support for faceted navigation is now standard in content management systems. Dr. Hearst has also acted as a consultant for a wide range of search companies. Dr. Hearst has advised more than 50 masters-level interface design projects, from problem formation and needs assessment through three rounds of evaluation. She has also taught Information Organization and Retrieval and a course called Search Engines: Technology, Society, and Business, which includes a set of popular video lectures (also available on YouTube).

KEITH INSTONE is the information architecture lead for IBM's digital presences. He is also active in various user experience community efforts. You can find him online at instone.org.

ERIN MALONE is currently a Partner at Tangible UX and has over 20 years of experience designing applications, social experiences and best practices for companies like Intuit, Yahoo!, AOL, AltaVista, Ask, and a host of startup companies. She was the founding editor-in-chief of Boxes and Arrows and a founding member of the IA Institute. She co-authored *Designing Social Interfaces* (O'Reilly Media / Yahoo Press, 2009) with Christian Crumlish.

PETER MORVILLE is a writer, speaker, and consultant. He is best known for helping to create the discipline of information architecture. His bestselling books include *Information Architecture for the World Wide Web* (O'Reilly, 2006) and *Ambient Findability* (O'Reilly, 2005). Peter's latest book, *Search Patterns: Design for Discovery*, was published by O'Reilly Media in 2010. He advises such clients as AT&T, Harvard, IBM, the Library of Congress, Microsoft, the National Cancer Institute, Vodafone, and the Weather Channel. His work on experience design and the future of search has been covered by Business Week, The Economist, Fortune, NPR, and The Wall Street Journal. Peter lives in Ann Arbor, Michigan with his wife, two daughters, and a dog named Knowsy. He blogs at findability.org.

AHMED RIAZ is a user experience designer with a background in industrial design and design research, an expertise in visual thinking and a passion for making objects that dissolve into behavior. When not designing, he can be found searching for and eating at the best hole-in-the-wall restaurants and street food in the world. His past design experiences include time spent researching air craft interiors for Gulfstream Aerospace, honing his skills as a professional napkin sketcher for the visual thinking company XPLANE, and reinventing ecommerce for the internet pioneer eBay. Currently he is working as a senior designer for frog design, thinking of strategies that lead to sustainable success for clients of all shapes and sizes. His personal site is: ahmedriaz.com

MARIJKE RIJSBERMAN is a design anthropologist with Cisco's Collaborative Software Group, studying virtual collaboration in all its incarnations, including the mobile experience. Before joining Cisco, Marijke was an independent user researcher and interaction designer with clients in health care, financial services, ecommerce, and productivity, both Fortune 500 and startups. She has a long-standing interest in the anthropology of work under global capitalism and cultivates a passion for the anthropology of waste during her off-hours. For more information, see www.interfacility.com.

CHRISTIAN ROHRER is a veteran of Web user experience design and research, having participated directly in the development of some of the world's most popular Web destinations, including Yahoo!, eBay, and Realtor.com. In his most recent role as Senior Director of User Experience Design at Move, Inc., he led a talented team of designers and researchers in developing top real estate Web sites and applications., including the #1 consumer real estate Web site and the top-rated real estate iPhone app, both under the Realtor.com brand. He previously served as eBay's Director of Customer Intelligence for Products and was a founding member of the eBay Research Council, an executive-sponsored body that advises the company on best research practices and synthesizes insights from market research, community outreach, international research, Web analytics, and user experience research. Prior to that, he was Director of User Experience Research at Yahoo!, where he was also a founding member of the Yahoo! Research Council. Both at Yahoo! and eBay, he served on the User Experience Design leadership team, reporting directly to the VP of the department. Before joining Yahoo!, Rohrer conducted design research and ethnographies for NCI (now Liberate), focusing on the strategies employed by people learning to use interfaces on TV-based Internet appliances. He also spent five years as an independent UNIX consultant and two years as a support engineer at SCO. Rohrer has a PhD in symbolic systems in education (cognitive science) from Stanford University and a BA in computer and information sciences with honors from the University of California, Santa Cruz. He is an active member of various industry organizations and maintains a blog and site at www.xdstrategy.com.

LOUIS ROSENFELD is an independent information architecture consultant for Fortune 500 corporations and other large organizations, and founder and publisher of Rosenfeld Media, a publishing house focused on user experience books. He has been instrumental in helping establish the fields of information architecture and user experience, and in articulating the role and value of librarianship within those fields. Lou is co-author of *Information Architecture for the World Wide Web* (O'Reilly; 3rd edition 2006) and the forthcoming *Site Search Analytics,* co-founder of the Information Architecture Institute, and a former columnist for *Internet World, CIO,* and *Web Review.* He blogs regularly and tweets (@louisrosenfeld) even more so.

JAIMIE SIROVICH is the author of the technology-oriented search marketing reference, *Professional Search Engine Optimization with PHP* (Wrox, 2007). Doubling as Web developer and search marketer at SEO Egghead, Inc., he focuses on helping ecommerce clients succeed. He does this with multi-channel integration, marketing know-how, and building navigation and search solutions conceived with both humans and robots in mind. Jaimie can be reached at jaimie@seoegghead.com or via www.seoegghead.com/about/contact-us.seo.

PETE STAHL has made technology less frustrating at Cisco, eBay, America Online, Microsoft, Netscape, and Entrust, among others. His designs touch areas as diverse as ecommerce, 3D social environments, network management, online conferencing, and gesture-based pen computing. He is a highly rated speaker on interaction design at conferences, such as IxDA, IA Summit, and Web 2.0 Expo. A specialist in design patterns and component libraries, he led eBay's notorious Pattern Optimization Squad and was impresario of Polynesian-themed Page Parsing Parties, where designs are deconstructed into their constituent components. While there, he and Josh Damon Williams pioneered a new methodology for Interaction Audits. More recently, he has written and presented on "The Rhythm of Interaction," urging colleagues to design pacing and tempo into what are increasingly dynamic and cinematic user experiences. He holds a degree in music theory and composition from Harvard.

DANIEL TUNKELANG is a leading industry advocate of human-computer information retrieval (HCIR). He was a founding employee of faceted search pioneer Endeca, where he spent ten years as Chief Scientist. During that time, he established the HCIR workshop, which has taken place annually since 2007. Always working to bring together industry and academia, he co-organized the 2010 Workshop on Search and Social Media and has served as an organizer for the industry tracks of the premier conferences on information retrieval: SIGIR and CIKM. He authored a popular book on faceted search as part of the Morgan & Claypool Synthesis Lectures. In November 2009, he moved to Google, where he works on local search quality. Daniel holds degrees in math and computer science from MIT and a PhD in computer science from CMU, where he worked on information visualization. He blogs at The Noisy Channel (http://thenoisy-channel.com/) about information science and retrieval.

LUKE WROBLEWSKI is currently Chief Design Officer and co-founder of a stealth start-up. He is also an Entrepreneur in Residence (EIR) at Benchmark Capital. Prior to this, Luke was the Chief Design Architect (VP) at Yahoo! Inc. where he worked on product alignment and forward-looking integrated customer experiences on the Web, mobile, TV, and beyond. Luke is the author of two popular Web design books (*Web Form Design* (Rosenfeld Media, 2008) and *Site-Seeing: A Visual Approach to Web Usability* (Wiley, 2002)) and many articles about digital product design and strategy. He is also a consistently top-rated speaker at conferences and companies around the world, and a co-founder and former Board member of the Interaction Design Association (IxDA). Previously, Luke was the Lead User Interface Designer of eBay Inc.'s platform team, where he led the strategic design of new consumer products (such as eBay Express and Kijiji) and internal tools and processes. He also founded LukeW Ideation & Design, a product strategy and design consultancy; taught graduate interface design courses at the University of Illinois; and worked as a Senior Interface Designer at the National Center for Supercomputing Applications (NCSA), the birthplace of the first popular graphical Web browser, NCSA Mosaic.

Credits

ACQUISITIONS EDITOR
Mary James

PROJECT EDITOR
W. Jason Gilmore

TECHNICAL EDITOR
Pabini Gabriel-Petit

SENIOR PRODUCTION EDITOR
Debra Banninger

COPY EDITOR
San Dee Phillips

EDITORIAL DIRECTOR
Robyn B. Siesky

EDITORIAL MANAGER
Mary Beth Wakefield

FREELANCER EDITORIAL MANAGER
Rosemarie Graham

MARKETING MANAGER
Ashley Zurcher

PRODUCTION MANAGER
Tim Tate

VICE PRESIDENT AND EXECUTIVE GROUP PUBLISHER
Richard Swadley

VICE PRESIDENT AND EXECUTIVE PUBLISHER
Barry Pruett

ASSOCIATE PUBLISHER
Jim Minatel

PROJECT COORDINATOR, COVER
Katie Crocker

COMPOSITOR
Chris Gillespie,
Happenstance Type-O-Rama

PROOFREADER
Nancy Carrasco

INDEXER
Robert Swanson

COVER IMAGE
Wiley in-house design

COVER DESIGNER
Ryan Sneed

Acknowledgments

ANY PROJECT OF THIS MAGNITUDE is well beyond the scope of individual effort. Literally scores of people are involved, and thanking them all properly is bound to be an imperfect process. Sorry if I missed anyone!

First, I'd like to thank my UXmatters editor, Pabini Gabriel-Petit. Pabini was instrumental in making this book happen and supported and encouraged my writing through the UXmatters Search Matters column, tirelessly weeding out imperfections from my sentences. I'd also like to also thank a fantastic editing and creative team at Wiley—Scott Meyers, Mary James, Jason Gilmore and everyone else involved in producing this book. Likewise, I want to thank my fantastic agent, Neil Salkind and the great folks of Studio B.

I also want to thank all my fantastic co-writers who have contributed a great deal of their personal time and expertise to producing this book: Frank Guo, whose knowledge of eyetracking and ads research was invaluable in writing the ads chapter; Tricia Clement, whose expertise in behavioral psychology, information architecture, and help systems is second only to her ability to bring out the best in people; Ahmed Riaz, one of the most creative and visually gifted interaction designers I ever had the privilege to work with. Special thanks to Peter Morville for writing such a kind foreword at short notice and for his continual support and inspiration.

I also want to thank the amazing writers, designers, and UX practitioners who contributed their unique perspectives that so enriched this humble work: Pete Bell, Josh Clark, Christian Crumlish, Brynn Evans, Frank Guo, Marti Hearst, Keith Instone, Erin Malone, Peter Morville, Pabini Gabriel-Petit, Marijke Rijsberman, Christian Rohrer, Lou Rosenfeld, Jamie Srorovich, Peter Stahl, Daniel Tunkelang, and Luke Wrobleski.

Finally, I want to acknowledge many of the amazing professionals who have greatly inspired me: Dan Norman, Jared Spool, Edward Tufte, Bill Scott, Phil Bartholo, Larry Lynch, Ranjit Mavinkurve, Chris Baum, Simona Brusa-Pasque, Larry Hannigan, Rian Van Der Merwe, Jeralyn Reese, Michael Manning, and Dirk Gonzales. This book stands on the shoulders of giants.

—GREG NUDELMAN

Contents at a Glance

Contents

Foreword

THE COLORFUL, BUSTLING BAZAARS of Europe, South America, and Asia have earned a special place in my heart. Fresh fruit, warm bread, exotic flowers, antiques, books, toys and trinkets: To wander the street markets of Barcelona or Santiago is to feel alive. And who could resist browsing the tiny stalls and massive stores of electronics, anime, and manga in Tokyo's Akihabara? It's shopping you'll never forget.

While *bazaar* derives from the Persian *baha-char* meaning "the place of prices," the finance is lost in the romance. We travel great distances to see these sights, and then buy needless things, simply to be part of the action. The exchange of goods and services is elevated into an experience that's entertaining, educational, and inspiring.

These vibrant markets offer stark contrast to the suburban shopping mall, an odious place I avoid like the plague. On a rare visit, as I physically drag my cadaver from rack to rack, store to store, anchor to anchor, I am painfully aware of the search costs of modern meatspace, which is why I do most of my shopping online.

Of course, a similar spectrum exists in ecommerce, with many more bad stores than good. The difference is in the distance. On the Web, every shop is just a click away. Location isn't what it used to be. And, since low cost often leads to low profit, smart sellers have learned that insanely great user experiences, especially in search and discovery, are the new keys to the kingdom of sustainable competitive advantage.

That's why you must read this book. In *Designing Search*, Greg Nudelman brings tremendous insight and experience to the challenges of ecommerce, drawing upon rich illustrations and examples to explain user behavior and design patterns. By exploring such diverse topics as faceted navigation, liquid layout, pearl growing, and third-party advertising, Greg reveals today's best practices from Amazon to Zillow.

And, from multi-channel to multi-touch, Greg tackles the bleeding edge. His analysis of why we can't apply mobile patterns to tablets—"the iPad is NOT a large iPhone"—weaves ergonomics and ethnography into a story that's compelling and convincing. Even better, despite the high-tech focus, Greg's empathy for the user shines through in the way he frames searching and shopping as high-touch social experience.

In short, whether you and your team are carefully refining cross-channel integration for established brick and mortars like REI and Wal-Mart, or innovating like madmen for new brands like Groupon and Zipcar, this book will help you to escape the death of the mall and embrace the vivacious, pleasurable, and profitable life of the bazaar.

—Peter Morville

Introduction

WITH ALL THE BOOKS on search and finding, why do you need yet another one? Because search is one of the oldest, most fundamental, yet challenging and rapidly evolving problems facing humanity today. This book focuses on one specific application of search: ecommerce search—whether on the Web, smartphones, or tablet devices such as the iPad. Rather than covering larger questions involving frameworks and search-related theories, I've decided to focus on helping you improve your ecommerce search user experience in direct and measurable ways. You learn all about the most effective design patterns and tips which can cause your customers to buy more, leave your store happier, and tell their friends and social networks about the positive experience they had using your site or mobile app.

Some of the design approaches introduced in this book have earned their reputation through repeated successful application. Others are novel applications of fundamental design principles—or new design ideas just waiting for their opportunity. Both the time-tested design patterns, and the new design ideas flow directly from a rich source: the hundreds of lab studies and field observations I've carried out over the years. In short, I've written this book for UX designers, engineers, and product managers who are ready to take their ecommerce search user interface to the next level and win in the marketplace.

I hope this book inspires you to look beyond the obvious, have fun designing innovative solutions, and experiment with what you learn. Designing effective ecommerce search solutions presents a truly wicked design challenge, which is what makes it so interesting!

How This Book Is Structured

This book is broken into three parts comprising 17 chapters.

Part I: Optimizing eCommerce Search Results Pages

Part I discusses ways to optimize the layout and content of ecommerce search results pages. It also covers the importance of no search results pages; provides a quick but useful framework for understanding why shoppers behave as they do, taken from different perspectives of industry's thought leaders and a construct of shopper roles; describes how to avoid pogosticking; discusses the use of thumbnail images; and provides answers to the important but difficult question of how to deal with ads on search results pages.

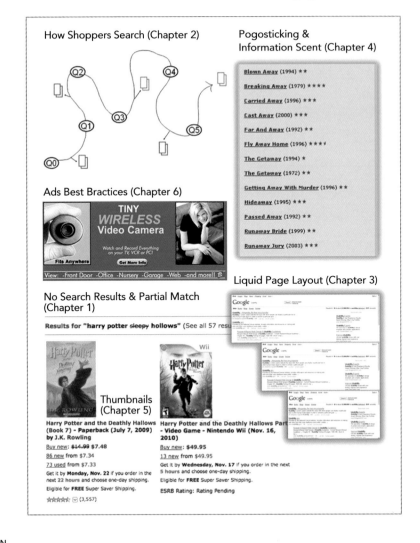

Part II: Designing eCommerce Search Interactions

Part II covers a wide array of topics related to the design of intuitive and effective ecommerce search interactions. It discusses interaction design for faceted search filters, with particular emphasis on the most challenging filtering problems: numeric filters and date filters; sorting; query disambiguation; offers a useful but under-used More Like This design pattern; and closes with a chapter on breadcrumbs.

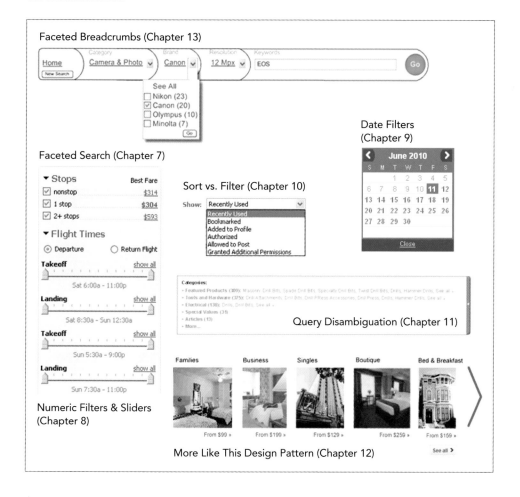

Part III: The Future of eCommerce Search

Part III discusses current and near-future opportunities for innovative design in the realm of ecommerce search. It covers diverse topics such as visual browsing; limitations and opportunities in designing mobile search user interfaces, with particular attention to the challenges of faceted search results on mobile devices; and designing search for ecommerce help systems. The book closes with search strategies specific to tablet devices.

Case Studies

Several chapters include one or more case studies that discuss a real-world search application and explain how to redesign a problem interface using the techniques shown in the book. Case studies are important because they are meant to summarize the chapter material and explain how to use what you learned in a practical application.

Perspectives and Excerpts

In addition to the case studies, selected chapters include perspectives by leading UX practitioners and excerpts from a variety of notable UX books. Perspectives are meant to enhance your knowledge by expanding the chapter topic, providing an interesting angle or example, or taking a deeper look at a specific aspect of the material discussed in the chapter.

Conventions

Throughout the book you'll encounter several icons which you can use to quickly refresh your memory each time you revisit the material.

The pattern icon identifies approaches you should consider when implementing concepts discussed throughout the chapter.

The antipattern icon identifies approaches which should be avoided when implementing concepts discussed throughout the chapter.

Note—The note icon indicates notes, tips, hints, tricks, and asides to the current discussion.

Exploring Beyond This Book

If you want more information about ecommerce search, visit its companion Web sites for more resources and inspiration in the form of my articles and blog posts:

- **DesignCaffeine**—DesignCaffeine.com/DesigningSearch
- **UXmatters Books**—www.uxmatters.com/ux-books/uxmatters-books/designing-ecommerce-search.php

How to Contact the Author

You can reach Greg through his Web site, DesignCaffeine.com which also houses his blog and links to useful resources.

OPTIMIZING ECOMMERCE SEARCH RESULTS PAGES

Search is a wicked problem of terrific consequence... the defining element of user experience. It changes the way we find everything... It shapes how we learn and what we believe.

—PETER MORVILLE

CHAPTER 1

STARTING FROM ZERO:

Winning Strategies for No Search Results Pages

Search, more than any other activity, is a living, evolving process of discovery—a conversation between a customer and the Web site. Unfortunately, this conversation is often fraught with miscommunication, and so it is critical for you to keep this conversation going even when the customer has initiated a search that yielded no results.

Unfortunately, the typical product team has no coherent strategy for cases when there are no search results, generally treating such occurrences as a "user error." Most teams spend the bulk of their design phase working on the search results pages for a successful search. Then in the harried moments prior to launch, the engineers hurriedly slap something together for the no search results page. Such an approach is detrimental to the success of a customer's search experience.

In my experience, the effort and ingenuity a product team invests in the no search results page is indicative of its overall dedication to customer success. Ignoring this special kind of search results page virtually guarantees a mediocre search experience and contributes to obscurity in the ecommerce marketplace. On the other hand, if a team thinks creatively about the case when there are no search results and focuses on customer needs, it can turn a temporary snag in communication into an opportunity for deeper connection and a source of tremendous competitive advantage.

THE NO SEARCH RESULTS PAGE: YOUR KEY TO COMPETITIVE SEARCH ADVANTAGE

To see how original thinking about the no search results page can revolutionize an entire industry, consider the history of Google. Although a relative latecomer to an already saturated search market, Google blew away all competition through an unapologetic dedication to customer success. One critical innovation was the Google *Did you mean…* feature, which gave the process of discovery a safety net and made exploration more fun. This feature was the result of deliberate and original thinking about how to help people correct the misspellings that were a common cause of the appearance of the no search results page. Controlled vocabulary substitution redefined the way Google does search, and today, the *Did you mean…* feature shown in Figure 1.1 is a virtual necessity for a successful search implementation.

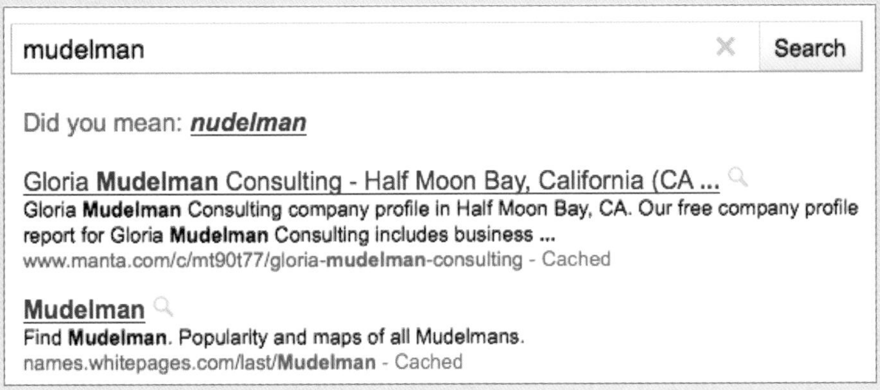

FIGURE 1.1

The Google *Did you mean...* feature

If you want to create a killer search app, begin with the no search results page. Starting from zero forces your team to address the most difficult design questions up front and honestly assess your engineering budget and capabilities. More important, your team can define the entire search user interface design problem more precisely—in a compelling and possibly even original way.

No Search Results Strategy: Not a Zero-Sum Game

No simple set of rules exist that guarantees a successful implementation of a no search results page. However, the following four broad design principles provide a useful starting point:

1. Don't be afraid to say *I did not understand.* Clearly indicate there are no search results, so your customer can recover.

2. Focus on providing a way out. Make sure every control on the search results page does something productive to help resolve the no search results condition.

3. Create a robust partial match strategy. Over-constraining is the most frequent mistake people make when searching ecommerce sites. Having a robust partial match strategy is critical.

4. Employ multiple content strategies. Draw from multiple sources to provide the most relevant content first to aid recovery from the no search results condition, while staying true to your customer's original intent.

Now look at some examples of how you can combine these design principles creatively to develop both compelling customer experiences and opportunities for business success.

Don't Be Afraid to Say *I Did Not Understand*

Clear communication of system state forms the foundation of all human-computer interaction. In his *Alertbox* blog post "Ten Usability Heuristics," Jacob Nielsen put "Visibility of system status" at #1. If customers cannot understand that a search system did not find what they asked for, they can't take the appropriate corrective action. Yet many search applications do not display the no search results condition clearly or accurately.

Figure 1.2 shows an example of a search results page from a leading financial information site, Morningstar.com. Can you tell whether the system found what the customer searched for?

FIGURE 1.2

Morningstar.com does not communicate zero search results effectively

On the Morningstar search results page, there is no explicit message that states **No results found**. The only zero on the page appears in the black bar in the form of **1-0 of 0**, which does not make much sense. Compare the Morningstar page with the Google page shown in Figure 1.3.

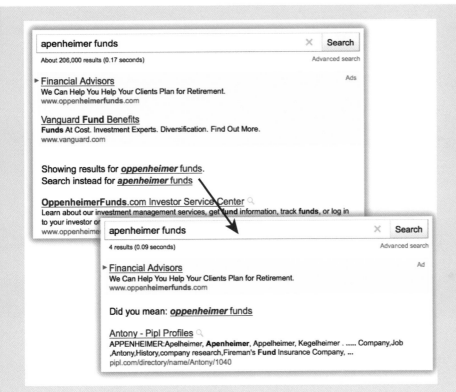

FIGURE 1.3

Google clearly communicates a zero search results condition and often takes appropriate corrective action automatically

The status message on the Google search results page is clear and straightforward: **Showing results for oppenheimer funds. Search instead for apenheimer funds**, making it obvious that the system assumed a misspelling and made the most likely substitution automatically. In case the person actually did want to search for **apenheimer**, Google also makes the original query available. Clicking **Search instead for apenheimer funds** yields the result shown in Figure 1.3 in the lower right.

If you look carefully, you noticed that this Google system behavior is a little different than the **Did you mean:** implementation shown in Figure 1.1. In the case of the search for **Mudleman**, the system merely suggested the substitution

but still ran the original query. On the other hand, in the case of **apenheimer**, the system performed the substitution automatically. The words **Did you mean:** appear in red font in Figure 1.1, whereas they are less prominent in black ink in the lower right in Figure 1.3. This system behavior demonstrates another key principle: The best design for your application is the one that works best for a particular query, your audience, and your business model. There are no hard-and-fast rules for implementing any of the strategies that handle no search results conditions. Even the industry's best sites work tirelessly to make continuous, small improvements. No search results pages are critical to your site's success, so it pays to keep a particularly close eye on any design changes to make sure that they are indeed providing a better experience for your customers. That is why it is important to continuously test and evaluate the performance of your no search results pages using A/B testing (see sidebar).

A/B TESTING AND MULTIVARIATE TESTING

To ensure you create successful design solutions that meet both business and customer goals, your team should conduct frequent, quantitative A/B testing of your no search results page and other search results pages. Follow up with qualitative lab and field testing to help you make sense of your A/B testing results and suggest ideas for future improvements.

The central idea behind A/B testing is to have two different user interface designs running on your site at the same time, while collecting key performance metrics (KPMs) that enable you to measure desired customer behavior.

For example, say you want to introduce some improvements to your current no search results page, which you can call variant A. To determine whether your redesigned version of the page, variant B, offers any improvement, you can deploy variant B and send a small percentage of site visitors—for example, 1% to 10%—to that server and observe the metrics for variant B:

- Did those visitors buy more stuff?
- Did they stay on your site longer?
- Did they add more things to their favorites or wish lists?
- Did they come back to your site sooner to make additional purchases—showing loyalty to your site?

Of course, these are ecommerce metrics, but you can set up your own relevant KPMs and figure out whether variant A or B is more successful.

Most successful companies use multivariate testing, which can be thought of in simple terms as numerous A/B tests performed on one page at the same time. Whereas A/B tests are usually performed to determine the better of two content variations, multivariate testing can theoretically test the effectiveness of limitless combinations. In practice the number of combinations is limited by the amount of time it will take to get a statistically valid sample of visitors and computational power. However, it can be substantial, with some of the larger multivariate tests including 40 or more combinations.

Multivariate testing is the primary method by which Netflix decides whether any new user interface design is an improvement and should go live on its site. Netflix regularly displays new user interfaces to a small percentage of its customers for a few hours or days at a time. If customers are more successful using a new user interface, variant B, according to the KPMs, that new variant goes live on the site for all customers. If not, the new design is rejected. By doing this type of testing, Netflix can remain confident that its site is continuously improving because the key metrics tell that it is. This improvement strategy has certainly worked well for Netflix. Since 2005, the company has consistently ranked #1 in customer satisfaction across the entire ecommerce industry!

Focus on Providing a Way Out

After the system indicates that the no search results condition occurred, it must now help the customer recover. Whenever you display a no search results page, always provide a helpful way forward to get your customer back on track as quickly as possible. Virtually every control on the page should be focused on doing *something* to help the customer recover from the no search results condition, and any extraneous controls for filtering and sorting search results should be removed.

On the Morningstar.com no search results page, the most prominent controls on the page are the links on the gray bar, shown in Figure 1.4, which include **Analyst Reports & Data**, **Morningstar Articles**, and **Tools**. At first glance, it seems that clicking these links would enable customers to browse content relevant to their query. Unfortunately, the links are actually *filtering* controls that serve only to further constrain a search that already has no results. Instead of providing a way out, filter links on a no search results page actually suck the customer deeper into the quagmire of the no search results state, now requiring the customer to click the Back button multiple times to get back to some useful content.

Morningstar is not the only site that is guilty of providing unproductive and confusing links that do not give customers a way out. Can you spot some useless filtering controls on the Endless.com no search results page shown in Figure 1.5?

FIGURE 1.4

Misleading links on the Morningstar no search results page

FIGURE 1.5

Endless.com no search results page

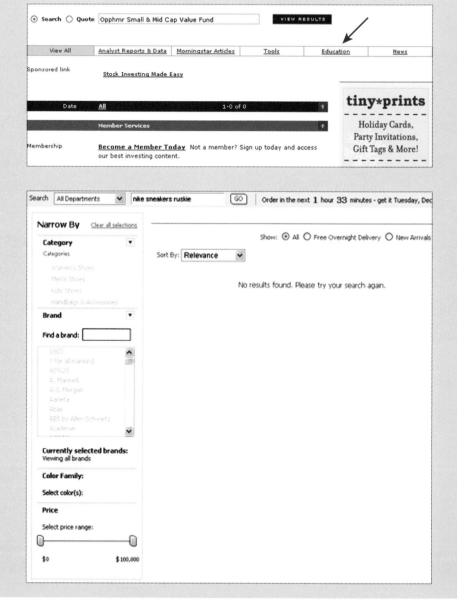

If you answered *The entire page except the search box,* you are correct. Further constraining already nonexistent search results to those with Free Overnight

Delivery, changing the sort order, narrowing by category, or using a fancy price slider would all yield an endless stream of no results. Such system behavior is confusing to customers who are already frustrated by getting no search results.

Instead of providing controls that further constrain a customer's query on your no search results page, make sure every control gives the customer a productive way out. Compare these endless nonproductive results to the page in Figure 1.6, which shows the result of the same query on Amazon.com.

FIGURE 1.6

Amazon.com shows customers the way to find Nike sneakers

Amazon.com's no search results page succeeds in a big way, because of its very prominent and useful links and content that helps customers find their way to Nike sneakers and get away from the no search results page.

CREATE A ROBUST PARTIAL MATCH STRATEGY

Many of the user research participants I've observed over the years have leaned toward over-constraining their queries by entering too many search keywords.

Note—After misspelling, over-constraining is probably the most common cause of no search results pages on ecommerce sites.

Because over-constraining search results is so common, partial match strategy deserves special consideration for most ecommerce sites.

Partial match is a strategy that shows some relevant content that matches a viable part of the customer's query, while also indicating which keywords were omitted from the search results. Showing partial matches is important because what people find often changes what they seek by giving them additional clues about the target content. Effective partial match strategy gives your customers the best chance to recover and succeed in finding what they are looking for on your site.

Adding more information to explain what you mean is also a common human response when you are feeling misunderstood. Thus, a natural human response to a no search results page is to add more keywords to the original search query. Unfortunately, for most ecommerce search engines, this strategy works poorly, because additional keywords only constrain the query further without fixing the original reason for getting zero search results.

Note—The problem of over-constrained searches is especially prevalent when people are searching for an item of particular interest to them, so you will not always be able to observe this behavior in a usability test with predefined search tasks and made-up items for which participants are to search.

This makes field studies one of the most instructive environments in which to observe how people interact with your no search results pages.

For example, during one field study I conducted for one of the top ecommerce sites, a particularly representative participant mistakenly searched for the book titled *Harry Potter and the Sleepy Hollows* and, as a consequence, received no search results. This person then attempted to recover from the no search results condition by adding more keywords—a misspelled author name *J.K. Rawlin,* thus, inadvertently multiplying the confusion. Unfortunately, the site I was studying did not, at the time, provide any partial matches to show which of the keywords was the problem. When this participant came up empty after several search attempts involving incorrect or misspelled keywords, she concluded that the site must not carry any *Harry Potter* books and moved on to another site to make her purchase, never coming back to the original site that failed her. It is interesting to note that this behavior is typical.

Note—In most studies I've observed, even after participants have figured out which part of the query they've gotten wrong, not a single person has ever come back to the site that originally failed to deliver partial matches that would in some way guide them to the product they were seeking.

Several participants have commented that the lack of guidance as to which keyword was the problem "made them feel stupid" and adversely affected their perception of the site. Thus, an effective partial match recovery strategy is critical for ecommerce no search results pages.

Few sites do a better job at partial match than Amazon.com. As Figure 1.7 shows, the Amazon.com no search results page shows not just one, but *two* partial match results that use some of the customer's original keywords, while at the same time clearly indicating which keywords were omitted from the partial match query by using effective strike-through font.

FIGURE 1.7

Amazon.com uses an effective partial match strategy

Not every company can afford to create a partial match strategy as robust as that of Amazon.com, but even a small step in the right direction can lead to a better customer experience. Often, over-constrained searches involve picking the wrong category in a filter set, so an easy place to start developing your partial match strategy might be with omitting a category (if the customer has selected one) from a query that led to a no search results page.

Note—Picking a wrong category need not be the result of any confusion about the category structure. It is very common for customers to forget to change the category when they switch gears and start searching for a different product or when they start their search via an external link that catapults them deep into your search results with a category filter applied.

Thus, a basic keyword-only search of **All Categories**, with no other constraints, should form a basis of your partial match strategy.

For example, the top of Figure 1.8 shows Ketera Network's no search results page that resulted from picking the wrong category "Plastics and Rubbers" while looking for manufacturers of "gold-leaf paper."

FIGURE 1.8

Ketera Network's rudimentary no search results page

As a rudimentary recovery mechanism, the page provides a link that enables the customer to rerun their original keyword query in All Categories. Clicking this partial match search link yields the search results page containing "Gold Leaf Embossing Co" (bottom of Figure 1.8).

Although this approach works, it forces the customer to take action (click a link) without indicating in any way that a link would yield a useful result. A better experience would be to run the keyword-only query automatically on the back end, and, should it yield any search results, to display these results as partial matches within the body of the no search results page using a "More Like This" design pattern described in Chapter 12. Of course, the resulting page needs to indicate to customers clearly how the query was changed to create these results so they may respond accordingly.

EMPLOY MULTIPLE CONTENT STRATEGIES

Good content is a key to helping people recover from a no search results condition. In providing content for no search results pages, you need to keep in mind the customer's original goal and stick as closely as possible to the spirit of the original query. Typically, in addition to the partial match discussed in the previous section, successful sites employ multiple content strategies. Normally, what is judged to be the most relevant content is provided first, followed by less relevant content shown lower on the page.

In addition to an "All Categories" partial match link, the Ketera Networks no search results page in Figure 1.8 contains a variety of simple but useful content designed to help the customer recover from a no search results condition. The page includes a link that enables customers to browse their original category, "Plastics and Rubbers," and all of the 28 other categories of suppliers in the column on the left. Below links directly relevant to the customer's query, the page displays a list of featured suppliers. If customers still can't find what they are looking for, the page enables them to create their own Request for Information (RFQ) so the right services can find *them* instead. The Ketera Network no search results page is a simple, albeit rudimentary example of employing multiple content strategies to deal with a no search results condition.

Following is a list of some useful ideas for no search results content strategies, in order of their relevance to the customer's original query:

1. Spelling correction and substituting a customer's original keywords with different keywords from a controlled vocabulary
2. Removing some of a customer's original keywords, or making partial matches
3. Matching only categories or aspects, without the keywords
4. Top searches, featured results, or most popular results
5. Third-party resources and ads

You already looked at a good example of controlled vocabulary keyword substitution: the Google *Did you mean...* feature shown in Figure 1.1. To provide relevant content, Google draws upon its enormous list of the indexed keywords for which people have previously searched, which forms its controlled vocabulary, to suggest the closest matching available keyword.

Successful content strategies for handling cases when there are no search results are not limited to the five just mentioned. Google's brilliant auto-suggest feature, another industry-defining innovation shown in Figure 1.9, is an excellent example of a successful marriage of two content strategies: making partial keyword matches and using a controlled vocabulary for keyword substitution.

FIGURE 1.9

Google auto-suggest prevents a no search results condition from occurring

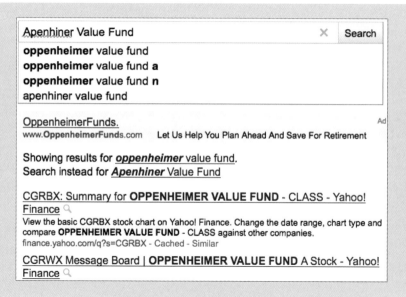

When automatically suggesting search keywords, Google chooses the top keywords from its controlled vocabulary of the most popular keywords. By matching the beginning of a string the customer begins to type with popular search keywords, Google ensures a successful search, forestalling the no search results condition before it ever occurs. In doing so, Google has devised another tremendously useful and industry-changing search tool. The point: Don't stick with just one specific type of search assistance. Instead combine design features and content creatively to meet the goals of your partner in conversation on the other side of the human-computer interface.

CASE STUDY: HOTMAIL NO SEARCH RESULTS PAGE

Now take a look at the Hotmail no search results page, following a scenario in which I'll try to look up Luke Wroblewski's email address by searching for any email messages I've recently sent or received from him. But I've inadvertently misspelled Luke's last name, so my search query is *Luke Wroblwski*. This situation is, unfortunately, all too common. (I personally experience it almost daily with people's creative spellings of my own last name.) Indeed, it is likely that millions of people experience the Hotmail no search results page on a daily basis.

Unfortunately, the Hotmail no search results page, shown in Figure 1.10, completely misses the mark, violating *all* the design principles discussed so far and thus, committing the three deadly sins of no search results pages, as follows:

1. There is no indication of the no search results condition. Instead, the central message seems to be **No message is selected**, which is technically true, but hardly useful in this situation, because there are no messages to select.

2. Instead of focusing on providing a way out, the page presents several completely useless and confusing controls—like the **Sort by** check box with no options and the **Change Your Reading Pane Settings** link.

3. There is absolutely no content that helps me reach my goal. The **Return to inbox** link and the various filter links on the left do nothing to help me connect with Luke.

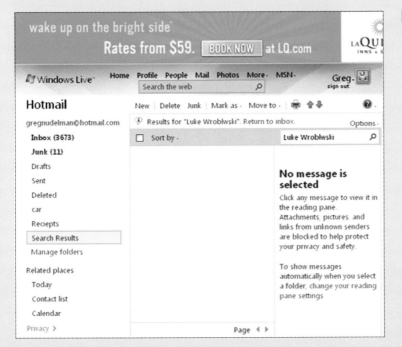

FIGURE 1.10

The Hotmail no search results page commits all three deadly sins

What can you do to improve this page? Obviously, removing some of the confusing controls and improving the no-results messaging would help. Further, you could think about the search problem creatively and try applying a social networking model to email. For example, if Luke and I have ever corresponded in the past, we could remain connected in the system, which would automatically remember Luke's email address. If we've never connected before, the system could helpfully offer to introduce me to Luke for a fee. Of course, we also need robust controlled-vocabulary matching, so the system always finds my existing connections first—no matter how badly I've misspelled their names. In Figure 1.11, my simple wireframe shows how a redesigned Hotmail no search results page might look. It employs the three design principles described earlier and uses sample content borrowed from LinkedIn.com.

FIGURE 1.11

Employing the three design principles to improve the Hotmail no search results page

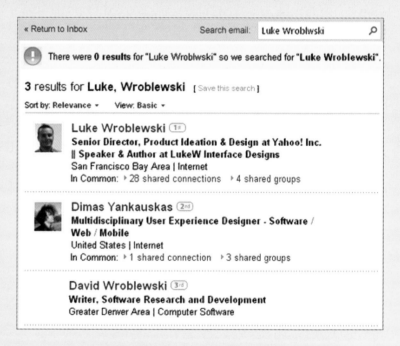

By neglecting to give its no search results page the attention it deserves, Hotmail has quite possibly lost a massive opportunity to launch a social networking revolution. However, its loss resulted in a huge opportunity for LinkedIn, to the tune of millions of dollars.

No search results conditions provide a precious opportunity to go the extra mile to connect your customers to the content they are looking for. You can greatly deepen the customers' connection with your brand, create legions of loyal followers, and blow away your competition, but only if you pay attention to what your customers are trying to do and address their problems with creativity and the care they deserve.

HOW CAN YOUR SITE-SEARCH ANALYTICS HELP YOU?

Not sure whether people searching on your Web site are getting what they need from your search system? There's good news: Your organization is probably logging searchers' queries. Find that data and use it. It's a gold mine for user research and insights, and you *already own it.* Unlike other types of Web analytics, this is *semantically rich data*—it records users' needs, not just their actions. And most important, users can express their information needs in *their own words.*

You can benefit from this data in many ways, including the following:

- You can identify gaps in your offerings. Do people keep searching for a product you don't currently offer? Maybe you should reconsider your product mix.

- You can determine ways to improve your site's user interface design for search and search results, leading to better conversion rates. At minimum, you know how wide that search box should be.

- You can discover the points at which navigation and search fail and remedy the problems you identify.

- You can learn the tone and flavor of your users' language and make sure your content—titles, metadata, and copy—matches up well with their language.

- You can devise a variety of search-related metrics you may not have considered before. In turn, you can integrate these into your organization's Key Performance Indicators (KPIs), enabling you to do a better job of assessing how well your organization meets its goals. So, your managers should like site-search analytics.

Ironically, as useful as all this sounds, many organizations don't bother to analyze their users' search queries. They may just be ignorant of the potential of site-search analytics, or perhaps their query data is buried in some corner of their organization that seems too hard to reach. But it's likely that the biggest barrier to the adoption of site-search analytics is simply that it sounds like it would be hard to do.

That's a misconception: Even free analytics applications such as Google Analytics now provide at least minimal site-search analytics features. Spending an hour a month reviewing even the most basic reports can yield some great insights that can immediately help your organization—and ideally, pave the way to going further with site-search analytics. Following are two types of reports that are great starting points:

⠶ **Most frequent queries**—Study this at least once a month to get a sense of what your users' most important information needs are—and how they change over time. Test those queries out yourself: Do they retrieve relevant results?

⠶ **Most frequent queries with zero results**—Assuming no results means failure, which kinds of queries go wrong the most? Is the content there, but mistitled or rife with jargon? Or do you need to create new content?

In all cases, start with the most frequent queries—the *short head* to the *long tail* you may have heard of—because frequent queries *really* occur frequently, much more often than you might expect. If you sorted all your site's queries by frequency and stacked them from most frequent to least frequent, you'd get a distribution that looks like that shown in Figure 1.12, which depicts the *Zipf Distribution*, in which a few frequent queries—the ones in the *short head*—account for a huge volume of all search activity.

FIGURE 1.12

Typical distribution of site queries by frequency

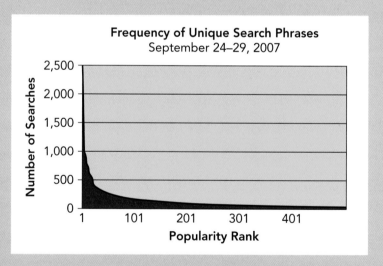

Named after economist George Kingsley Zipf, the *Zipf Distribution* curve describes just about every Web site's search activity and is at the core of site-search analytics. This graph makes a simple, but powerful point: *A few unique queries go a really long way.* So, if you start by analyzing short-head queries, your efforts can also go a really long way.

This point is so important I want to illustrate it in yet another way: through a *Zipf Distribution* rendered in text. Table 1.1 shows that the most frequent query on the Michigan State University Web site, *campus map*, accounts for 1.4% of all searches during the time period they studied. To reach 10% of *all* search activity on their Web site, look at only the *14* most frequent queries—*not* a big number. (In this table, #14 is *housing*.) To get to 20% of all search activity takes only 42 queries; 50%, 500 queries; and so on.

RANK	CUMUL. %	COUNT	QUERY
1	1.40	7,218	campus map
14	10.53	2,464	housing
42	20.18	1,351	webenroll
98	30.01	650	computer center
221	40.05	295	msu union
500	50.02	124	hotels
7,877	80.00	7	department of surgery

TABLE 1.1

The Zipf Distribution of Search Activity. Rendered in Text

Depending on your available time, your efforts to analyze search queries can scale quite nicely. Have only an hour this month? Analyze your top-ten queries; they'll account for a good chunk of all search activity. Have twice as much time next month? Keep going, picking off the most common queries, one by one. As long as you let the Zipf distribution drive your priorities, your work can have a huge impact.

Searchers on your Web site want to have a conversation with your organization. If people do not find what they need, they may go to your competitors' sites. If they had no alternatives and are stuck with you, their poor experience would make them unhappy and damage your brand. Through their search queries, people are asking you—in their own words—for products, information, help, and ideas. Site-search analytics are one of the best ways to understand what your customers are looking for and ensure you give them the answers they need.

—Louis Rosenfeld

REFERENCES

Gill, Judith. "Effective Internet Search: Search Help." *SearchHelpCenter*, March 2004. Retrieved January 31, 2009.

Mondosoft. "Web Site Usability Metrics: Search Behavior—Search Trends." May 2004. Retrieved January 31, 2009.

Nielsen, Jakob. "Search: Visible and Simple." *Alertbox*, May 13, 2001. Retrieved January 31, 2009.

Nielsen, Jakob. "Eyetracking Research." *Alertbox*, April 17, 2006. Retrieved January 31, 2009.

Nudelman, Greg. "The Timestamp-Based Caching Framework." *JavaWorld*, January 3, 2005. Retrieved January 31, 2009.

Nudelman, Greg. "Improve the Usability of Search-Results Pages." *JavaWorld*, January 23, 2006. Retrieved January 31, 2009.

Spool, Jared M. "Producing Great Search Results: Harder than It Looks." *UIE*, July 09, 2008. Retrieved January 31, 2009.

HOW SHOPPERS SEARCH

Before talking about designing the perfect search user interface for custom-ers on your ecommerce site, it would help to understand how people search. Search is a fundamental activity for descendants of hunter-gatherers, so explaining how and why you and I manifest various search behaviors is an interesting and complex problem. Building on the general principles govern-ing our search behaviors, this chapter introduces a framework of search roles that provides a useful foundation for understanding the basics of the ecom-merce search process. This role-based framework is a powerful and flexible tool that you can use throughout the design process of the ecommerce Web site or mobile app.

HOW PEOPLE SEARCH

Search is not a predictable, step-by-step activity. For instance, it wouldn't be unusual for a shopper's search to start on Google, move to Amazon.com, jump to a brand site such as Pottery Barn, and then to eBay or Craigslist—where people look for lower prices—and finally to return to Amazon.com. Searches can also span multiple devices, physical locations, and both virtual and physi-cal networks. A single search might start on a mobile phone; continue by asking for friends' advice, and then explore various social networks on a computer at work—and finally end with making a purchase on a computer at home. (See Pete Bell's perspective on this matter towards the end of this chapter.) One thing is clear: What you find often determines the next step. As information architecture and search expert Peter Morville has eloquently said, "What we find changes what we seek."

Despite the high variation and lack of predictability of the individual search behaviors, the search industry's leading user experience (UX) professionals have identified and documented several general search behavior patterns such as Quit, Narrow, Expand, and Pearl Growing, and antipatterns such as Pogosticking and Thrashing that seem to reappear in different contexts. (See the perspective by Peter Morville on the next page.)

PATTERNS OF BEHAVIOR

The following excerpt is taken from Chapter 3 of the book *Search Patterns* by Peter Morville.

Quit

Search ends with an exit. Users always quit. The question is why? Did they find what the need or simply give up? Was it the information or the interface? Too little, too much, too slow? Quit is a pattern that demands analytics. We must know the reason they're leaving.

Narrow

When users don't quit, they refine. Narrow is the second most common pattern around. Our initial query casts a wide net. Upon seeing the results, we pull back. Sometimes, we can avoid such initial imprecision. A wider box invites more words. So does experience with large (and growing) bodies of content. In fact, the average number of keywords per query in Web search has moved from 1-2 to 2-3 in recent years. However, advance query specification is difficult, because we don't know the size or structure of the index. When we are searching without a map, even a traditional search engine results page (SERP) tells us a lot. The nature of snippets and the number of results lets us judge how (and how much) to narrow. Even better, faceted search puts metadata on the map, and even Sort provides a way to limit what we see.

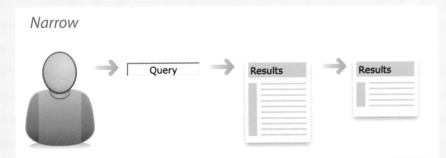

continues

PATTERNS OF BEHAVIOR *(continued)*

Expand

The opposite pattern is rare. Expand is uncommon, partly because users often cast a wide net to begin, and partly because it's a harder problem. Of course, users can try a broader query. When "low fat lemon bar" returns no results, we omit "low fat" and try again. We can also relax constraints by undoing facet value selections. We can always take a step back. However, explicit support for expand is rare. It's most commonly seen in the thesaurus browsers of library databases. Rather than a formal hierarchy, search applications often let users expand (or at least explore) by showing related terms within matching categories.

Pearl Growing

Independent of interface, expert searchers employ a singular strategy for expansion known as pearl growing. Find one good document, then mine its content and metadata for query terms and leads. We might look for more articles about this topic, by this author, or from this source. In ecommerce applications, we might find a product we like and explore similar products in this product type or brand. Pearl growing is an old trick that's taught in library school. Fortunately, pearl growing is also a strategy we can spread by embedding it with the interface. Google's Similar link is the most ubiquitous example. Although algorithms can be complex, the user needs only to click a link.

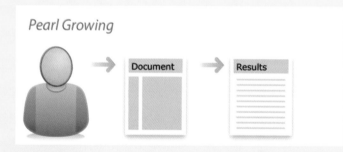

continues

PATTERNS OF BEHAVIOR *(continued)*

Pogosticking

The patterns of behavior we've covered so far—quit, narrow, expand, and pearl growing—are time-less. They are inherent to search. Other patterns (or antipatterns) are produced by bad design. For instance, repetitive bouncing between the SERP and individual results is known as pogosticking. A little pogosticking means users are sampling the results. That's to be expected, but when it happens a lot, it's not sampling; it's a symptom. Perhaps our snippets and metadata lack the scent users need to effectively scan results, so they must visit each one in turn. Or, if sequential viewing of results is a desirable pattern, we need solutions that support this behavior, such as iPhone's touchscreen, to let users flick through image results in a linear fashion.

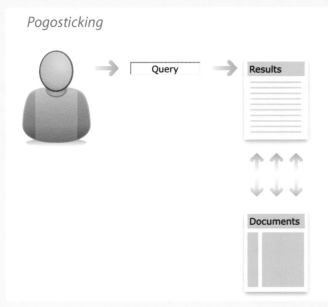

Pogosticking

Thrashing

Another common antipattern is thrashing. In thrashing, a design flaw resides in users' heads in the form of the anchoring bias. We set the anchor with our initial query, and then, despite poor results, we insist on small variations of the flawed search phrase rather than trying new approaches. For instance, a user searching for a concert may try many queries that begin with the (misspelled) nickname rather than switching to the performer's full name. Autocomplete and Autosuggest offer two ways to break this pattern. First, autocomplete helps users avoid typos and get the query right to begin with. Second,

continues

PATTERNS OF BEHAVIOR *(continued)*

autosuggest can recommend related queries that don't include the original search term. This feature taps query reformulation data, the terms user enter after their first search fails, to make the semantic leap and help users who start in the wrong place weigh anchor and move on.

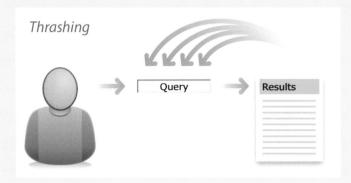

A typical search process involves fluidly moving between activities such as typing in a query and then refining that query; browsing search results, product categories, or brand catalogs; navigating tag folksonomies; or expanding a search by following breadcrumbs. Most likely, these patterns reflect human species' relatively nascent adaptation of the ancient food- and shelter-seeking behaviors to the fast-moving, multifaceted digital world. To describe these complex human behaviors, multiple theoretical models for information seeking have been developed. These models include the Standard model, Cognitive model, Dynamic (Berry-Picking) model, and many others. At the end of this chapter, you can find a brief excerpt from the book *Search User Interfaces* by Marti Hearst, which includes a brief discussion on the Dynamic (Berry-Picking) model and of search and browse strategies that most readily pertain to ecommerce. Fully exploring the theoretical aspects of search would go far beyond the scope of a single chapter. If you are interested in the subject, I highly recommend reading Marti's book and checking out some of the many excellent resources on this subject mentioned at the end of the chapter.

The ecommerce search roles discussed in this chapter adapt broader search behavior patterns and theories specifically to the design of ecommerce search. This set of refined roles presents a modeling tool that can help designers apply their understanding of people's search behaviors to create more effective and more enjoyable interfaces that perform well in multiple contexts and for a variety of ecommerce search tasks.

HOW SHOPPERS SEARCH

Over the course of my user research and UX design work in the ecommerce domain, I have identified five ecommerce search roles that apply almost universally across ecommerce search design projects. Even in cases in which only some of the roles apply, they serve as a great starting point for discussion. The five roles are as follows:

:: Explorer

:: Casual Shopper

:: Targeted Shopper

:: Fun Seeker

:: Committed Shopper

People acting in each of these roles have a specific set of goals, concerns, and assumptions that determine their behaviors.

Note—During a search process, a person's ecommerce search role can change fluidly.

For instance, a customer might start out as an Explorer, checking out an ecommerce site a friend told him about and become interested in a particular product and take on a Targeted Shopper role, reading the product reviews and learning more about shipping costs. At this point the customer's role might again change, becoming a Committed Shopper who is ready to buy. It is helpful to think of these ecommerce search roles as hats. Although a person would be likely to wear only one hat at one time, these hats are fairly easy to change.

Because search is such a dynamic activity, this kind of role-based user modeling is helpful. Similar to using personas, employing these ecommerce search roles lets a design team judge how a particular page or sequence of pages on an ecommerce site would support each role and whether it would provide adequate opportunities for customers to *switch* roles and enter a deeper level of engagement with the site and, ultimately, commit to making a purchase.

Now review each of these roles in detail.

Explorer

Any visitor who is not familiar with a site or its features assumes the Explorer role. A person may not be familiar with a Web site or application for many reasons: A friend might have suggested they try the site. They might have clicked an ad or a link and ended up on a new site or a new part of a site. Whenever this happens, people naturally adopt the Explorer role.

Goals

The person in the Explorer role might have one or more of the following goals:

:: "I want to learn and understand enough about this site to make a judgment about its value for my product search process."

:: "I want to know whether this site carries products in which I'd be interested."

:: "I want to learn and understand enough about a particular feature of this site, so I can judge its value to me in my product search process."

Concerns

The person in the Explorer role might have one or more of the following concerns:

:: "This site might be a waste of my time."

:: "This site's inventory might not match what I'm looking for."

:: "This site might be difficult to learn, so I'd look stupid."

Assumptions

The person in the Explorer role might assume one or more of the following:

:: "I expect this site to be easy to understand, so I can quickly determine whether it's worth my time."

:: "I can learn about this site while finding what I'm looking for."

:: "Learning about this site should be reasonably easy and could even be fun."

Behaviors

Explorers are likely to begin by typing in a general category query such as *Chairs*. Depending on the site they're on, 10% to 20% of Explorers are likely to browse if its category structure looks reasonably inviting and the information scent is strong enough to catch their wandering eye.

Note—Generally, someone in an Explorer role does not complete tutorials, but instead tries to get along through satisficing.

SATISFICING

Satisficing is a term made up through the combination of *suffice* and *satisfy*. It was coined by Herbert Simon in 1956. He pointed out that human beings lack the cognitive resources to maximize: We usually do not know the relevant probabilities of outcomes, and we can rarely evaluate all outcomes with sufficient precision. Instead, we employ a decision-making strategy that attempts to meet criteria for adequacy, rather than to identify an optimal solution.

Casual Shopper

People who are reasonably familiar with a site but do not yet have a clear idea of the product they want to investigate can take on a Casual Shopper role. Typically, people adopt this role when they are searching for gifts, looking for ideas on what to buy, or just starting to investigate a costly, long-term purchase such as a stereo system or a new roof.

Goals

The person in the Casual Shopper role might have one or more of the following goals:

- "I want to find a high-quality, popular product that would make a great gift and purchase it—preferably at a small discount."
- "I'm planning to make a large purchase, so I need to gather preliminary information about the product's possible features and options."

Concerns

The person in the Casual Shopper role might have one or more of the following concerns:

- "What if my friend doesn't like my gift?"
- "I wonder if this product is well made? I don't want to buy something cheap and impractical."
- "I don't want to be forced to make a large purchase before I've done enough research. I want to make sure I pay for only the exact features I actually need."
- "Shopping presents so many temptations. I don't want to get caught up in a shopping spree."

Assumptions

Typically, the person in the Casual Shopper role might assume one or more of the following:

- "I expect to find popular products, gifts, and decorating ideas without working too hard."
- "Appealing images and discounted prices should pique my interest."
- "I expect to find informational pages that are fun to use, explain my options, and have lots of images that show available products."
- "I expect to find customer reviews and editorial content that can help me decide between competing products."
- "The site's category structure should make sense."

Behaviors

Casual Shoppers typically browse using a site's category structure or search using category queries such as *Gifts*.

Note—Casual Shoppers are also likely to search for *decorating ideas* on Google and click a link in the search results that land deep within your site's hierarchy.

Expect Casual Shoppers who are thinking about making a large purchase to come back to your site several times—over a few days or even months—before they commit to purchase.

Targeted Shopper

People who know exactly what product they're looking for take on the Targeted Shopper role and its associated behaviors. Targeted Shoppers have taken their time and narrowed their choice to one or two alternatives. They're in the process of weighing their options and finalizing their decisions about price, accessories, delivery options, and bundles because they're ready to make a purchase.

Note—This is a critical stage, just before someone completes a purchase.

Goals

The person in the Targeted Shopper role might have one or more of the following goals:

- "I want to find a product I've already decided to buy."
- "I want to find the best price and delivery options for the product I'm purchasing."
- "I know what I want, so this site should just get out of my way!"
- "I need to decide between a few competing products and delivery options on one or more sites."

Concerns

The person in the Targeted Shopper role might have one or more of the following concerns:

- "I'm concerned that there might be hidden costs such as high shipping charges."
- "What if the item I buy is not actually new?"
- "I'm worried I might miss something and end up overpaying. I want to find the best price."

Assumptions

The person in the Targeted Shopper role might assume one or more of the following:

:: "Finding the product I want should be straightforward."

:: "I don't want to be pestered with useless and distracting advertising for things that don't relate to the product I'm purchasing."

:: "I expect to get clear and complete pricing information."

:: "I want free shipping—but if I can't get it, I at least want to see instructions on how to get a shipping discount."

:: "I expect to find useful accessories for the product I'm purchasing, which can help me get the most out of my purchase from the time it arrives at my door."

:: "I expect to see powerful product or option comparison tools whenever I might need them."

Behaviors

People in a Targeted Shopper role almost always search.

Note—Targeted Shoppers usually type precise and complete queries—even including model numbers when appropriate, such as *Canon EOS Digital Rebel T1i.*

This lets them conveniently jump directly to whatever product they're looking for. Targeted Shoppers usually try to compare a product's *complete* price on your site—including the available shipping options and their costs—with its cost on another site before making a purchase. They also look at the available accessories and perhaps some related products—so they find upsells helpful. If Targeted Shoppers have not yet made a decision to buy, they might browse competing products. However, they may not trust a site's recommendations and are more likely to read reviews and consider features that indicate what fellow customers ultimately purchased after viewing a particular product to seek out more powerful or cheaper alternatives that offer better value.

Note—Targeted Shoppers that have made a committed decision to buy a specific product and are seeking the best price often become annoyed by cross-sells such as competing brands and models or any advertisements unrelated to their purchase.

Fun Seeker

Fun Seeker is a role that, at first glance, might not seem to belong in this list of ecommerce search roles. Yet, on most of the ecommerce search projects in which I've been involved, some people tend to exhibit Fun Seeker behaviors. Fun Seekers tend to take actions for their own amusement rather than engaging in purposeful shopping activities with the intention of actually buying anything or even acquiring information about a potential purchase. Instead, Fun Seekers just want to have fun. They're looking for entertainment.

Goals

Fun Seekers typically have one or more of the following goals:

- "I just want to have fun and enjoy myself."
- "I'd like to find interesting content my friends will be interested in."
- "I want to see what's new or popular."

Concerns

Fun Seekers often exhibit one or more of the following concerns:

- "I'll get bored."
- "I won't find any interesting content my friends will be talking about."
- "I might pursue something that looks interesting at first glance but turns out to be lame, so spending time reading about it would be a waste of my time."

Assumptions

Fun Seekers typically assume one or more of the following:

- "I expect to be entertained by extremes of human behavior, interesting stories, great content, and user-generated reviews."
- "I'm just going to go with the flow."
- "I'm looking for entertainment, not going shopping. But, if I happen to find something I love, I might buy it."

Behaviors

The Fun Seeker role often spontaneously manifests itself in two ways. First, this role may emerge when people click an external link and discover interesting content their friends or news sources have judged to be entertaining or worthy of consideration. Second, this role may appear when people become distracted by content that has nothing to do with the reason why they came to a Web site in the first place.

For instance, Fun Seekers might look at funny or colorful ads, read interesting content—perhaps a human-interest story about donations or a sponsorship campaign—browse content or traffic aggregation features such as "Top 100 items on the site," or look at features such as "Items popular in my geographic location." People in the Fun Seeker role often read top-rated reviews—even for products they have no interest in—simply because the reviews are popular and might be entertaining. They might read the content in the most active discussion groups, too, and if they become engaged, they might add comments of their own. Fun Seekers tend to consume gossip and other content on a site that has nothing to do with shopping.

Committed Shopper

People assume the Committed Shopper role when they have found the products they want and are ready to check out. Because ecommerce sites rely on selling goods and services, and people in the Committed Shopper role are the ecommerce site's most valuable visitors, it is essential that they be successful in using a site's features.

Goals

A Committed Shopper typically focuses on the following goals:

- :: "I need to find the products I've decided to purchase."
- :: "I need to add products to my shopping cart."
- :: "I need to check out quickly, securely, and with a minimum of fuss."

Concerns

Committed Shoppers may be concerned about one or more of the following:

- :: "I want to be sure my credit card information is secure."
- :: "I don't want to fill out a long and complicated form."
- :: "I don't want to have to remember whether I've already registered with a site—and what email address I gave them."

- ∷ "I don't want to have to remember my password or go through password recovery."
- ∷ "I don't want to be bothered with ads and last-minute offers."
- ∷ "I want to make sure I receive free shipping or the best shipping discount, if available."
- ∷ "I want to make sure I don't get swindled at the last minute."
- ∷ "I want to avoid doing anything wrong, like entering an old address."

Assumptions

Committed Shoppers assume one or more of the following:

- ∷ "Checkout will be fast, easy, and secure, and the system will guide me through it."
- ∷ "I'll get to confirm my total purchase price and shipping charges. If a shipping discount is available, the site will tell me how to get it."
- ∷ "The check-out form will not ask me unnecessary questions."
- ∷ "I will have access to content that answers my questions about returns, shipping dates, and so on."

Behaviors

People in a Committed Shopper role just want to check out quickly. They become impatient with site features that prevent them from doing that—so they prefer to avoid long check-out forms, sites that require them to register and check their email for a confirmation message before they can check out, and sites that make them remember their username and password. Committed Shoppers are usually interested in getting free shipping, so they seek out shipping discounts.

Roles and Personas

You can use ecommerce search roles on their own or integrate them into other user-centered design approaches. One particularly useful User Centered Design (UCD) modeling tool that complements roles well is personas. For those unfamiliar with personas, they are fictional characters, composite models of archetypical types of users—for example, different types of customers that will be using the ecommerce site. Personas were popularized by software design expert Alan Cooper in his 1999 book, *The Inmates are Running the Asylum* to model specific goals and behaviors of people as they interact with the system and help the project team to better relate to a specific type of customer. For this reason, personas are typically given familiar human names, pictures and fictional biographies.

The project team can use personas and ecommerce search roles together to model people's behaviors. The best way to do that is use the roles to *augment* personas. Doing so can enrich your understanding of ecommerce search design requirements for a particular persona or user profile and help your team to better understand how a particular persona might interact with a system.

Roles also help you to think about personas interacting with the site, in real-life, multistep scenarios. For example, a technology-savvy, 16-year-old high-school student would have different goals, concerns, and behaviors from a 40-year-old nurse who is a mother of two, even when both of them are acting as Explorers. In other words, a particular role augments each persona differently, resulting in a unique set of behaviors and scenarios.

Perhaps the biggest benefit of using ecommerce search roles—even in the absence of UX data of any kind—is that they foster a common understanding and team consensus. These roles have the potential to uncover misunderstandings and highlight areas of disagreement as the design project challenges you can constructively resolve using data. As for personas, the primary value of ecommerce search roles is team empathy toward the customers interacting with the site.

Finally, it is important to note that, although this framework can be helpful and these five ecommerce search roles apply to most ecommerce projects, this generalized framework is not precise. For any framework to be maximally useful for a specific project, you should refine it through direct observation of customers and careful study of key performance metrics. As the prominent philosopher and the father of General Semantics Alfred Korzybski so eloquently stated, "The map is not the territory." You can neither camp on the little triangles that represent mountains on a map nor go swimming in those blue patches of ink that represent lakes. Rather than viewing this role framework as "reality," use it as you would a map—to help you navigate your ecommerce search design projects, and as the foundation for developing your own approach—subject to change as you get more data and gain a better understanding of the needs and behaviors of your customers.

SEARCH AS A MULTICHANNEL EXPERIENCE

Mario's grill has rusted through, and he's ready to upgrade to a more durable one. He begins with a Web search engine and clicks through to a store whose brand he likes. On that site, he uses a faceted search (see Chapter 7 for more on faceted search) to refine the results to a handful of models whose attributes might meet his needs. He scrolls through the user reviews on those grills to see which ones other buyers trust and then prints out the reviews for the two he likes best. He checks the local inventory online and finds a branch nearby that has both.

Mario uses his mobile phone to get directions to the store. When there, he goes to the grill aisle and inspects them in person, reviews in hand. He discovers another model on clearance that he hadn't noticed online. He looks up the model on a store kiosk, whose design is similar to the Web site, but it has no user reviews. He turns to his mobile phone instead and reads some user reviews. Now, he has a top pick. He uses his mobile phone one last time to sanity check the in-store price against that of a Web-only superstore. Feeling good, he drives home with a new grill.

This ethnography exemplifies an increasingly common multichannel search experience. As people do product research and make purchases, they mix channels. In the report titled *Profiling the Multichannel Consumer*, Patti Freeman Evans of Forrester Research reported that 70% of consumers research products online and then purchase offline. And in an earlier report from Forrester titled *Multichannel: In-Store Pickup Gains Importance*, Brian Walker estimates that the Web influences $397 billion of store sales per year, projected to grow to $1 trillion by 2012, or one-third of all retail sales. Freeman Evans broke down what constitutes online consumer research. For example, 60% read customer reviews and 42% checked in-store availability before going to the store to buy.

Multichannel no longer means just online and brick-and-mortar stores. Even Web-only stores need to consider mobile and call-center use. And increasingly, people are accessing the Web from new channels such as their gaming console and connected TV. Each channel brings its own expectations to search.

If you were to do more multichannel, search-behavior ethnographies like this, you would eventually find a pattern:

- People use multiple search features, across multiple *modes* of discovery.
- People's expectations of search features vary according to the context of the channel.

Modes of Search

One helpful model of search behavior places modes of search on a continuum ranging from fact finding to discovery. And within that continuum, people use a variety of search features to support the different modes.

In *fact finding*, users know in advance what they're looking for. For example, they already know the specific brand and model of grill they want. Some search features that might support fact finding include the following:

- **alphanumeric string correction**—which uses fuzzy matching so users can mistype a model name and still find it
- **autophrasing**—which detects when multiword combinations are likely compounds, automatically boosting the relevancy of those results
- **barcode or QR code scanners**—which use a mobile phone's camera to directly retrieve product information

At the other extreme of the continuum is *discovery*, where people don't yet know what they want or even how to describe it. For example, they know they want a more durable grill, but they don't yet know the attributes that make a grill durable or the brands they trust to build a reliable one. Some search features that support discovery include the following:

- **faceted search**—which shows people results having particular attributes and lets them browse and refine the results
- **user-review search**—which lets people read the frank feedback of other consumers and possibly exposes the attributes of the reviewers through faceted search
- **buying guide, product-info sheet, or demo video search**—which incorporate features of document search like text mining and advanced relevancy to show supplemental information alongside results from the product catalog

Context of the Channel

People's expectations of search features vary according to the context of the channel. For example, they expect mobile to be location-aware, and in-store kiosks to be inventory aware. On the Web, they expect pages to be optimized for a big screen; on mobile devices, for a small one. And they also expect a store to know which channel they've used. For example, a call center should have different return information for an online shopper than for someone who shopped at a brick-and-mortar store.

Although the multichannel search experience is already common, it is not yet a well-designed experience. It's a kluge. People face unnecessary gaps across channels, often because the channels aren't aware of each other. For example, Mario couldn't pass his shopping cart from his laptop computer-based search to his mobile environment, which would have let him bring user reviews to the store without printing them out. And the in-store kiosk Mario used didn't include user reviews at all because a brick-and-mortar store's team, with little connection to the online store, managed it.

There's a reason the multichannel experience is still poor. Retailers are not yet organized to make multichannel work. Typically, different groups own the different channels, and they have no incentives for cooperation and sometimes even have counterincentives. Even when groups do try to coordinate across channels, they still have difficulty knowing when a shopper crosses from one channel to the next or even measuring how the channels affect each other. For example, in the aforementioned report *Multichannel: In-Store Pickup Gains Importance,* Brian Walker found that "Only 13% of Web managers at multichannel retailers view driving sales to their brick-and-mortar stores as a top priority."

As an experience design discipline, multichannel search is still in its infancy, and investment in it lags actual user behavior. That means there are still no best practices. However, there are early adopters whose experimentations might point the way toward the future.

:: **Home Depot**—Given the nature of the home-improvement business, it was one of the first to recognize that its shoppers frequently do research online and buy from a store. In response, it added extensive sets of how-to guides and product-info sheets to its Web site and were one of the first vendors to let people search online for local, in-store inventories.

:: **Borders**—It has a strong loyalty program that carries across channels. It coordinates email promotions with its online search, so an offer in a promotional email clicks through seamlessly to its Web site. And its in-store kiosks are also closely tied to its online channel, so users can pass information from their online shopping cart to a store.

:: **B&H**—With a loyal audience comprising professionals, B&H was one of the first to launch a smartphone app that helped buyers working in the field to order replacement supplies or research emergency substitutes. Its merchandisers order replacement supplies using the same tools as B&H online customers, helping to coordinate the two.

Multichannel-search experience design is still in its early stages, but we already have a good idea of how to go about it. The key is to understand how the context of each channel sets a user's expectations of its search features. Retail stores need to understand how its customers transition from one channel to the next, and design their search in a way that helps customers complete their tasks, even as they switch channels.

—Pete Bell

MODELS OF THE INFORMATION SEEKING PROCESS

The following excerpt is taken from Chapter 3 of the book *Search User Interfaces*, by Marti Hearst.

When designing new search interfaces, a potentially fruitful strategy is to notice the gaps in support of the information seeking models, or the aspects that are not well-served in current designs. Additionally, many types of information needs are not currently supported well in search algorithms and interfaces. The next breakthrough in search interface design could arise from finding new techniques that better support how people are naturally inclined to conduct their searches.

Information Seeking Models

Major theoretical models of information seeking include:

:: The Standard model

:: The Cognitive model

:: The Dynamic (Berry-picking) model

:: Information seeking in stages

:: Information seeking as a strategic process, including:

    :: Strategies as sequences of tactics

    :: Cost structure analysis and foraging theory

    :: Browsing versus search

    :: Orienteering and other incremental strategies

    :: Sensemaking

Although most of these models are beyond the scope of this excerpt, the following points merit particular consideration when designing for information seeking in ecommerce context.

Dynamic (Berry-Picking) Model

The standard model of the information seeking process contains an underlying assumption that the user's information need is static and the information seeking process is one of successively refining a query until all and only those documents relevant to the original information need have been retrieved. However, observational studies of the information seeking process find that searchers' information needs change as they interact with the search system. Searchers learn about the topic as they scan retrieval results and term suggestions, and formulate new subquestions as previously posed subquestions are answered. Thus, while useful for describing the basics of information access systems, the standard interaction model has been challenged on many fronts (Bates, 1989, O'Day and Jeffries, 1993, Borgman, 1996b, Hendry and Harper, 1997, Cousins, 1997).

continues

MODELS OF THE INFORMATION SEEKING PROCESS *(continued)*

Bates, 1989 proposed the *Berry-Picking* model of information seeking, which has two main points. The first is that, in the process of reading and learning from the information encountered throughout the search process, the searchers' information needs, and consequently their queries, continually shift (see Figure 2.1).

FIGURE 2.1

Berry-Picking
information
seeking process

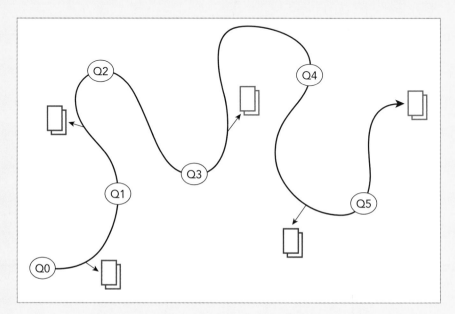

Information encountered at one point in a search may lead in a new, unanticipated direction. The original goal may become partly fulfilled, thus lowering the priority of one goal in favor of another. The second point is that searchers' information needs are not satisfied by a single, final retrieved set of documents, but rather by a series of selections and bits of information found along the way. This is in contrast to the assumption that the main goal of the search process is to hone down the set of retrieved documents into a perfect match of the original information need.

The Berry-Picking model is supported by a number of observational studies (Ellis, 1989, Borgman, 1996b), including that of O'Day and Jeffries, 1993, who interviewed 15 business analysts about their typical search tasks. They found that the information seeking process consisted of a series of interconnected but diverse searches. They also found that search results for a goal tended to trigger new goals, and hence search in new directions, but that the context of the problem and the previous searches was carried from one stage of search to the next. Finally, the main value of the search was found to reside in the accumulated learning and acquisition of information that occurred during the search process, rather than in the final results set.

continues

MODELS OF THE INFORMATION SEEKING PROCESS *(continued)*

Search Strategies as Sequences of Tactics

Bates, 1979 suggests that a searcher's behavior can be characterized by search strategies which in turn are made up of sequences of search *tactics* that she groups into four categories:

Term tactics: Refer to tactics for adjusting words and phrases within the current query. These include making use of term suggestions provided by the search system and selecting terms from an online thesaurus.

Information structure tactics: Are techniques for moving through information or link structures to find sources or information within sources. An example of an information structure tactic for an academic researcher is looking at the research articles that cite a given paper, and following the citation chain. Another example is, when searching within an online collection or Web site, following promising hyperlinks or searching within a category of information—for example, searching only within the technology section of a news Web site.

Query reformulation tactics: Examples include narrowing a given query specification by using more specific terms or gaining more control over the structure of the query by using Boolean operators.

Monitoring tactics: Monitoring refers to keeping track of a situation as it unfolds. Bates discusses several high-level monitoring tactics, including making a cost-benefit analysis of current or anticipated actions (weighing), continuously comparing the current state with the original goal (checking; note the similarity to Norman, 1988's gulf of evaluation), recognizing patterns across common strategies, and recording incomplete paths to enable returning at a later time. Bates also notes that one of the fundamental issues in search strategies is determining when to stop; monitoring tactics can help with this determination.

A question arises as to how a searcher who is monitoring their search knows to stop following one strategy and take up another. O'Day and Jeffries, 1993 defined a number of *triggers* that motivate a seeker to switch from one search strategy to another. These triggers include the following:

- The completion of one step and beginning of the next logical step in a plan
- Encountering something interesting that provides a new way of thinking about a topic of interest, or a new, interesting angle to explain a topic or problem
- Encountering a change or violation of previous expectations that requires further investigation
- Encountering inconsistencies with or gaps in previous understanding that require further investigation

continues

MODELS OF THE INFORMATION SEEKING PROCESS *(continued)*

O'Day and Jeffries also attempted to identify stop conditions—circumstances under which people decided to stop searching. These were fuzzier than the triggers for changing strategies, but they did find that people stopped searching when:

:: There were no more compelling triggers.

:: An "appropriate" amount of material had been found.

:: There was a specific inhibiting factor (such as discovering a market was too small to be worth researching).

These stop conditions can be cast in terms of a cost-benefit analysis, which was subsequently expanded into *information foraging theory* by Pirolli and Card, 1999.

Browsing versus Search as an Information Seeking Strategy

A bedrock psychological result from cognitive science is *recognition over recall*; that is, it is usually easier for a person to recognize something by looking for it than it is to think up how to describe that thing. A familiar example is experienced by learners of a foreign language; it is usually easier to read a sentence in that language than to generate a sentence oneself. This principle applies to information seeking as well. Rather than requiring the searcher to issue keyword queries and scan retrieval results, the system can provide the searcher with structure that characterizes the available information.

A number of theories and frameworks contrast *querying/searching* and *browsing/navigating,* along several dimensions (Belkin et al., 1993, Chang and Rice, 1993, Marchionini, 1995, Waterworth and Chignell, 1991). One way to distinguish searching versus browsing is to note that search queries tend to produce new, ad hoc collections of information that have not been gathered together before, whereas navigation/browsing refers to selecting links or categories that produce predefined groups of information items. Browsing also involves following a chain of links, switching from one view to another, in a sequence of scan and select operations. Browsing can also refer to the casual, mainly undirected exploration of navigation structures. Hertzum and Frokjaer, 1996, phrase the contrast as follows:

"Browsing is a retrieval process where the users navigate through the text database by following links from one piece of text to the next, aiming to utilize two human capabilities ... the greater ability to recognize what is wanted over being able to describe it and ... the ability to skim or perceive at a glance. This allows users to evaluate rapidly rather large amounts of text and determine what is useful."

---

continues

MODELS OF THE INFORMATION SEEKING PROCESS *(continued)*

Aula, 2005 writes the following:

"Considered in cognitive terms, searching is a more analytical and demanding method for locating information than browsing, as it involves several phases, such as planning and executing queries, evaluating the results, and refining the queries, whereas browsing only requires the user to recognize promising-looking links."

Thus, in principle, in many situations it is less mental work to scan a list of hyperlinks and choose the one of interest than it is to think up the appropriate query terms to describe the information need. But there are diminishing returns to scanning links if it takes too long to find the label of interest, and there is always the possibility that the desired information is not visible. That is, browsing works only so long as appropriate links are available, and they have meaningful cues about the underlying information.

For more information see *Search User Interfaces*, by Marti A. Hearst, published by Cambridge University Press, 2009.

REFERENCES

Cooper, Alan. The Inmates are Running the Asylum, SAMS, 1999.

Evans, Patti Freeman. "Profiling the Multichannel Consumer," Forrester Research, July 29, 2009 (updated August 6, 2009).

Hearst, Marti A. *Search User Interfaces*, Cambridge University Press, 2009.

Korzybski, Alfred. "A Non-Aristotelian System and its Necessity for Rigour in Mathematics and Physics," a paper presented before the American Mathematical Society at the New Orleans, Louisiana, meeting of the American Association for the Advancement of Science, December 28, 1931. Reprinted in *Science and Sanity*, 1933, pp. 747–761.

Morville, Peter and Callender, Jeffery. *Search Patterns,* O'Reilly Media, Sebastopol, 2010.

Simon, H. A. "Rational choice and the structure of the environment." *Psychological Review*, Vol. 63 No. 2, pp. 129-138. 1956.

Walker, Brian K. "Multichannel: In-Store Pickup Gains Importance," Forrester Research, February 5, 2009 (updated February 9, 2009).

PERSPECTIVE REFERENCES

[Bates, 1989]
M.J. Bates. The design of browsing and berrypicking techniques for the on-line search interface. *Online Review*, 13(5): pp. 407–431, 1989.

[O'Day and Jeffries, 1993]
Vicki L. O'Day and Robin Jeffries. Orienteering in an information landscape: how information seekers get from here to there. In *Proceedings of the INTERCHI Conference on Human Factors in Computing Systems (CHI'93)*, Amsterdam, April 1993. IOS Press.

[Borgman, 1996b]
C.L. Borgman. Why are online catalogs still hard to use? *Journal of the American Society for Information Science*, 47(7): pp. 493–503, 1996.

[Hendry and Harper, 1997]
D.G. Hendry and D.J. Harper. An informal information-seeking environment. *Journal of the American Society for Information Science*, 48(11): pp. 1036–1048, 1997.

[Cousins, 1997]
S.B. Cousins. "Reification and Affordances in a User Interface for Interacting with Heterogeneous Distributed Applications." PhD thesis, Stanford University, May 1997.

[Ellis, 1989]
D. Ellis. A behavioural model for information retrieval system design. *Journal of Information Science*, 15: pp. 237–247, 1989.

[Bates, 1979]
M.J. Bates. Information search tactics. *Journal of the American Society for Information Science*, 30(4): pp. 205–214, 1979.

[Norman, 1988]
D.A. Norman. *The Psychology of Everyday Things*. Basic Books, New York, 1988.

[Pirolli and Card, 1999]
P. Pirolli and S.K. Card. Information foraging. *Psychological Review*, 106(4): pp. 643–675, 1999.

[Belkin et al., 1993]
N. Belkin, P. G. Marchetti, and C. Cool. Braque – design of an interface to support user interaction in information retrieval. *Information Processing and Management*, 29(3): pp. 325–344, 1993.

[Chang and Rice, 1993]
Shan-Ju Chang and Ronald E. Rice. Browsing: A multidimensional framework. *Annual Review of Information Science and Technology*, 28: pp. 231–276, 1993.

[Marchionini, 1995]
Gary Marchionini. *Information Seeking in Electronic Environments*. Cambridge University Press, 1995.

[Waterworth and Chignell, 1991]
J.A. Waterworth and M.H. Chignell. A model of information exploration. *Hypermedia*, 3(1): pp. 35–58, 1991.

[Hertzum and Frokjaer, 1996]
Morten Hertzum and Erik Frokjaer. Browsing and querying in online documentation: A study of user interfaces and the interaction process. *ACM Transactions on Computer-Human Interaction (ToCHI)*, 3(2): pp. 136–161, 1996.

[Aula, 2005]
A. Aula. "Studying user strategies and characteristics for developing web search interfaces." PhD thesis, University of Tampere, Finland, Ph.D. Dissertation, "Dissertations in Interactive Technology," Number 3, 2005.

CHOOSING THE RIGHT SEARCH RESULTS PAGE LAYOUT

Your layout decisions for search results pages will have tremendous impact on user experience (UX). For instance, choosing the right width for search results is important, and the optimal width for search results may be a great deal narrower than some people using big monitors would believe.

Figure 3.1 shows a Starbucks search results page made virtually unusable through some very poor page layout choices. At a screen resolution of 800 × 600 pixels, most of what you see is the left margin of the layout and a large logo.

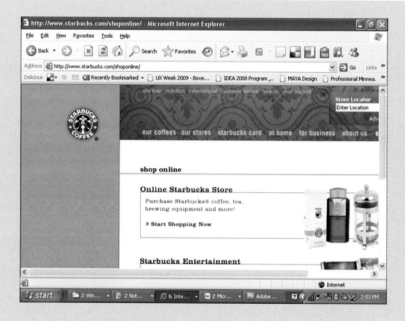

FIGURE 3.1

Starbucks search results at 800 × 600 pixel resolution

Although there are many ways to use horizontal space on search results pages, you can generally distinguish between liquid and fixed-width layouts. Each style of layout offers a unique set of challenges and opportunities.

USING LIQUID LAYOUTS

In a liquid layout, the width of the search results on a Web page shrinks and expands to fill the available space as a user changes the screen resolution or the width of the browser window. Not surprisingly, many top sites such as Google effectively utilize liquid layouts to create top-notch user interfaces that perform well at any screen resolution or window width, as shown in Figure 3.2.

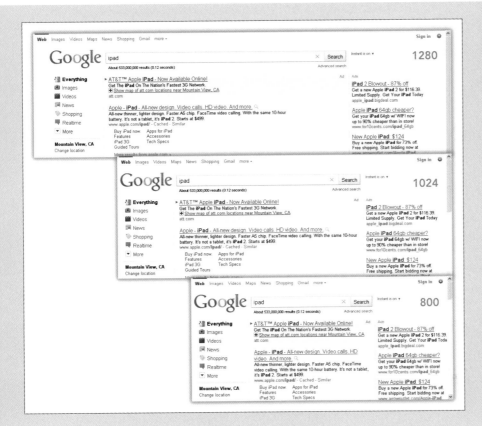

FIGURE 3.2

Google uses a liquid layout

Note—Search results pages receive the majority of the ecommerce site's traffic, and key purchase decisions often happen here. Small improvements in quality of search results pages often have tremendous positive impact on the company's bottom line.

Industry best practice is to format search results using liquid layout and spend the extra time optimizing your HTML and CSS so that search results use all of the available screen space. Unfortunately, few sites follow this recommendation. Many developers argue that liquid layouts are harder to achieve in such a way that the search results maintain visual consistency. The reality is that creating liquid layouts is not that difficult. If you need some help, you can find several great resources for creating liquid layouts at the end of this chapter.

No matter the reason, neglecting this recommendation is unfortunate because this is a good way to generate additional revenues from fairly simple

HTML/CSS modifications. All search results pages on a Web site use the same basic HTML structure and CSS styles, so after you optimize a liquid layout for your search results, all search results pages across your entire site should behave consistently across various screen resolutions and window sizes. Using a liquid layout is the best practice for search results pages.

USING FIXED-WIDTH LAYOUTS

If, for any reason, a liquid layout is not feasible, the other option is to use a fixed-width layout, and the majority of consumer Web sites—including top ecommerce retailers Amazon and Staples—do exactly that. To use a fixed-width layout effectively, you must understand your audience well and be aware of the screen resolutions your customers use. One of the best examples of search results pages that have a fixed-width layout is on Staples.com, pictured in Figure 3.3.

FIGURE 3.3

Staples fixed-width layout

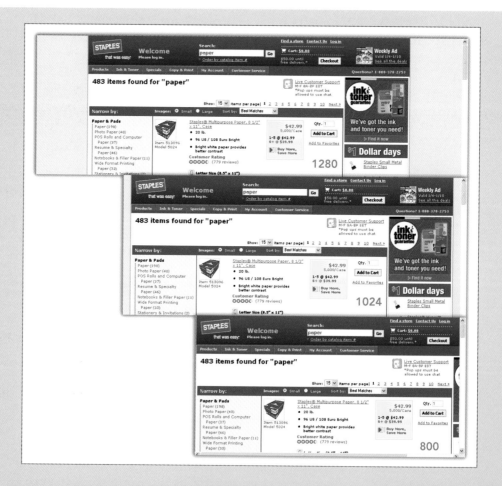

Many Staples.com customers work for large enterprises, which continue to use older desktop monitors or small notebook computers with an 800 × 600 resolution. As a result, search results pages, the hardest working pages on the Staples.com site, are optimized for the lowest common denominator—800 × 600 screens.

In addition to displaying search results, Staples wants to make sure the ads in the column on the right are visible to all customers. With a fairly extensive filtering system found in the left navigation bar, you get one of the narrowest search results spaces on the Web. It's only 560 pixels wide! This, of course, makes it necessary for each search result to comprise several lines to provide sufficient information for users to avoid unnecessary pogosticking—that is, successively clicking links to view item details, finding they're not the right item, and returning to the search results page again and again.

Compare the narrow, fixed-width layout on Staples.com to the much wider search results layout on Amazon.com. As you can see in Figure 3.4, Amazon customers using an 800 × 600 screen have to frequently scroll from one side to another. Even customers using the most popular 1024 × 768 screen resolution have to scroll search results pages from side to side to see entire items!

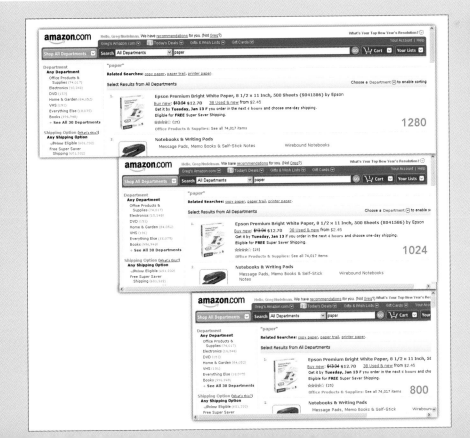

FIGURE 3.4

Amazon requires horizontal scrolling at 1024 × 768

Horizontal scrolling at 1024 × 768 resolution stems from the fact that Amazon .com affords a royal fixed width of 815 pixels for its search results—a whopping 45% more space than Staples! Partly as a result of using such a wide layout, each of the Amazon's individual search result rows comprises fewer lines than Staples, making each individual row slightly thinner.

Why is this significant? At a 1024 × 768 screen resolution, Staples can display only three products per page, whereas Amazon can display four products— 33% more.

Note—Having fewer search results on a page affects both the available showroom floor and the customer's perception of the overall relevance of search results on a site.

Does this mean Amazon is better than Staples? Not necessarily. Both sites offer excellent potential for a great finding experience. However, the page-layout dimensions do indicate that each site's fixed-width layout is optimized for their best customers—those that make the company most profitable. And, simply put, optimizing for your best customers is the best practice for a fixed-width search results page layout.

OPTIMIZING FOR YOUR BEST CUSTOMERS

The take-away here is that only you and your customers can determine the best fixed-width layout for your site. If your site is like most ecommerce or content sites, the overall share of 800 × 600 page views is anywhere between 1% to 5%. Can you ignore these customers and optimize for higher resolutions? That depends on your business model.

If you are a content provider, you may want to ignore that 1%, because you get paid by page impressions. However, if you are a retailer, you may discover that those 800 × 600 page views are coming from large enterprise companies that buy often and in large bulk orders. So, that 1% to 5% of page views may actually be responsible for a whopping 5% to 20% of your sales! Thinking about optimizing revenues, it makes perfect sense that Staples has made its search results narrower, for 800 × 600 screens, whereas Amazon search results pages are wider, for screens with widths of 1280 pixels and above. Presumably, Amazon has discovered that its biggest profits come from affluent consumers who have wider screens with higher resolutions.

Note—It's up to you what fixed-width layout you choose, but make sure the metric you use fits your revenue model and optimize for your most profitable customer base. Of course, you can alternatively do what Google does and choose to invest in a good liquid layout that is optimized at every screen resolution that is important for your customers.

HANDLING MARGINS IN FIXED-WIDTH LAYOUTS

When choosing a page layout, you need to ensure your pages behave gracefully on all popular screen widths. Liquid layouts like the one shown in Figure 3.2 are usually left aligned and handle extra width gracefully by increasing the white space between columns or increasing the width of the primary column on a page. Fixed-width layouts, on the other hand, are generally centered and absorb any extra space by adding neutral margins or panels at the left and right of a page's fixed-width main content area.

For a usable, fixed-width search results layout, there are only two optimal choices: centered or left aligned. A centered layout, like the one found on Staples. com, divides the extra space at the margins in half, as shown in Figure 3.3. In contrast, sites with left-aligned, fixed-width layouts—such as the StubHub Web site pictured in Figure 3.5—put all the extra space on the right side of the screen.

At first glance, a left-aligned, fixed-width page layout might seem like a logical choice. The search results start at the upper left on each page, which seems desirable, because in the West, you read from the upper left to the lower right. However, in fixed-width layouts, the margin on the right quickly becomes disproportionately large in comparison to the rest of the page.

In my field research, I've observed people's reactions to the large, empty spaces that appear on the right in fixed-width layouts. All that space devoid of content causes what I can describe only as pixel agoraphobia. When that space first opens up, people usually grimace and attempt to reduce the width of the window to remove some of the empty space. Most Windows users who have maximized their browser window do this by clicking the Restore Down button on the window title bar. This sometimes results in a window size too small for a site, so users must then adjust the window size manually.

FIGURE 3.5

StubHub has a single, large, white margin on the right

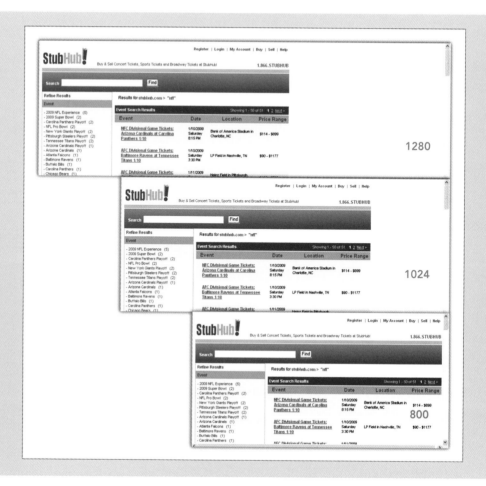

Note—When your customers are busy fiddling with the width of the browser window, they're not shopping or looking at ads on your site. They're usually becoming more and more irritated—and that's before they've even begun interacting with your Web site's fabulous functionality!

In contrast, a centered layout—especially one that uses a neutral or darker color for its margins or side panels—divides the blank space into two halves, thus reducing the effect of pixel agoraphobia. So, if you insist on using a fixed-width layout, opt for a centered layout for your search results pages, with darker or neutral-colored side panels, especially if a significant percentage of your customers have wide, high-resolution screens.

REFERENCES

Budd, Andy. *CSS Mastery: Advanced Web Standards Solutions*. London: Friends of ED, 2006.

Griffiths, Patrick. "Elastic Design." *HtmlDog*, January 2003. Retrieved March 6, 2009.

Koblentz, Thierry. "One Clean HTML Markup, Many Layouts." *TKJDesign*, October 2005. Retrieved March 6, 2009.

Olsson, Tommy. "Relatively Absolute." *AutisticCuckoo*, December 2004. Retrieved March 6, 2009.

Shea, Dave. *The Zen of CSS Design: Visual Enlightenment for the Web*. Berkeley: Peachpit Press, 2005.

Shea, Dave. *Zen Garden*. Retrieved March 6, 2009.

Weakley, Russ. "Liquid Layouts the Easy Way." *MaxDesign*, December 2003. Retrieved March 6, 2009.

BALANCING POGOSTICKING AND PAGE RELEVANCE

When designing the data and layout for search results pages, the design strategy boils down to a single key principle: Show the greatest number of results possible, without increasing pogosticking. In other words, the challenge is finding the right balance between the following:

:: Provide enough information in individual search results, so customers can make informed decisions about whether to view product detail pages—that is, click product links.

:: Provide enough relevant search results on each page of results to warrant further exploration of the site.

On the one hand, if your search results do not provide enough summary product information, you force customers to jump to individual product detail pages and then cycle back and forth between product detail and search results pages, like a child bouncing on a pogo stick. On the other hand, if you do not provide enough information, customers may not find relevant results. The tension between these two opposing design forces is what makes the problem of creating search user interfaces so interesting.

POGOSTICKING IS NO FUN

Although pogosticking may sound like a fun activity, it is usually counterproductive to your customers' finding the content and products they need. As usability expert Jared Spool discovered in his many studies of search results gallery pages:

"In our studies of ecommerce sites, for example, 66% of all purchases happened without any pogosticking at all—the users purchased the first selection they chose from the gallery two-thirds of the time. And when users did pogostick, the more they did so, the less they purchased. We've found this extends to non-ecommerce sites as well: Our studies show that users who don't pogostick find their target content 55% of the time, whereas those who do pogostick end up only succeeding 11% of the time."

—JARED SPOOL

We can define *Pogosticking Score* as the average number of product detail pages viewed during each search—that is:

```
Pogosticking Score = (# detail page views - # detail page views from
search engines) / # of search queries
```

Now look at a real-life example to see how damaging pogosticking can be. A customer is looking for Roger Ebert's review of a particular Japanese film. Searching by director's last name, *Miyazaki*, yields no results. (No results condition was covered in detail in Chapter 1.) Fortunately, the customer remembers that the film's title has the word *away* in it. Figure 4.1 shows the search results for the word *away* on RogerEbert.com.

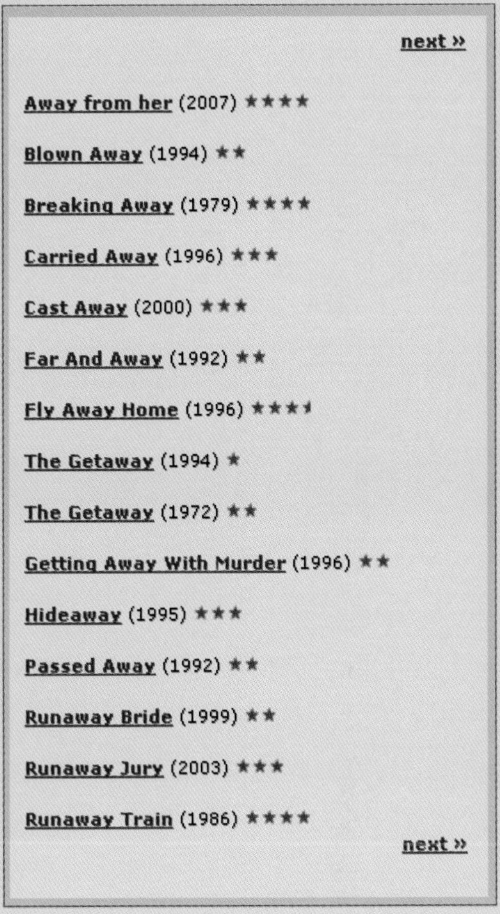

next »

Away from her (2007) ★★★★

Blown Away (1994) ★★

Breaking Away (1979) ★★★★

Carried Away (1996) ★★★

Cast Away (2000) ★★★

Far And Away (1992) ★★

Fly Away Home (1996) ★★★⁴

The Getaway (1994) ★

The Getaway (1972) ★★

Getting Away With Murder (1996) ★★

Hideaway (1995) ★★★

Passed Away (1992) ★★

Runaway Bride (1999) ★★

Runaway Jury (2003) ★★★

Runaway Train (1986) ★★★★

next »

FIGURE 4.1

Can you tell which film is Miyazaki's masterpiece?

Although the customer decides "Getting Away With Murder" is probably not the film he's looking for, "Carried Away," "Far And Away," "Fly Away Home," "Hideaway," and about ten other links all present possibilities. One choice looks as good as another, because this page provides only three bits of data: title, Ebert's rating, and the year a film was released. Certainly, this is not enough information to make an informed decision. Then, he notices the next **»** links and quickly realizes that there are potentially many similarly structured results pages to browse. The next **»** links actually prove helpful in making his decision: He is now absolutely sure searching on this site will be a total waste of his time. So, he heads over to Netflix, shown in Figure 4.2, to search instead.

FIGURE 4.2

Netflix provides good summary information in search results

Flushed Away
(2006) PG
In this lively comedy from DreamWorks Animation and Aardman Features (Wallace & Gromit), London high-society mouse Roddy (voiced by Hugh Jackman) is flushed down the toilet by Syd, a common sewer rat. Hang on for a madcap adventure deep in the bowels of Ratropolis, where Roddy meets the resourceful Rita (Kate Winslet), the rodent-hating Toad (Ian McKellen) and his faithful thugs Spike and Whitey (Andy Serkis and Bill Nighy).
Add
★★★★☆

Spirited Away
Sen to Chihiro no kamikakushi
(2001) PG
Adapted from the Japanese original, director Hayao Miyazaki's adventure tale won the Best Animated Feature Oscar for its story of 10-year-old Chihiro (voiced by Rumi Hiragi). During her family's move to the suburbs, Chihiro wanders into a magical world where a witch rules -- and those who disobey her are turned into animals. When her parents are turned into pigs, Chihiro must find a way to help them return to their human form.
Add
☆☆☆☆☆

Breaking Away
(1979) PG
After graduating from high school, Dave Stohler (Dennis Christopher) dreams of becoming a champion bicyclist. Posing as an exchange student to mask his working-class roots, he frustrates his parents (Paul Dooley and Barbara Barrie) and charms a local college girl (Robyn Douglass). Peter Yates's Oscar-winning coming-of-age drama culminates when Dave gets a chance to leave his past behind and race against the Italian riders he worships.
Add
★★★★☆
Available Formats: DVD and also available to watch instantly with Netflix unlimited plans. Learn more >

Swept Away
Travolti da un insolito destino nell'azzurro mare d'Agosto
(1974) R

On Netflix, the customer can effortlessly pick out the right film in the search results because it includes a beautiful picture in animé style. Notice, however, that even if the search results had no pictures, he would could still find the right result. He can find all the information he needs to correctly identify the particular movie for which he is looking by quickly scanning the film's short description—which includes keywords such as *Japanese* and *director Hayao Miyazaki*, and its *PG* rating. Thus, he's spared from having to pogostick between search results pages and multiple product detail pages.

OVERLY RICH SEARCH RESULTS CAN BE UNHEALTHY FOR YOUR SITE

There are no general guidelines about what summary information your customers might actually need in search results or how much information is healthy for your particular application. More summary information in each result is generally better because this decreases pogosticking. However, it's possible to include too much information. It's a balancing act. Take a look at the Expedia hotel search results in Figure 4.3.

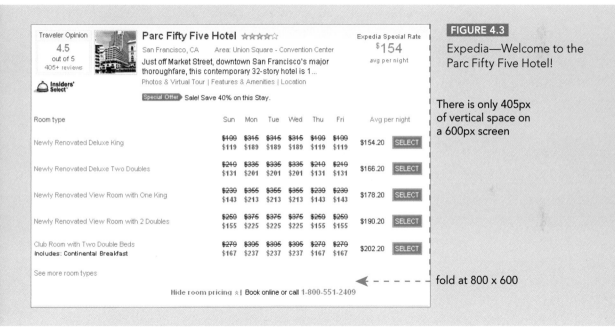

FIGURE 4.3

Expedia—Welcome to the Parc Fifty Five Hotel!

There is only 405px of vertical space on a 600px screen

fold at 800 x 600

At an 800 × 600-pixel screen resolution, Expedia customers can see *only a part of one* magnificent search result for the Parc Fifty Five Hotel. That's right! Some customers will have to scroll just to see one entire search result! This is an extreme case of overly rich information in search results.

In general, displaying a smaller number of search results on each results page impacts your site's user experience (UX) in two critical ways:

:: Fewer products on each page of results expose less of your site's inventory to customers, at a given resolution.

:: Results pages that show fewer products are less likely to be relevant to customers.

To understand this issue better, contrast the Expedia search result with the Orbitz search results shown in Figure 4.4.

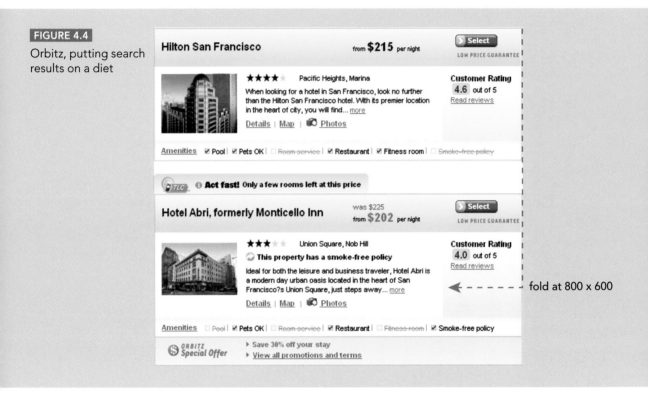

FIGURE 4.4

Orbitz, putting search results on a diet

fold at 800 x 600

Placing more products on each search results page requires using less screen real estate for each result. On 800 × 600-pixel resolution screens, Orbitz shows almost two full search results, whereas Expedia customers can barely see a single result. This means the Orbitz showroom floor has approximately 200% the capacity of that found on Expedia.

The number of search results on a page is also significant from the standpoint of the overall page relevancy. Often, business people and designers alike forget that their site is not the only site on the Web, and consumers have many choices. Your customers continuously collect and evaluate your Web site's information scent—the cues your site gives them to estimate how much useful information they are likely to get on a given path. When the information scent keeps getting stronger, people continue exploring. But when they no longer expect to find useful additional information they are interested in, your customers can be gone, just like that. But can't users just scroll down to what's relevant?

It is true that they *can*.

Note—Research shows people actually have no problem scrolling. However, people will scroll only if they feel they have a hope of finding something relevant to them lower on the page.

In a search world dominated by Google, this hope quickly diminishes if what customers see on the page above the fold is not relevant. There is a strong mental model at work here: The most relevant stuff is at the top, and the further down you go, the less relevant the content is likely to be.

For example, if a customer looks for a historic, boutique bed-and-breakfast in San Francisco, she is not likely to find an Expedia page dominated by the Parc Fifty Five Hotel particularly relevant. In contrast, Orbitz shows two results, so that *doubles* the chances that one of those results might be the historic boutique jewel the customer is looking for. No search engine is perfect at understanding customers' desires, which they often express in vague and over-generalized terms. But, by exposing a greater number of search results on a page, you maximize the chances for your customers to quickly find something of relevance and either make a purchase right away or continue scrolling. Conversely, if you show only a few results and force your customers to scroll to find something relevant, you are risking their giving up after a quick glance and going somewhere else.

OPTIMIZE RESULTS FOR YOUR BUSINESS AND YOUR CUSTOMERS

For individual search results, the basic design tension is between two opposing forces:

:: How much summary information would enable your customers to make the right decision without pogosticking?

:: How many search results can you show on a single page to capture the interest of your customers?

Include *too little* summary information, and you get pogosticking. Include *too much* summary information, and customers get too few results—and perhaps no relevant results at all.

Note—Although important, pogosticking is but one attribute of the search experience. Peter Stahl describes many other useful metrics such as Interactive Density and Jack-in-the-Boxiness in his perspective at the end of this chapter.

Most often, the best solution lies somewhere in the middle between these two extremes. However, it is possible that practical factors that are unique to your Web site may complicate the matter still further. For instance, the absence of pogosticking is not the only determinant of successful search results. Your search results may get an excellent, low pogosticking score, but you still might not sell anything because customers don't find your search results relevant. What's even more incredible is that some Web applications succeed despite having high pogosticking scores. As long as people become emotionally engaged with your search results and product detail pages load reasonably quickly, they don't mind picking up and trying on individual items.

On the other hand, detailed summary results, such as those from Expedia, seem cumbersome on 800×600 screens. But what if I told you that all Expedia customers care deeply about the price per room per diem—perhaps because of corporate travel policies? Do those Expedia results still seem too rich? What if I also told you that all Expedia customers use 1920×1200-pixel resolution screens? Suddenly, the design of the search results pages on Expedia begins to make a lot of sense.

Now, I don't actually claim to know anything about Expedia customers. The point I am trying to make is that only your customers can tell you what level of summary information is appropriate for your search results. You have to think through all the use cases and then experiment with including or excluding various pieces of information in the search results to see how the changes impact your completion metrics, click-through behavior, and pogosticking score.

Search has always been a field that was traditionally dominated by hard-core metrics and marketing research. Those are great methodologies that yield reliable results. However, qualitative research data and, in particular, field research, combined with metrics, can give your design team a wealth of insight about your customers' pain-points and a much-needed fresh look at the problem and possible creative solutions. When it comes to thinking out of the box, field research is simply the best tool you have.

CONDUCTING FIELD RESEARCH

Field research—observing your customers in their "natural habitat"—is a rich subject, well beyond the scope of this book. To conduct field research it pays to get professionally trained usability researchers who will collect maximum data quickly from the fewest possible subjects and help you make sense of your findings, thereby putting your research budget to best possible use. However, oftentimes simply going out to the place where the customers typically conduct their searches, such as their home or office, and watching your customers use yours or your competitor's system (while muttering choice curse words) can be invaluable. While you watch, it helps to make sure your customers are shopping for items they actually intend to buy—this makes peoples' behaviors more realistic. Be sure to ask your research subjects to think out loud and *show* you what they mean. Remember that you can get extra information by asking non-leading clarifying questions after the participants complete their task.

There are lots of fantastic books that can serve as a great introduction to field research:

- *Observing the User Experience: A Practitioner's Guide to User Research* by Mike Kuniavsky
- *Contextual Design: Defining Customer-Centered Systems* by Hugh Beyer and Karen Holtzblatt
- *Rocket Surgery Made Easy: The Do-It-Yourself Guide to Finding and Fixing Usability Problems* by Steve Krug

People working for large corporate design teams or well-funded startups are often well insulated from customers who browse the Web on 12-inch notebook monitors, with 800 × 600-pixel resolutions, and their font size turned way up. Try always to be mindful of your customers' hardware requirements and how many of your search results might actually show up on their screens.

When deciding what summary information to include, keep in mind this key design principle: Show the greatest number of search results possible, without increasing pogosticking. Always take the time to optimize your search results pages for your business and your customers' unique goals and needs. Your customers will make it well worth your time and effort.

THE "FEEL" OF SEARCHING

When people talk about the "look and feel" of a user experience, they usually mean just the "look"—the colors, shapes, typography, and other visual design elements. Of course "look" is an important aspect of user experience. But what about "feel"? What is that?

At a literal level, feel is the tactile sensation of operating a system: the way your finger slides across the glass surface of a touch screen, how you move your hand from mouse to keyboard and back, the cramp you get from holding down the mouse button as you drag something to just ... the ... right ... spot.

But "feel" can also describe how systems *invite and respond to* physical input. A set of extra-large buttons and sliders onscreen feels like a children's toy. Digital physics, such as the realistic deceleration of scrolling on mobile devices, feels natural. A Web page filled with menus and callouts that pop up as you mouse over them feels like a minefield of jack-in-the-boxes.

Josh Damon Williams and I have developed the beginnings of a vocabulary to describe feel: a collection of "feel attributes." Some of these can be measured objectively, for example by dividing the number of interactive elements by the size of a page or screen. Others are more subjective, such as how often the governing metaphor or paradigm changes as users move through an experience. Here are a few feel attributes:

Objective

:: **Dimensions (height, width)**—The area users have to work in can be cramped or expansive

:: **Number of interactive elements**—How many hyperlinks, scrollbars, buttons, text fields there are

:: **Interactive density**—A simple formula: Number of interactive elements dimensions

:: **Jack-in-the-boxiness**— Number of interactive elements ÷ dimensions

Semi-objective

:: **Number of syntactic actions in a task**—How many clicks, taps, key presses, mouse targetings, and so on are required to complete a task.

:: **Reloadiness**—How frequently users encounter latencies, and how long they have to wait. For Web pages, how often they reload.

:: **Tool-switchiness**—How much users must move from mouse to keyboard and back. On touchscreens, how much users must enter and exit typing mode.

:: **Flatness/bumpiness**—Flat = uses only basic interactions. Bumpy = uses advanced techniques.

:: **Responsiveness**—The amount (or lack) of pop-up layers, animation, video, mouse-over responses, device vibration, and audio, as opposed to more traditional, unchanging display.

Subjective

:: **Fickleness**—How often the governing metaphor or paradigm changes as users move through an experience

:: **Simplicity/complexity**—The degree to which the experience feels simple to grasp and operate, or is subtle and complex

:: **Forgiveness**—The degree to which the experience invites exploration and guessing, or penalizes mistakes

:: **Grooviness**—How much the experience allows users to get into a groove, forgetting about the mechanics of operating the system and becoming absorbed in the experience itself

:: **Wordiness**—How much text users must read

:: **Cognitive load**—How much users must think

Using these measures (and any others you care to invent), it's possible to characterize user experiences in a way that allows comparisons and goal-setting. You can measure whether an iteration of a design feels denser, flatter, or wordier than a previous one, and whether that's enough to satisfy your users' needs.

Most important, the measures give designers the vocabulary they need to have productive conversations about what the feel of their experience is and should be. If it's true that nothing is actually real until there are words to describe it, then these measures make "feel" real.

—PETER STAHL

REFERENCES

Hotchkiss, Gord. "Tales of Pogo Sticks, Bouncy SERPs, and Sticky Pages." *Enquiro Full Service Search Engine Marketing,* September 7, 2006. Retrieved February 20, 2009.

Schwartz, Tal. "ClickTale Scrolling Research Report V2.0." *ClickTale,* October 5, 2007. Retrieved February 20, 2009.

Spool, Jared. "Galleries: The Hardest Working Page on Your Site." *UIE Brain Sparks,* November 30, 2005. Retrieved February 20, 2009.

Spool, Jared. "Utilizing the Cut-off Look to Encourage Users To Scroll." *UIE Brain Sparks,* August 2, 2006. Retrieved February 20, 2009.

Tarquini, Milissa. "Blasting the Myth of the Fold." *Boxes And Arrows,* July 24, 2007. Retrieved February 20, 2009.

CHAPTER 5

MAKING $10,000 A PIXEL:
Optimizing Thumbnail Images in Search Results

The old adage *a picture is worth a thousand words* rings just as true when referring to search results. To make your search results more efficient to use, more
relevant, and more attractive, images reign supreme. Nothing else on your
search results pages can come close to offering the same potential as thumbnail
images for dramatically increasing your conversion rates and revenues.

Although your Web site's image requirements are likely unique, you might
encounter some common pitfalls when using images in your search results. The
good news is that you can easily avoid most of these mistakes with awareness
and a little foresight.

A PICTURE IS WORTH A THOUSAND WORDS

Why do most Web sites use thumbnail images in search results? Following are
two good reasons:

:: Helping users identify relevant search results

:: Reducing pogosticking—that is, customers' bouncing back and forth
between search results and the items at their links' destinations

Research consistently shows that well-crafted images make excellent use of
the limited screen real estate on search results pages and play a crucial role in
providing the information scent people need to navigate search results effectively. Simply put, pictures sell content.

Are thumbnail images in search results appropriate for every Web application? Not by a long shot! The majority of the information on the Web is still
text, and for text-based pages, it's better to display search results as text-only
summaries or keyword metadata. Some search results are just so varied that
it's difficult to predict whether a thumbnail image would be appropriate—as
for the majority of the results retrieved by the Google search. However, if good
thumbnail images would better communicate your search results' relevance or
make navigation easier, they're worth including.

When including thumbnail images in search results, you have two layout
choices:

:: **List view**—Flush left at the beginning of each search result

:: **Gallery view**—Two or more images appearing side-by-side in each row on
a page

Although there are guidelines that are specific to each image layout, general guidelines include the following:

:: Make thumbnail images large and informative.

:: Include supporting text.

:: Go easy on the borders.

:: Maintain focus on the image content.

:: Help customers judge an item's actual size.

:: Be creative in choosing informative images.

Let's explore each of these best practices in more detail.

MAKE THUMBNAIL IMAGES LARGE AND INFORMATIVE

When search results pages feature thumbnail images, the key to their success is making sure the images are big enough to carry sufficient detail so that customers can easily tell items apart. Unfortunately, most images on search results pages are too small.

Book covers and the packaging for CDs and DVDs serve an important promotional role in that they help people to easily distinguish between items. In addition to their title and the name of the author or artist, they usually carry rich visual details denoting the genre, intended audience, and content. To take full advantage of such rich image content when displaying image-based search results, you need to choose an image size that's big enough to get the job done. On IMDb, the images shown in Figure 5.1 are too small for anyone to distinguish between "Spirited Away" and "Fly Away Home." People can't reliably tell these movies apart.

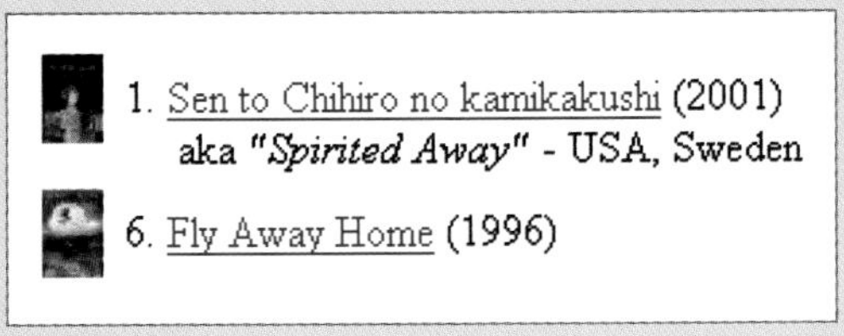

 1. Sen to Chihiro no kamikakushi (2001)
   aka "Spirited Away" - USA, Sweden

 6. Fly Away Home (1996)

FIGURE 5.1

IMDb images are too small

Contrast the small images on IMDb with the big images on Netflix. In Figure 5.2, can you tell which movie is about birds and which is in the style of a Japanese anime? Yes!

FIGURE 5.2

Netflix provides large images to help identify movies easily

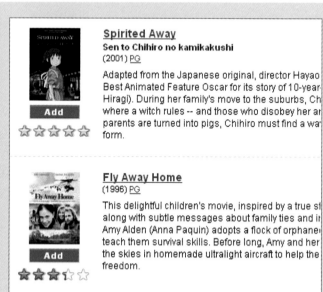

If the items you show in search results are fairly large or have a lot of detail, you must make your images even larger. Unfortunately, most sites do exactly the opposite. Looking at Figure 5.3, you can guess, with some degree of certainty, that IronPlanet.com sells heavy industrial equipment.

FIGURE 5.3

Aggregate Screen versus Terex Telehandler

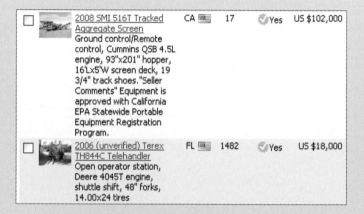

However, based on these pictures, can you tell what an Aggregate Screen is or how you might use one in your building project? Probably not. Then, what about a Terex Telehandler? Small images make it impossible to tell the two machines apart, much less enable customers to guess their functions.

Small thumbnail images are not merely impractical.

Note—My research experience indicates that small thumbnail images are actively harmful to your customers' search experience and possibly your bottom line.

If your images are too small, people waste a lot of time squinting and staring at the page, trying to squeeze some information out of the images. Ultimately, they fail to do so and end up clicking images anyway, at which point they realize they've clicked the wrong items. So, the consequence of overly small images is pogosticking, which wastes customers' time, reduces their success in finding what they need, and on an ecommerce site, reduces revenues. Small images, therefore, act like false advertisements, teasing and frustrating your customers with what look like the right items but actually are nothing of the sort.

INCLUDE SUPPORTING TEXT

In some cases, thumbnail images contain the bulk of items' information scent, so it makes perfect sense to use a gallery design like the one on Etsy. Just make sure you show enough supporting text to ensure customers can make sense of what a thumbnail image portrays. As shown in Figure 5.4, without the item's complete title, you can't tell whether Etsy is selling a photo, framed graffiti, or the entire scrumptious caboose.

Urban Color no.1 - ...
NestaHome $18.00

graffiti train car ...
voodooointhehills $3.00

FIGURE 5.4

What's for sale at Etsy—graffiti or caboose?

To make matters even worse, titles sometimes seem to get cut off randomly. Although including an ellipsis at the end of any cut-off text is a widely recognized best practice, it can eat up space that might show two or three more characters of a title instead. As shown in the redesign in Figure 5.5, good visual design can help improve the appearance of text when screen real estate is limited.

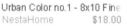

FIGURE 5.5

Fading out a title

Urban Color no.1 - 8x10 Fine   graffiti train car photo 8x10 pr
NestaHome $18.00   voodoointhehills $3.00

In this redesign, not only is the title text extended all the way across the bottom of each photo, a fade-out effect is used instead of an ellipsis at the end of the text to indicate that the title's full text is not visible, while making full use of the space. If a title exceeds a certain character count and must be cut off, you can easily achieve this fade-out effect by assigning different styles to the last two or three letters of the title, using progressively lighter colors for successive characters. The fade-out effect is certainly not appropriate for every Web site; however, it can be useful, particularly in tight spaces where every letter counts. For example, it can be used for data-intensive mobile applications that need to deliver the content that has to match a corresponding Web application.

Note—Although fade out is a pretty good technique, you can't always count on visual design alone to bail you out. If the text of titles in your search results is consistently getting cut off, it might be time to consider an interaction design solution.

For example, artists posting their items on Etsy could be alerted when they exceed a certain character count. Alternatively, it might be appropriate to have a short title specifically for search results and an additional, longer description field for display on item detail pages. Finally, if a single line of text does not provide enough information, search results can show several lines of text, as necessary.

GO EASY ON THE BORDERS

Most business people and designers have figured out that images with heavy borders do not convert as well as those surrounded by simple white space. Actually, I was hard pressed to find a good example of thumbnail images with heavy borders—though they were quite common until a few years ago.

You can remove borders completely as a best practice, using only white space to separate items on search results pages. If you absolutely must have thumbnail borders, in the words of novelist Jennifer Stone, "Go easy, and if you can't go easy, go as easy as you can." As data visualization expert Edward Tufte has so eloquently advocated:

"Gray grids almost always work well and, with a delicate line, may promote more accurate data reading and reconstruction than a heavy grid. Dark grid lines are chartjunk... [Ideally, information should be] transparently organized by an implicit typographical grid, defined simply by the absence of type."

If you do use borders, be sure to center your images—both horizontally and vertically—within them. Otherwise, you might end up with a strange effect like that shown in Figure 5.6, which shows Nordstrom search results for shoes. On this page, each shoe appears to be perching on the bottom edge of its box, like a bird on a windowsill. If the designers simply took away the borders, there would be no distracting perching effect.

FIGURE 5.6

Perched shoes on Nordstrom

KEEP THE FOCUS ON THE IMAGE CONTENT

When showing thumbnail images on search results pages, strive to provide an actual, detailed picture of each item, and keep the images simple. Although a small, light-gray drop shadow might be appropriate, it's usually best to ignore the temptation to add funky backgrounds and distracting visual effects.

Note—In search results, the primary goal of thumbnail images is to provide clear pictures of the items, so customers can determine which item to click. Anything that does not contribute to their success in reaching this goal simply does not belong in a thumbnail image.

Figure 5.7 shows two examples of thumbnail images from ecommerce sites. On the left, an image from JCPenney's Gift.com has a noisy background that is highly distracting and will likely prevent shoppers from being able to compare Fit Flops with other items effectively. On the other hand, the image from REI, on the right, provides a powerful information scent with unadorned, high-quality images of a shoe shown at different angles. It's hard to believe both thumbnails occupy virtually the same amount of screen real estate!

FIGURE 5.7

Fit Flops versus NorthFace
Ultra Gore-Tex XCR

Calorie Burning Sandals: Fit
Flops
See 5 more like this

The North Face Ultra 104
Gore-Tex XCR Trail-Running
Shoes - Men's
Price: $110.00
(15 Reviews)
☐ compare

When REI took these pictures, they took the extra trouble to turn one of the shoes in such a way as to show its sole. This image is a great example of the effective use of real estate to improve an item's appeal. As usability expert Jared Spool reported in his lecture at the 2007 Computer-Human Interaction Society Symposium, high-performance athletic shoes sell better if the image shows the sole of the shoe and the traditional side view. If it helps lead your customers to the right item, provide multiple views of each item if the image real estate allows it.

HELP CUSTOMERS TO JUDGE AN ITEM'S ACTUAL SIZE

It is helpful to depict an item in a way that indicates its actual size. Many people might struggle with the purchase of a digital gadget online because they are looking for something small that can fit in their pocket but can't judge size from the images. Unfortunately, most etailers do not make it easy to determine the size of gadgets based on their thumbnail pictures. For example, the search results from Best Buy, shown in Figure 5.8, feature two digital cameras of completely different sizes, but the two pictures do not convey this information.

FIGURE 5.8

Which camera is bigger?

Looking at the search results, you cannot tell that the camera on the right would easily fit in a jeans pocket, but the one on the left would barely fit in a large purse!

Note—Showing pictures of many similar-looking electronic gadgets without indicating their size tends to confuse people, who often walk away from the purchase saying, "These all look the same. I guess I just need to go to the store to hold them in my hand before I can decide."

Fortunately, there is an easy way to solve this problem. In thumbnail images of products for which size does matter, show an item that has a known size—such as a coin, a dollar bill, or a soft drink can—next to each item to make size comparisons easy. This should help remove any confusion your customers might have about size and help them make the right purchase.

BE CREATIVE IN CHOOSING INFORMATIVE IMAGES

Sometimes, an actual image of an item is just not that helpful. Look at the bags of coffee beans, for example, as shown on the Peet's Coffee & Tea search results page in Figure 5.9. Can you spot the difference between Sumatra and French roast? Probably not.

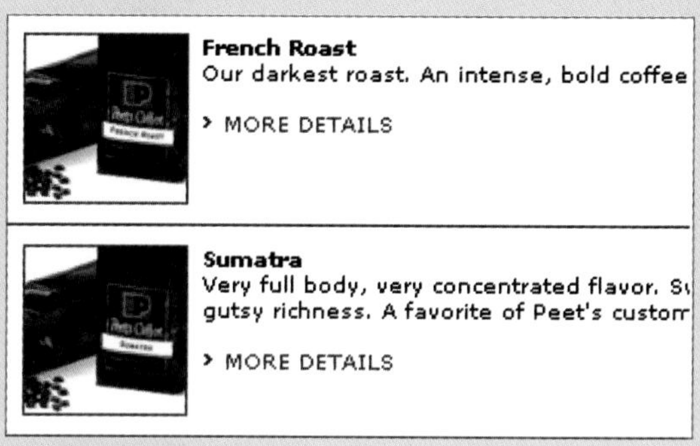

FIGURE 5.9

Can you tell the difference?

French Roast
Our darkest roast. An intense, bold coffee

> MORE DETAILS

Sumatra
Very full body, very concentrated flavor. S(
gutsy richness. A favorite of Peet's custom

> MORE DETAILS

Each picture showing a generic coffee bean bag reveals hardly anything about the products. In this case, a map of a coffee-growing region, a close-up of a single bean, or even a thumbnail-sized bar graph of flavors, sweetness, color, and acidity might help to reduce the amount of navigation it takes to find the right item. So, if literal images don't work, go ahead—get creative!

If you give thumbnail images the attention they deserve and optimize them in all the ways this chapter has suggested, your images can be worth $10,000 a pixel—or at the very least, a thousand words!

REFERENCES

Armitage, Linda H. and Peter G.B Enser. "Analysis of User Need in Image Archives." *Journal of Information Science*, Volume 23, Number 4, 1997.

Fogarty, James, Desney Tan, Ashish Kapoor, and Simon Winder. "CueFlik: Interactive Concept Learning in Image Search." Proceedings of the SIGCHI Conference on Human Factors in Computing Systems CHI 2008, Florence, Italy, 2008.

Hu, Jianying and Amit Bagga. "Categorizing Images in Web Documents." *IEEE MultiMedia*, Volume 11, Issue 1, January–March 2004.

Lam, Heidi and Patrick Baudisch. "Summary Thumbnails: Readable Overviews for Small Screen Web Browsers." Proceedings of the SIGCHI Conference on Human Factors in Computing Systems CHI 2005, Portland, OR, USA, 2005.

Maekawa, Takuya, Takahiro Hara, and Shojiro Nishio. "Image Classification for Mobile Web Browsing." Proceedings of WWW 2006, Edinburgh, Scotland, 2006.

Miller, Andrew D. and W. Keith Edwards. "Give and Take: A Study of Consumer Photo-Sharing Culture and Practice." Proceedings of the SIGCHI Conference on Human Factors in Computing Systems CHI 2007, San Jose, CA, USA 2007.

Tufte, Edward. *Envisioning Information*. Graphics Press, Cheshire, Connecticut, 1990.

Vaughan, Misha W. and Marc L. Resnick. "Best Practices and Future Visions for Search User Interfaces." *Journal of the American Society for Information Science and Technology*, Volume 57, Number 6, April 2006.

Woodruff, Allison, Andrew Faulring, Ruth Rosenholtz, Julie Morrison, and Peter Pirolli. "Using Thumbnails to Search the Web." Proceedings of the SIGCHI Conference on Human Factors in Computing Systems CHI 2001, The Hague, The Netherlands, 2001.

Woodruff, Allison, Ruth Rosenholtz, Julie B. Morrison, Andrew Faulring, and Peter Pirolli. "A Comparison of the Use of Text Summaries, Plain Thumbnails, and Enhanced Thumbnails for Web Search Tasks." *Journal of the American Society for Information Science and Technology*, Volume 53, Number 2, January 2002.

CHAPTER 6

BEST PRACTICES FOR ADS IN SEARCH RESULTS

COAUTHORED WITH FRANK GUO

Conflicting demands have left UX professionals concluding online advertising is a necessary evil. Customers frequently go out of their way to say they detest ads, whereas marketers always seem to try their hardest to stuff as many of them as they can on every page of a Web site, including the search results page. This leaves many UX design professionals stuck trying to balance the ad equation—and frequently failing to fully satisfy either customers or marketers. This chapter describes real-world strategies for successfully integrating ads into your search results.

DON'T KILL YOUR GOLDEN GOOSE

Online advertising is increasingly seen as a legitimate way to boost revenues on an ecommerce site—in part, because of the currently rocky economy. Every penny counts, and every stream of potential revenue demands careful consideration. However, research and experience show that, for an online business to succeed and thrive, it is important to balance any temptation to boost short-term revenues through advertising with the long-term goals of boosting UX, customer loyalty, and brand attributes. If you are not careful, trying to squeeze out a few more eggs can kill your golden goose.

However, following a few simple guidelines—while listening carefully to your customers—can help your business make money with ads, without compromising either long-term customer loyalty or your brand image.

INTEGRATE AD DISPLAYS WITH THE REST OF YOUR SITE

In recent years, Google has emerged as the Web's leading supplier of ads. Indeed, Google AdSense makes it easy—and often profitable—for you to sign up and host ads on your Web site. Most of the time, the ad content is fairly well targeted, so many retailers, bloggers, and developers of social networking sites have taken advantage of the opportunity to boost revenue through this service. Unfortunately, few have made the effort to customize the boxed ads to make them look like the rest of their site. Figure 6.1 shows the social networking site Fishing.net, which carries Google ads just as they come out-of-the-box, without any customization.

FIGURE 6.1

On Fishing.net, Google ads have no customization

Neglecting to customize third-party ads is, of course, easier, but there are consequences to this approach:

:: Customers frequently perceive your entire site as cluttered and disorganized.

:: Customers mostly ignore the ads because they look different from the rest of your content.

This is a situation that negatively impacts both the marketers and your customers. Your customers lose out because their experience of your site is degraded. Your marketers lose out because customers click their ads less often—if at all.

Experience shows that a small amount of visual design and programming effort that makes your ads look like the rest of your site can yield tremendously positive responses from your customers. They stop seeing ads as clutter and instead perceive them as content. Google, of course, provides a superb example of this strategy in practice, as shown in Figure 6.2.

FIGURE 6.2

Google sets the standard for ad placement and integration

Google has carefully crafted its customer experience, paying strict attention to everything from page balance and spacing to tweaking even the smallest visual design elements. On January 26th, 2007, Search Engine Land magazine interviewed Marissa Mayer, Google's VP of Search Products & User Experience, on the subject of Google ads. In this interview, Marissa Mayer, described how replacing the box that used to contain ads on the right side of search results pages with a vertical line separator improved ad traffic because of the ads' closer integration with the content.

MAKE SURE CUSTOMERS CAN EASILY DISTINGUISH ADS FROM CONTENT

When taken to the extreme, the guideline to better integrate ads and content becomes a design antipattern. Customers' inability to distinguish ads from content becomes especially painful and disruptive when a Web site carries a large number of ads. For example, on Fishing.com, as pictured in Figure 6.3, there are so many closely integrated ads that they become virtually indistinguishable from the content—to the extent that it becomes difficult to understand what service the site actually provides.

FIGURE 6.3

Ads on Fishing.com are overwhelming and confusing

However, even if the number of ads on your site is not overwhelming, customers can have difficulty distinguishing them from content. One common problem is providing different types of search results—some of which stay on the same site, whereas others take customers elsewhere. (Surprising customers about where links go is never a problem for Google or other Web search engines because both their ads and their search results take searchers to other sites.)

On the other hand, for destination sites that sell their own merchandise or provide a branded service while also hosting third-party ads, it is important to positively differentiate between ads, legitimate content, and featured—that is, paid—results. Autotrader.com, pictured in Figure 6.4, mixes many different types of search results together, so it's hard to tell what clicking each result might do. Orange results are actual, "organic" search results, whereas the slightly padded results in blue are paid advertisements.

FIGURE 6.4

Autotrader.com mixes many different types of search results

When clicking a search results link takes searchers somewhere surprising or, by mistake, they click a featured result, their reaction is often quite negative. Yet, to the extent that a link satisfies a customer's need, clicking it can be a positive experience—finding exactly what the customer was looking for. The key to solving this problem is grouping the different kinds of content, while making it clear what are paid advertisements or featured results and clearly differentiating paid content from organic search results through subtle, but telling visual cues.

Colin Ware, in his book *Information Visualization: Perception for Design* describes so-called preattentive attributes, which involve the early stage of visual perception that occurs mostly below the level of conscious thought, at a high speed. He distinguishes four categories of preattentive attributes: form, color, spatial position, and motion. You can apply the grouping strategies for all four categories of these attributes to ads, typically using line size, shape, hue, and enclosure to subtly differentiate ads from content. Motion applies mainly to animated ads, which can be an appropriate differentiation strategy, depending on their content, as we discuss later in this chapter.

Google's search results provide a great example of subtle preattentive differentiation. As shown in Figure 6.2, Google displays three kinds of results on search results pages:

:: **Ads at the top**—Their subtle, yellow background hue differentiates them from the organic results.

:: **Organic search results in the middle**—These are the actual content.

:: **Ads in the column on the right**—Their placement and narrow column format differentiate them from the organic results, plus a vertical line sets them off.

Overall, the results on this page fit together and flow well, whereas the ads' formats subtly, but unequivocally differentiate them from the content.

Note—Customers' ability to effectively differentiate various types of content diminishes as the numbers of different types and sources of content appearing on a page increase—even when the content is grouped appropriately and visually integrated, using the site's colors and fonts.

At some point, a search results page simply reaches its point of saturation, and it becomes impossible for customers to tell the different types of search results apart. When doing usability studies for a major retailer that provided ten different types of search results, Greg found that most test participants could not distinguish one type of result from another when scrolling through search results pages. Thus, the experience became overwhelming for people using the site, who were often frustrated, because they never knew where they were about to go when they clicked a search result.

Buy.com is another site oversaturated with different types of search results and ad content. As called out in Figure 6.5, Buy.com hosts at least 13 different formats for third-party ads on a single page! No surprise; the site rating service Internet Retailer commented, "The site all but overwhelms its visitors with information and options."

For your search results pages to be effective, they must display only a limited number of different types of content and ad formats. Otherwise, with no clear guidance, your main content gets lost and customers become confused because they are overwhelmed by the number of things competing for their attention. The key to integrating ads into your search results, without destroying the search experience, involves being clear about what generates the most site revenue. Is it the ads? Or the content? Does it depend on the query? Have you made the costly mistake of serving as many ads to your top customers as you do to window-shoppers and people who just happen to drop by? After you answer these key questions, you must remain disciplined and stay focused on your core earning potential. Though you can provide occasional, helpful third-party content on the side—particularly, if it helps a customer make a decision.

For example, can you tell whether Buy.com makes more money if people buy the headphones shown on the page—or instead investigate how to make their sandwiches moist and juicy with Best Foods Mayonnaise? Or maybe Buy.com really rolls in the dough when people buy its headphones from eBay or Dell instead? From its page content and layout, it is impossible to tell. You get the impression that Buy.com may be somewhat confused about where the bulk of its revenue comes from.

FIGURE 6.5

Buy.com's 13 different types of ads and third-party content are overwhelming

KEEP ADS RELEVANT AND APPROPRIATE

Note—Although many people are, at best, only dimly aware of ads, some ads are so toxic that hosting them can damage your brand perception and destroy the entire UX of your site.

Although everyone, no doubt, has their own list of the annoying advertisements, one particularly educational example is the infamous animated pop-up ads featuring the X10 spy cam that became popular in the early 2000s. The ad was, at once, so annoying and so ubiquitous that X10 bears the dubious distinction of having been one of the first companies to get people to register on the company Web site just to opt out from seeing its ads for 30 days. Figure 6.6 shows one version of the X10 ad.

FIGURE 6.6

The infamous X10 pop-up ads were some of the most annoying ever

Even though most ads may not be entirely obnoxious, they can nevertheless be completely inappropriate. Ad placement is often the key. FoxNews.com, which is pictured in Figure 6.7, shows just how insensitive and inappropriate some ads can be.

The news story on the page describes the accidental death of a Marine, yet ads for yellow teeth litter the page. Putting politics aside, how do you think the dead person's family felt when viewing this story? How about all the other families who have fathers, husbands, sons, or daughters serving overseas? Please, make sure your ads are appropriate to the content on a page. One way of doing that is to conduct user research and learn how your customers react to particular ads.

FIGURE 6.7

The insensitivity of inappropriate ads on FoxNews.com is striking

UNDERSTAND HOW YOUR CUSTOMERS INTERACT WITH ADS

Although usability studies and field research can give you important clues about how people interact with ads, eyetracking research can be especially helpful. Eyetracking studies help you to understand how customers perceive and interact with ads, and then depending on your objectives, design ads intelligently—to either catch or not catch their attention.

Note—Ad research is quite different from the usability research. Customers definitely don't come to a site just to look at ads, so they pay attention to them only in a spontaneous but not intentional way.

Thus, it's hard to ask them about whether they paid attention to ads because they probably won't be 100% sure. Eyetracking can fill this gap in your knowledge.

By meticulously tracking all eye movement during a test, you can tell whether and how a participant pays attention to the ads on a Web page, what visual search pattern he uses, and how he either skips or focuses on particular information on the page. When running eyetracking studies, spontaneity is key. If you interrupt a participant, ask questions, or have a broken prototype that doesn't let a participant interact with it naturally, your eyetracking data gets contaminated with all sorts of noise. For more information on eyetracking, see Frank Guo's perspective at the end of this chapter.

So, what does eyetracking methodology tell you about ads? You can observe the well-documented banner blindness—that is, customers typically ignore static banners, which are often located at the top of a Web page—even if they are of a ridiculously large size such as those on the Tutorialized.com frame that "captured" another site, HTMLGoodies.com, as shown in Figure 6.8. Though research clearly shows people usually ignore banner ads, the banner ads on the Tutorialized.com frame combined with the ads on HTMLGoodies.com site take up almost the entire area of the page above the fold, negatively impacting the UX and forcing customers to scroll to see any of the actual content.

FIGURE 6.8

Banner ads on Tutorialized.com take up the entire window

As Jakob Nielsen wrote in his August 20, 2007 Alertbox, "The most prominent result from the new eyetracking studies is not actually new. We simply confirmed for the umpteenth time that banner blindness is real."

UNDERSTAND WHAT MAKES A GOOD AD

Based on the findings of eyetracking studies, users spontaneously pay attention to things that are

:: Concrete

:: Actionable

:: Not like marketing

These findings apply to both typical search results and third-party ads. Thus, a good ad is concrete and to the point rather than full of generic, marketing jargon. For example, it might present a picture of the actual item being advertised or indicate clearly that there's free shipping rather than saying something like "We have thousands of cheap items in stock!" As shown in Figure 6.9, the ads on Cars.com are actually quite good.

FIGURE 6.9

Good ads with appropriate content on Cars.com

This ad on Cars.com follows an important principle: It is highly relevant to the search results on the page, calling customers' attention to the specific item in the search results. Even though the ad at the top of the page is a banner ad, it doesn't have the drawbacks of typical banner ads—such as presenting irrelevant content or being positioned too far away from the main content. The price quote, showing good value, is prominent and provides a good call to attention. The presentation of the ad is straightforward, with concrete information and little marketing language or visual noise.

Is it enough that an ad's content be appropriate? Although content is important, it is just one aspect of the marketing message. Another important principle of ad appropriateness is keeping an ad's style appropriate to the topic. Contrast the style of the Cars.com ad to the ad on the Yahoo! Movies page, pictured in Figure 6.10. Even without seeing the flashy animation, it is clear that the ad is quite vibrant.

FIGURE 6.10

An appropriate ad style on Yahoo! Movies is eye-catching

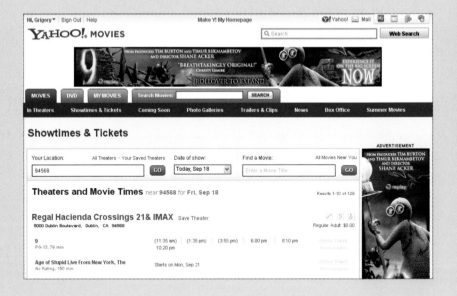

An ad with this animated style is highly appropriate if you expect customers to be getting ready for an action-adventure movie experience complete with special effects. In this case, tasteful, yet somewhat loud movie ads, providing links to previews, are not only appropriate, but also expected. This example shows how carefully chosen ads can form a large part of a Web page's useful content, making it unnecessary for Yahoo! to work so hard at keeping the page exciting.

For hosting ads, it definitely pays to get creative. The way an ad is presented matters a great deal in how customers perceive both the ad and the site hosting it. Creative, interesting presentations get extra points, especially if they are unobtrusive. For example, the peel-the-corner ad on EddieBauer.com, shown in Figure 6.11, is a great example of an ad that draws attention and invites participation, without obnoxiously dominating an experience. Peel corners work because they are unusual, visually interesting, and invite interaction; yet require very little space and do not draw undue attention in the same way loud animated banner ads do.

FIGURE 6.11

Getting creative with an interactive, peel-the-corner ad

Anecdotal evidence suggests that most people do not mind interacting with this kind of advertising and consider peel-the-corner style ads acceptable or even positive on a wide range of sites—if the ads contain appropriate content.

What kind of customer action should an ad invite? In Figure 6.9, the ad on Cars.com asks customers to purchase or consume a specific item on the same Web site—for example, purchase a Maxima. The ad in Figure 6.10 invites customers to participate in an offline interaction they can perform after viewing the ad—see a movie after reading a movie review and referring to a theater schedule on Yahoo! Movies. These are both examples of passive ads—that is, they do not invite customers to click, so much as capture eyeballs, with the purpose of instilling a subliminal desire to select a specific item among many that a site offers. This mirrors a classic bricks-and-mortar advertising strategy, in which certain companies pay stores to feature their brands on banners and place their products in prominent locations.

However, the Web is a dynamic medium, leading to all sorts of novel advertising models. One advertising model involves carrying your competitors' ads and advertising similar products for sale on a different Web site or in another store. On the one hand, customers' clicking these ads generates marketing revenue. On the other hand, this marketing revenue literally eats into the sales revenue from products and services your Web site provides. Thus, competitors' ads cause cannibalization.

LIMIT CANNIBALIZATION

Generally, carrying competitors' ads is a dangerous and losing proposition because cannibalization involves many hidden costs that are often hard to quantify. Most companies spend a lot of money on advertising to bring customers to their own Web sites.

Note—If customers click a competitor's advertisement, not only is there an opportunity cost—because those customers do not buy your own service or product—there is also a hidden cost—you've wasted your marketing dollars.

In addition to cannibalization threatening your bottom line, the experience of your customers' clicking your competitors' ads is likely to be disconcerting to them, leaving them less satisfied with your site as a result. Most competitors' ads just dump customers on the home page of their site or, at best, on a search results page, leaving them to figure out how to navigate to the one item they want—for instance, to compare a competitor's price for an item they were looking at on your site. Thus, clicking an ad almost always involves extra work for your customers. For this reason, if your customers get the results they want on your site, most do not click a competitor's ad—unless the ad makes an attractive offer or the competitor's brand is stronger.

Some sites understand their customers' reluctance to do extra work and consciously decide to exploit this fact by hosting competitors' ads—boosting their revenue without much cannibalization of their own sales. The key to doing this successfully is making rational judgments regarding which ads to host, based on your overall site revenue strategy and hard site traffic statistics. Some successful strategies for carrying competitors' ads include the following:

:: **Making competitors' ads look like advertising**—Customers deliberately ignore such ads, and they get few clicks. This strategy works great if you get paid for ad impressions, not by the number of clicks.

:: **Carrying only ads for weaker brands**—This limits the number of customers who click away from your site.

:: **Not allowing ads to display competitors' prices**—Displaying the actual prices for specific competing goods or services encourages customers to click ads.

The competitor ad on Yahoo! Cars, shown in Figure 6.12, provides a good example for all three of these strategies.

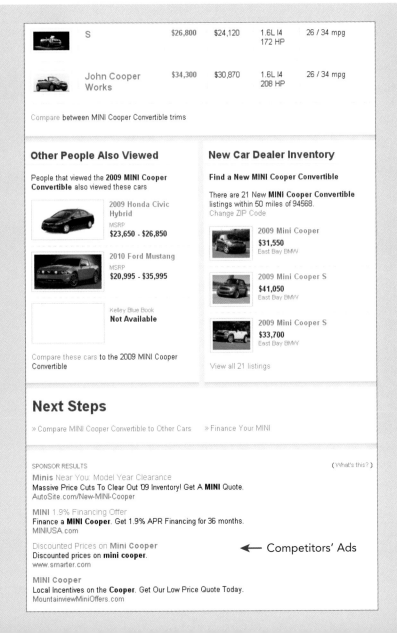

FIGURE 6.12

Competitor advertising on Yahoo! Cars

Another interesting strategy involves completely embracing the experience of offering the best marketplace price from whatever source and being fully committed to always carrying ads from various competitors. You can see one example of this strategy on Buy.com, which is shown in Figure 6.5 above. Buy.com shows prices from eBay and Dell, and the price for the product from its internal search engine. This strategy works well in any of the following cases:

:: Your site has the best price.

:: Differences in price are not significant.

:: Competitors' prices do not give a complete picture—for example, items for sale are used or have high shipping costs, but their ads do not communicate these details.

PROVIDE ADS FOR INTERNAL MERCHANDISE INSTEAD OF THIRD-PARTY ADVERTISING

Amazon.com uses an interesting variation of this strategy, carrying the same items from both its store and online marketplace, as pictured in Figure 6.13.

FIGURE 6.13

Ad for the Amazon.com marketplace

This is a scenario that allows for both Amazon.com and its customers to win. Amazon.com collects rich fees from sellers in its marketplace, so it makes money regardless of which items customers purchase. Having a marketplace also benefits consumers by providing multiple, highly relevant shopping options without presenting anything that looks or feels like an ad. This strategy is tricky because Amazon.com is essentially competing with its own sellers. However, despite the challenges, this strategy has been quite successful—in large part because Amazon.com has been proactive, constantly adjusting its price points and the inventory of items it carries to keep its marketplace thriving and provide customers with the comfort of knowing they are getting good prices from a brand they trust.

Amazon.com's strategy reflects a more general principle: Whenever possible, providing and upselling merchandise to customers is almost always better than hosting third-party ads. There are many good reasons to host your own merchandising rather than third-party ads, including the following:

:: **Control**—No matter how carefully you screen third-party ads, undesirable content sometimes slips through, harming your brand and sending your hard-earned customers to your competition.

:: **Visual design**—Despite your best efforts at ad customization, third-party ads look like, well, ads. On the other hand, you can fully integrate merchandising into your site, making the best use of your available space.

:: **Specificity**—Third-party ads are often not specific to a site's own products— nor would you want them to be because that would drive your customers to the competition. On the other hand, you can make merchandising as specific as necessary because in this case all ads ultimately drive traffic back to your own site, where transactions convert directly to your bottom line.

Merchandising simply offers a better UX. People like specific, targeted content that does not look like an ad but helpfully provides ideas and choices.

PAY SPECIAL ATTENTION TO ADS IF THERE ARE NO SEARCH RESULTS

Note—When there are no results, search results pages are an especially dangerous place to host advertising.

All the negatives of displaying competitors' ads discussed earlier become further exacerbated on a no search results page. Such a page is generally devoid of your own content, making third-party ads their primary calls to action.

As described in Chapter 1, "Starting from Zero: Winning Strategies for No Search Results Pages," no search results pages indicate to customers they've over-constrained their query and need to reformulate or broaden their search. Displaying third-party ads on a no search results page invites customers to abandon their natural behavior of iterative search in favor of following a fresh information scent. This interrupts the finding flow on your site and dumps your customers directly into your competitors' greedy hands.

Unfortunately, marketing folks often simply fail to grasp the iterative nature of the finding process and the critical role the no search results page plays in helping customers reformulate their queries. Some of them like to put ads on no search results pages, justifying their viewpoint by saying something like this: "We are simply meeting the customers' needs with our ads. The customers would leave our site anyway. We are just helping them and making some money along the way."

This thinking demonstrates a dangerous and fundamental lack of understanding of the differences between how search engines and ad-hosting services work.

Note—Search engines that are internal to a Web site typically combine keywords using an AND operator. Thus, they look for items or content that contains *all* the keywords a customer provides. This practice often leads to over-constrained queries, limiting the finding conversation between a person and a Web site.

Now contrast search engine results with hosted advertising results. Search engines providing hosted ads have no requirements for fidelity or specificity—the rules by which a site's own search engine usually abides. By using an OR operator instead of AND, hosted ad servers can cherry-pick ads, displaying only the most relevant ads or those matching the most profitable keywords in a customer's query, and ensure the ad server never fails to produce results.

Note—Even when the advertised product matches the customer's query only approximately, ad servers can still make the ad sound relevant by simply replacing the ad's title with dynamic text that exactly matches the keywords in the query.

For example, in one particularly memorable usability study Greg conducted, a task asked participants to find a ticket to a performance of the "Nutcracker" in San Francisco, during the holidays. After reading the task, one participant typed the query "Nutcracker Ballet in San Francisco December 1-31st," which, of course, matched no results on the site. However, the ad hosting engine produced a page similar to that shown in Figure 6.14.

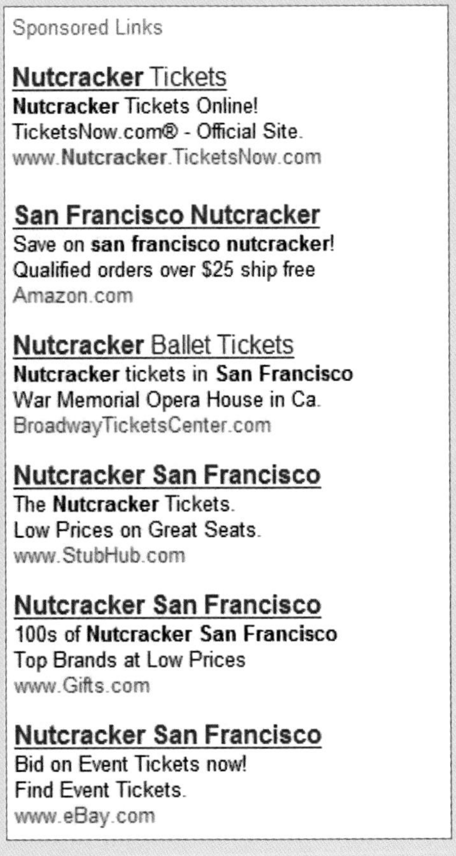

Sponsored Links

Nutcracker Tickets
Nutcracker Tickets Online!
TicketsNow.com® - Official Site.
www.**Nutcracker**.TicketsNow.com

San Francisco Nutcracker
Save on **san francisco nutcracker**!
Qualified orders over $25 ship free
Amazon.com

Nutcracker Ballet Tickets
Nutcracker tickets in **San Francisco**
War Memorial Opera House in Ca.
BroadwayTicketsCenter.com

Nutcracker San Francisco
The **Nutcracker** Tickets.
Low Prices on Great Seats.
www.StubHub.com

Nutcracker San Francisco
100s of **Nutcracker San Francisco**
Top Brands at Low Prices
www.Gifts.com

Nutcracker San Francisco
Bid on Event Tickets now!
Find Event Tickets.
www.eBay.com

FIGURE 6.14

Ads matching the query Nutcracker Ballet in San Francisco December 1–31st

Upon seeing the no search results page displaying these ads, the participant promptly clicked an ad and bought a ticket from a competing site, even though cheaper tickets were readily available on the site we were testing. If the participant had relaxed her query, she would have discovered this, but instead, the third-party advertising appearing on the no search results page led her down a different path. When there are no search results, that is the wrong place and time for displaying third-party ads.

As this story demonstrates, it is easy to lose customers on no search results pages, which represent a critical juncture in a conversation between a customer and a Web site—an opportunity for the customer to reformulate a query and gain a deeper connection with your brand. Host third-party ads on your no search results pages only as a last resort. Carefully calculate the cost of doing so. Which click would generate more long-term revenue: the ad or the tools for query reformulation? Which click would ultimately engender more long-term loyalty and a better relationship with your customers?

IN CONCLUSION

In his keynote speech at the 2008 Business Of Software conference, Seth Godin famously quipped, "Marketing is too important to be left to the marketing department." The same goes for hosting advertising in your search results pages. UX professionals should be actively involved in ad-hosting decisions to make sure your company's golden goose continues to thrive, well beyond the current quarter.

Use these ideas as a starting point for developing your own comprehensive merchandising and ad-hosting strategies. Making the tough choices that are necessary and getting creative with ad hosting is not easy, but it is an absolute must if your company is to survive and thrive in the current economic environment.

EYETRACKING TIPS AND TRICKS

Eyetracking is an increasingly popular research technique used by web design professionals to see how users interact with designs. It is traditionally used as a somewhat more "scientific" user research method than other research techniques. And therefore many practitioners ignore the "soft" or qualitative way of applying eyetracking. I'd like to offer a qualitative perspective of effective eyetracking research. To begin with, eyetracking is a very valuable technique to help us understand users' visual attention, answering questions such as what kind of content and visual treatment users attend to, the steps they take to find an object or explore the content, how long they stay focused on an object, and how effective their visual search is, and so on. Web design areas such as search, browsing, online ads, and Web content writing can greatly benefit from eyetracking research because in these contexts a big part of the design is to draw user attention and keep them engaged. Conventional usability testing techniques fall short of addressing this design objective. This is because during a conventional usability study, we understand user behavior by observing their mouse and keyboard movement and asking them to talk aloud as they go along. But oftentimes users interact with Web pages by just looking at the screen; therefore we can't tell what they are doing without the aid of an eyetracker. Also, it is very difficult for the user to accurately recall his or her own visual behavior, which consists of many random, unconscious spurts of eye movement, so the think-aloud protocol can't give us in-depth insight about the user's visual behavior. Eyetracking, in contrast, provides an ideal venue for understanding users' visual behavior.

As of today in the field of human computer interaction, a widely accepted approach of conducting eyetracking research is quantitative in nature. By quantitative, I mean, researchers look at eyetracking data at an aggregate level, typically in the form of a heat map and derive conclusions about where users pay attention to on a screen. I guess many of us in the human computer interaction field have heard of this type of eyetracking research, and some are great fans of it because it is perceived as cool and very "scientific." The problem with this approach is, eyetracking data is notoriously hard to interpret. For instance, users fixate on an area for a long period of time and therefore the heat map would look very "hot." This could mean that the area is well designed and attracts lots of user attention, or it could mean that it is ill designed and generates lots of user confusion. So a heat map in itself can't tell the entire story.

Based on my experience with conducting eyetracking research, I'd recommend an alternative approach of conducting eyetracking research, the qualitative way. To put it briefly, this means we observe users' eye movement on an individual basis and then cross reference this with other types of user data, such as user feedback collected by think-aloud protocol to produce a qualitative and in-depth understanding of user behavior. For instance, from one of the studies I conducted, the eye movement of a user suggested that her eyes traveled long distances, jumping from the top of the screen to the bottom and ignored all the page content in between. To understand what drove this kind of behavior, it was not just enough to look at the eyetracking data alone. From her verbal comments, I learned that she explored this Web page based on such an approach—she tried to calibrate how much content was there on the page before diving into any particular details; therefore she looked at the top of the screen and then immediately jumped to the bottom. In so doing she got a sense of what was there on the screen. That feedback, as combined with the eyetracking data, gave me a clear understanding of what she was trying to do when exposed to such a page the first time.

The same visual search pattern also emerged from other participants in the study. Here, the eyetracking data did not come from a large sample size and did not present itself as a heat map, which is only meaningful if the data comes from at least 20 plus participants. On the other hand, by synthesizing eyetracking and think-aloud protocol data across just 10 participants, I had a rather robust understanding of the typical visual search pattern for this type of Web design. This approach, by looking into the eye movement and comments of individual users on a case-by-case basis, allows us to tell a complete story of why users do what they do, as opposed to using quantitative techniques such as heat map, which doesn't provide this kind of in-depth understanding. The advantage of this approach relative to the quantitative approach also resides in the fact that to analyze eyetracking data quantitatively requires a very clean research design, some sort of experimental control, a very robust eye tracker hardware setup, and a large sample size, and only eyetracking experts with careful planning can pull off a quantitative eyetracking research study successfully.

On the other hand, the qualitative approach uses eyetracking as just another supplemental technique to be used on top of a conventional user evaluation study; therefore, it is more practical and cost effective. Of course, both methods have their respective areas of application. To generate clean and robust quantitative data in order to support executive decision making, for example, almost always requires a quantitative research approach. On the other hand, to generate in-depth learning for designers to uncover the secrets of effective Web design, qualitative eyetracking could provide richer insights.

Finally, let's talk more about the validity of qualitative analysis in the context of eyetracking. We typically think of eyetracking as a quantitative, scientific method of understanding human behavior—it captures eye movement in an accurate and quantifiable manner. And therefore we might be uncomfortable with hearing "eyetracking" in the same sentence as "qualitative" because this might suggest that the research is less valid. But let's think about a conventional user evaluation study, in which we interview a number of participants around their thoughts about some Web designs, and synthesize their feedback into a meaningful and coherent account of how well the design performs and how to improve the design. All of that is also qualitative in nature. The qualitative application of eyetracking is similar to that—we closely examine users' eye movement on an individual basis and perform synthesis across a number of users to get in-depth insights and uncover patterns. Therefore the qualitative approach of eyetracking research is informative and robust, just like the traditional qualitative user evaluation method.

—FRANK GUO

DESIGNING ECOMMERCE SEARCH INTERACTIONS

The overarching design goals... [are] to support flexible navigation, seamless integration of browsing with directed (keyword) search, fluid alternation between refining and expanding, avoidance of empty results sets, and at all times allowing the user to retain a feeling of control and understanding.

–MARTI HEARST

CHAPTER 7

BEST PRACTICES FOR DESIGNING FACETED SEARCH FILTERS

Faceted Search is a technique of accessing a collection of items by their multiple classifications, or facets. In contrast to hierarchical taxonomy classifications that allow the data to be ordered in a single, predetermined way, faceted search allows the data to be ordered in multiple ways, along the different facets. Each facet typically corresponds to the possible values of a property common to a set of digital objects.

Faceted search user interfaces for ecommerce sites are still fairly new, and potential design pitfalls abound. Fortunately, there are a few relatively simple and straightforward best practices that UX designers can follow to minimize cognitive friction and create search user interfaces that are easy to understand and use. This chapter describes some best practices for the design of search filters.

Recently, Office Depot redesigned its search user interface, adding attribute-based filtering and creating a more dynamic, interactive UX. Unfortunately, Office Depot's interaction design misses some key points, making its new search user interface less usable and, therefore, less effective. That's the bad news. The good news is that the implementation of filtering on the Office Depot site presents us with an excellent case study for demonstrating some important best practices for designing filters for faceted search results, as follows:

1. Decide on your filter value-selection paradigm—either drill-down or parallel selection.

2. Provide an obvious and consistent way to undo the selection of filtering options.

3. Always make all filters and filtering options easily available.

4. At every step in the search workflow, display only filter option values that correspond to the available items, or inventory.

5. Provide filter option values that encompass all items or the complete inventory.

By following the design best practices for attribute-based filtering this chapter provides, you can ensure your customers can take care of business without having to spend time struggling with your search user interface.

CHOOSE DRILL-DOWN OR PARALLEL SELECTION

There are two basic ways to select filter options: drill-down and parallel selection. Ignoring the various modalities of the many derivative mechanisms for these primary modes of selection, these two basic ways to specify a value for a filter essentially boil down to two choices: links and check boxes.

A link is the simplest way to select a filter option. By clicking a link, a customer can either select a single value for a specific filter or drill down a level in a taxonomy comprising a hierarchy of categories or departments. As shown in Figure 7.1, Amazon.com provides one of the best examples of a search results user interface that uses links to let customers select filter options. Links usually indicate a straightforward equals condition—for example, "I want to narrow my search results to Department equals Books"—as they do on Amazon.com.

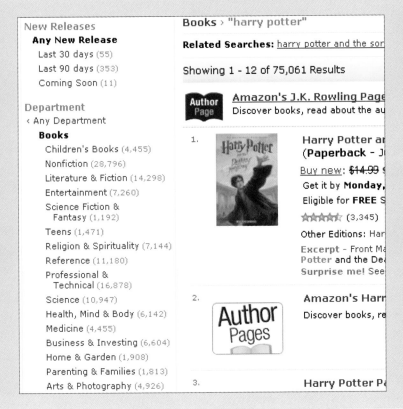

FIGURE 7.1

On Amazon.com, links enable customers to select a single filter option

In contrast to links, which enable customers to select only a single filter option, check boxes enable customers to indicate parallel selections of multiple filter options, limiting the scope of search results to those matching them. The KAYAK search user interface, shown in Figure 7.2, uses check boxes to limit search results to specific airlines. Check boxes typically indicate an additive "or" condition—for example, "I want to narrow the search results to: Airline equals American, Delta or United"—as on KAYAK.

FIGURE 7.2

On KAYAK, customers can narrow results to several airlines by selecting check boxes

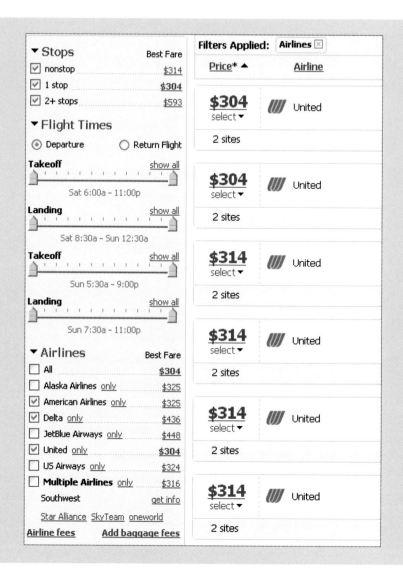

Links and check boxes complement one another very well. Links are great where customers need to display multiple levels in a hierarchy—for example, when there are multilevel category drill-downs. Check boxes are great for selecting one or more options for attributes like brand or size. Unfortunately, not all Web sites use these two value-selection paradigms correctly.

As shown in Figure 7.3, the Office Depot user interface uses check boxes for selecting values, leading customers to expect a parallel selection paradigm, in which they could indicate they want to search multiple price ranges by selecting several check boxes. For example, to find chair mats priced from $0 to $100, customers might expect to select the price filter's first two check boxes. Thus, after clicking the **$50–$100** check box to select it, they would expect to retain the ability to select the **$50 and below** check box.

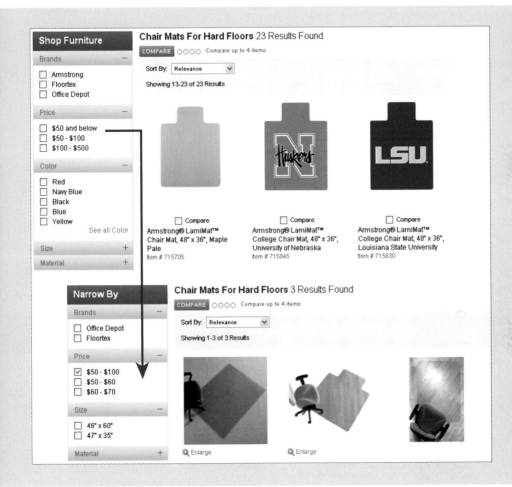

FIGURE 7.3

Office Depot confuses the drill-down and parallel selection paradigms

However, after a customer selects the **$50–$100** check box, the Office Depot search user interface does something completely unexpected. It drills down into the $50–$100 price range and *removes* the **$50 and below** check box, breaking the affordance of a group of check boxes that should let customers select multiple, parallel "or" values for a single filter. Instead, the user interface now displays **$50–$60** and **$60–$70** ranges, while still displaying the range of **$50–$100**

the customer originally selected as one of the available "or" values. Mixing the drill-down and parallel selection paradigms results in a confusing search user interface.

Another confusing thing about the Office Depot user interface is that it does not provide any obvious way to deselect filter options and return them to their original, prefiltered state. This brings us to the next best practice: providing an obvious undo mechanism.

PROVIDE UNDO FOR FILTER SELECTIONS

Make it as easy as possible for your customers to undo individual filter selections. Relying on the browser Back button as the sole interface device to undo a filter selection frustrates potential customers by forcing them to remove filters in the same sequence in which they were applied. Thus, someone looking at Large > Red > Hard Floor chair mats cannot switch to Small > Red > Hard Floor chair mats without first removing and then re-applying the Color and Floor Type filter selections, resulting in a large number of unnecessary clicks.

Both Amazon.com and KAYAK provide a clear, consistent way to undo the selection of a filter option and go back to **All** or **Any** for a specific filter. For example, as shown in Figure 7.4, Amazon.com provides a link to **Any Department**. Notice that the link is offset to the left, and a < symbol helps customers understand that this particular link goes back.

FIGURE 7.4

Amazon.com enables undo via a link to *Any Department*

Department
< Any Department
Books
    Children's Books (4,455)
    Nonfiction (28,796)
    Literature & Fiction (14,298)
    Entertainment (7,260)
    Science Fiction & Fantasy (1,192)
    Teens (1,471)

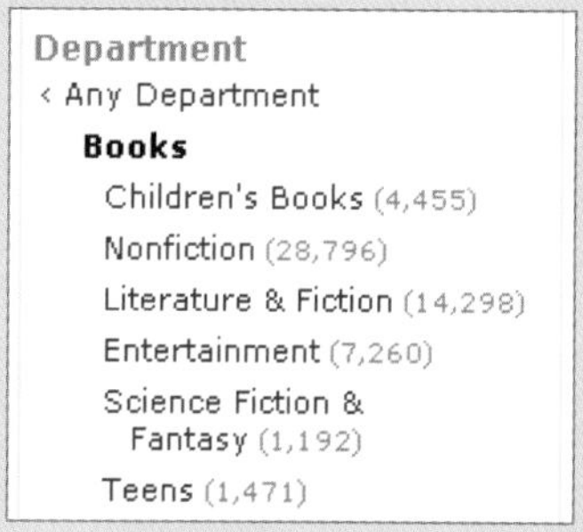

In Figure 7.5, you can see that KAYAK solves the undo problem by enabling customers to select an **All** check box, under **Airlines**, to view flights from all the available airlines. Note that the KAYAK undo is slightly less clear than that in the Amazon.com user interface, primarily because the **All** check box is neither highlighted in any way, nor separated from the rest of the check box options. Instead KAYAK highlights the airline that offers the best price. Although not standard, this is hardly something that would cause undue confusion.

FIGURE 7.5

KAYAK enables customers to undo airlines filter selection by checking All

On the other hand, the Office Depot user interface, shown in Figure 7.6, does not, at first glance, provide an obvious way of undoing the selection of the **$50–$100** price filter option. There is actually a mechanism that enables customers to do this, but it is not at all obvious. The way for a customer to return to **Any** price is to deselect all filter options. Although this design may be completely valid from the software's standpoint, requiring people to uncheck all of the selections to remove a filter creates two problems. First, it is very inefficient. In the above KAYAK example, it would require 3 clicks, each followed by a separate Ajax call and a refresh of the search results page—with the entire remove sequence taking at least 8-10 seconds. Second, and most important, this type of interaction conflicts with how most people think about filter selections, which makes this interface confusing. There is a strong mental model mismatch: to a person using the interface, *removing* a filter selection does not effectively communicate the concept of **All Prices**. It would be much more effective to provide an **All** or **Any** option.

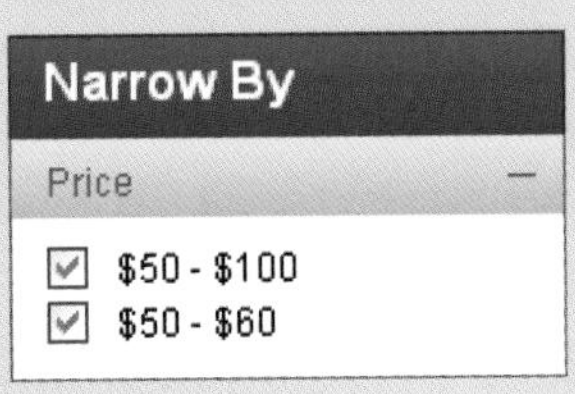

FIGURE 7.6

To undo, Office Depot makes customers deselect each filter option individually

Note—The discussion of removing filters through unchecking a check box vs. by selecting a **See All** option is covered in greater detail in the context of Breadcrumbs interfaces in Chapter 13.

Some sites use the deselect-to-undo paradigm successfully. One fine example is Yelp.com. However, sites that successfully implement deselect-to-undo typically make a concerted effort to ensure *consistency* in the values of filter options, which should not change based on other selections. For example, instead of removing options, the Yelp user interface makes certain filter options unavailable to indicate a lack of available inventory. Unavailable options appear dimmed, as shown in Figure 7.7.

FIGURE 7.7

Yelp ensures consistency for its deselect-to-undo paradigm

chinese San Jose
Browse Category: Chinese

▼ Hide Filters

Sort By	Cities	Distance	Features	Price
❯ **Best Match**	☐ Santana Row	Bird's-eye View	☐ Open Now (3:17pm)	☐ $$$$
Highest Rated		Driving (5 mi.)	☐ Good for Groups	☐ $$$
Most Reviewed		Biking (2 mi.)	☑ Outdoor Seating	☐ $$
		❯ **Walking (1 mi.)**	☐ Take-out	☐ $
		Within 4 blocks	... More features »	

❶ 1. Sino
Categories: Chinese, Asian Fusion

★★★☆☆ 670 reviews
377 Santana Row
San Jose, CA 95128
(408) 247-8880

« Mo' Map

Look, I don't particularly like being a jerk, but I gotta be honest with y'all... Sino is basically overpriced Americanized **Chinese** food that tastes OKAY at it's best. I know a lot of people

❶ 2. Panda Express

★★★☆☆ 14 reviews

However, in cases where consistency is difficult to achieve, it is a far safer approach to use **Any** or **All** to undo the selection of filter options, particularly where the values of the options for a filter are dynamic. As shown in Figure 7.8, when a customer deselects filter options out of sequence on the Office Depot site, even greater confusion results.

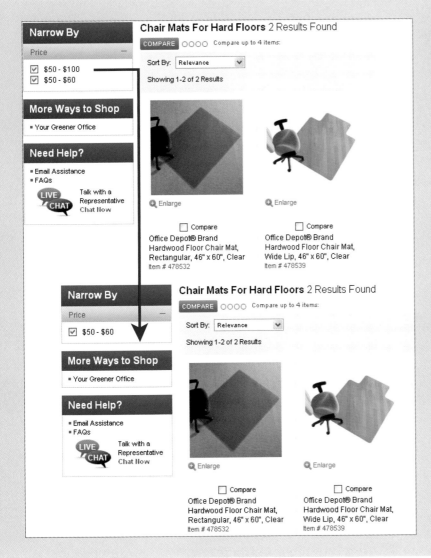

FIGURE 7.8

On Office Depot, the order in
which filter options are deselected
matters

The Office Depot user interface is particularly sensitive to the order in which
a customer deselects the check boxes for a single filter. For example, the price
filter option **$50–$100** simply disappears if the customer deselects it before
deselecting the **$50–$60** option. To undo the selection of both filter options, the
customer would have to click the browser's **Back** button twice because there is
no other way to return to the default state.

Typically, all the available filters and their options—plus the data that appears in the search results—are subject to change after each click. The key to providing a successful undo mechanism is to avoid completely removing options from a filter for which a customer has selected an option.

MAKE ALL FILTERS EASILY AVAILABLE

When designing faceted search filters, make sure all the filters always remain available to your customers. Please don't misunderstand me. I am not saying all filter options should remain visible at the same time. It is perfectly acceptable to collapse filters to just a label, providing a single link like **View All Filters** to expand them, or to display previously selected filtering options in a unique way. However, if at different steps in a search workflow, filters start randomly disappearing from the search user interface with no way to bring them back, bad things quickly start to happen.

Figure 7.9 shows what happens to the Office Depot search results when a customer selects the option **Red** for the **Color** filter. As you can see, when the customer selects a color, all the other filters disappear entirely.

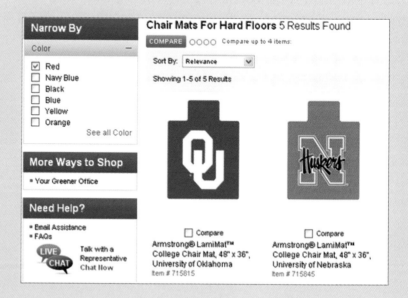

FIGURE 7.9

On Office Depot, filters disappear randomly

Does this system behavior make any sense? Say, for example, you want to buy a red chair mat. Under **Color**, you can select the **Red** check box and view a great variety of red chair mats. Is there actually a compelling reason for you to do anything else with the color filter? Will you, as a true connoisseur of all things red, perhaps drill down into shades of red for your chair mat, such as Burgundy, Farmhouse Red, or Ripe Tomato? Not likely—at least not for chair mats. Instead, you are more likely to say, okay, these are all the red chair mats. Great! Now, can you select a mat from a known brand? Or perhaps you would like a budget-priced mat, so you need to further constrain your search by price. Or maybe you are a fan of The Ohio State Buckeyes and want to find a chair mat with the team logo, leaving fans of the Michigan Wolverines blue with envy. Using other filters to continue tweaking your *red chair mats* query is a far more likely scenario.

Alternatively, consider a different use case: You just selected **Red** and now can see a bunch of red chair mats. Almost immediately, you realize these red chair mats are almost, but not quite, entirely unlike the mat you actually want to buy. So, you attempt to seek out a way to undo your most recent selection, and a way to view what other filters might be available for your use. Unfortunately, for both of these use cases, the Office Depot search user interface unhelpfully removed all other filters when you selected a color. This action would be tantamount to KAYAK's removing all other filters like departure and arrival times, number of stops, and price whenever a customer selected a particular airline. How helpful do you think that would be to someone trying to find a flight? Removing any previously selected filter is detrimental to customer success and is, therefore, not recommended. If you feel compelled, for some reason, to minimize the screen real estate you are devoting to filters, you can collapse individual filters or hide their options temporarily under a **More Options** link.

PROVIDE ONLY FILTER OPTIONS THAT REFLECT THE AVAILABLE INVENTORY

Chapter 1, "Starting from Zero: Winning Strategies for No Search Results Pages," touches on the idea of showing only options and links that actually point someplace useful. At every step in a search workflow, any available filtering options should reflect only the inventory that is currently available for purchase. The filtering options you display depend on a customer's previous actions—both the keywords in the original query and other filtering selections.

As shown in Figure 7.10, the chair mat color selections expand to reveal several color options including **Maple Pale** and **Cherry Spice**. Selecting **Maple Pale** and **Red** together should give you chair mats in both colors. Unfortunately, the user interface does not seem capable of supplying Maple Pale chair mats because when the page reloads, it displays the same five red chair mats. In reality, it's more likely those Maple Pale chair mats are just out of stock.

FIGURE 7.10

Office Depot shows color selections that are not applicable to a query

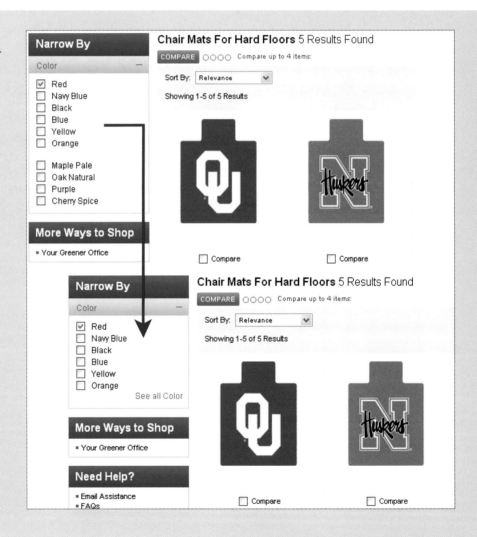

This idea seems obvious, but quite a few otherwise first-rate sites seem to miss it. Often, the underlying issue is technical. On many sites using Ajax search user interfaces, page calls retrieve and recompute all the summary data for every filter option in response to each change a customer makes to the filtering options, so speed becomes a primary concern. For many legacy systems, the demands of just-in-time data delivery are simply too much. At the end of their development cycle, developers are often frustrated to find that, despite their best efforts, their aging systems simply cannot deliver the speed necessary to retrieve the data for all filtering options, plus the items in the search results, plus the data for pagination, in a single Ajax call. In such an event, rather than redesigning the system from scratch to address the root cause of this problem, developers often end up taking shortcuts—either by caching all the filters, or by providing a generic list of options some of which, like the Maple Pale color option on Office Depot, may not be applicable to the specific query at hand.

Note—If demands of your design prove to be too much for the legacy system, try implementing caching and improving your database indexes. If the system still can't handle the demand, try scaling back. Experiment by replacing Ajax calls with human clicks, or reduce the total number of facets and filter options.

PROVIDE FILTER OPTIONS THAT ENCOMPASS THE COMPLETE INVENTORY

You must always strive to design every filter to include a list of options that encompasses the entire available inventory. Here's an example. As you can see in Figure 7.11, the color filter in the Office Depot search user interface does not display a filter option for finding the most common chair mat color, which is **Clear**. Therefore, even when a customer selects all of the color options, the site can display only a fraction of the available inventory—in this case, only 16 of 23 available items. The seven clear chair mats have no color attribute, so customers can never choose to view only those items using the Office Depot user interface. Instead, by choosing to engage with the color filter, they unknowingly remove clear mats from consideration. This system behavior is clearly not beneficial to someone looking for a chair mat—especially if they are looking for the most common, clear variety.

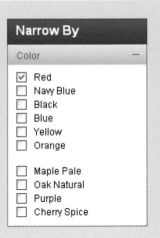

FIGURE 7.11

Office Depot doesn't let customers view clear chair mats

I am not sure what Office Depot's reason for omitting **Clear** from its color options might be, but it is reasonable to assume that the clear chair mats have the color attribute of empty, or null. Therefore, it is not possible to group these items and filter them by a valid color attribute. Fortunately, one fairly straightforward way to resolve any missing or inconsistent data is to include **Other** or **All Others** as a filter option. A SQL condition corresponding to the **Other** filter option should specifically capture any items for which the object's facet value is empty, or null, ensuring customers can always view the entire inventory by using some combination of the filter options available in the user interface.

Often, there are more options for a given filter than you can show at once. A basic rule of thumb is to display 4 to 7 options for each filter.

Note—the recommendation to include 4-7 filter options represents the average best practice that isn't right for every query. It is important to optimize the filter options for your specific use case. For example, depending on the query, Amazon.com sometimes displays a full list of all 29 categories, while KAYAK frequently shows a list of 12 or more airlines.

If there are too many options to display, it is often desirable to hide the rest of the options in a **More Choices** panel or pop-up. In this case, **Other** might be an option that shows up only when a customer views the additional options. Specific queries dictate where you should show each particular option. In the example, given the popularity of clear chair mats, **Other** should be at or near the top.

Note—Regardless of their order, it is critical to include all the options that encompass the complete inventory. This is especially important in cases in which there is no **All** or **Any** option with which customers can undo their selections—as in the Office Depot search user interface. Otherwise, you risk making some of the most popular items on a site unfindable.

TEST YOUR FACETED SEARCH INTERFACE

Be sure to test your search results user interfaces thoroughly with both potential and existing customers. It is important to test search user interfaces using realistic tasks. If your budget allows, avoid predefined search tasks. Instead, study how people find items they're interested in—preferably in an environment in which they would normally do the kind of searches you want to study. When designing search user interfaces, field studies are a crucial tool for continually making and validating design improvements—not just something you do merely as a formality at the end of a project.

THE DESIGN OF FACETED SEARCH UI CONTROLS

Throughout 2010, REALTOR.com® benefited from a change in the underlying search technology, and with it came the ability to present faceted search capabilities to those looking online for homes for sale. From a design perspective, we were able to provide users with an interface that gives them certainty about the number of results they would receive upon choosing a given facet, such as in the following screen shot, where clicking on "3+" under the Bedrooms section would result in seeing 72 homes for sale (with other search parameters still applied):

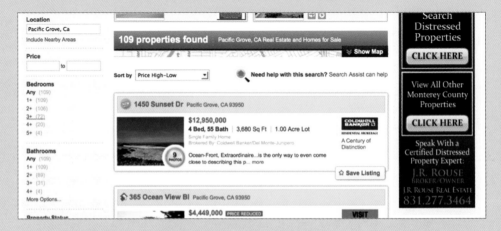

How to present faceted search UI controls became one of the more researched topics of the project. The preceding arrangement organizes facets into categories in a familiar left-hand-side placement. This is used quite widely, but has a few disadvantages. First, it uses up horizontal space, which could be otherwise used to show even more content on the search results page or a more standard 300 pixel-wide right column. (The preceding right-hand-side column is only 190 pixels, and cannot accommodate a small map of the area nor the more attractive 300 × 250 ad unit.)

Secondly, the connection between the search controls in the left-hand side and the results below were sometimes not clearly made in the minds of users. This is partly due to some of the content in the middle column having only an indirect relationship to the controls (e.g., featured placements) while other content is directly controlled by it. Also, the sheer number of elements on the page can be overwhelming, and there could be a stronger visual connection (through color and typography) between UI controls and the controlled content. Also the fact that the user must scroll so far to see all of the search controls meant that they often missed important options they wanted.

Finally, we noticed a negative effect on site speed with this arrangement as well. In this design, all the facets and their resulting numbers had to be computed and shown the preceding 3-column design shown.

One alternative we experimented with featured the faceted search UI controls arranged in a categorized horizontal bar above the search results page, such as in the following mock up:

One of the unexpected benefits of this arrangement was site speed. By putting the search UI controls under categorized layers, we could "lazy load" the facet information after the other elements on the page were loaded, which resulted in a snappier site. By the time users clicked on a category to reveal the facets, they were loaded and ready for use.

Another benefit from this arrangement was a clear understanding of how to control the search and what elements on the page it affected. This was partly due to a reduction in clutter and having only two columns on the page. Users clearly understood that the wider column on the left was the "primary" information, while the information in the wider 300 pixel right-hand side provided relevant but ancillary content.

The above design was not implemented in the first release of the REALTOR. com® redesign of 2010, primarily due to the ripple effect it had on several other aspects of the business and the underlying platforms that would need to be built to accommodate it. But from the standpoints of design, usability, and site speed, it proved to be a superior choice.

—CHRISTIAN ROHRER, PH.D.

NUMERIC FILTERS:
Issues and Best Practices

Faceted search (introduced in Chapter 7, "Best Practices for Designing Faceted Search Filters") has become the de facto standard for search on most ecommerce sites. Among the various types of facets that describe digital object collections for the purposes of conducting electronic commerce, numeric filters are quite common: They represent shoe size, camera resolution, price, rating, recommended age, and much more. Numeric filters help people make sense of their digital world and make better decisions. However, filters containing numeric values remain among the most confusing and difficult to use. The following three usability issues surface most often with numeric filters:

:: Representing discrete values for aspects as sets of ranges—for example, treating camera resolutions or shoe sizes as a continuum instead of a collection of discrete data points

:: Inadvertently emphasizing overly constrained filter states, which makes it too easy for people to select un-resourceful system states, such as products with a one-star rating

:: Being parsimonious with inventory information—using UI elements that do not report inventory amounts, which makes it difficult to predict the outcome of interacting with these elements

Recently, powerful user interface controls called *sliders* have become a popular approach to representing numeric filter attributes. Unfortunately, many companies have given little thought to usability of sliders and how these new controls integrate into the holistic search process. Rather than solving existing usability problems, poorly designed sliders create even more confusion among users attempting to use this feature. Fortunately, sliders that also show inventory as a histogram make this control much easier to use and more effective. The histogram slider design pattern is presented at the end of the chapter.

REPRESENTING DISCRETE VALUES FOR ASPECTS AS SETS OF RANGES

One of the most common pitfalls with numeric aspect filters is representing discrete values as sets of ranges. What makes a filter value discrete? Certain types of products are commonly identified by widely recognized, discrete values— for example, a digital camera might have a 10MP resolution and a lens with 3× zoom, and shoe sizes come in full and half-sizes such as 10 and 10.5. These discrete values tend to be consistent across competing brands and models and rarely change from one vendor to the next.

Many sites offering faceted search do not present discrete numeric values for aspect filters in the most useful fashion. Designers are often tempted to present such values to customers as sets of ranges, which typically results in a user interface similar to that in Figure 8.1, showing a camera-resolution filter on eBay.

☐ 14.0 MP & More (743)
☐ 13.0 to 13.9 MP (1)
☐ 12.0 to 12.9 MP (1,358)
☐ 11.0 to 11.9 MP (2)
☐ 10.0 to 10.9 MP (1,258)
☐ 9.0 to 9.9 MP (27)
☐ 8.0 to 8.9 MP (280)
☐ 7.0 to 7.9 MP (226)

FIGURE 8.1

eBay implements the camera-resolution filter with values presented as a set of ranges

My usability studies have shown that many people have trouble finding 10MP within a 9.9MP–11.9MP range and applying the filter correctly. The problem is a mental model mismatch. People don't think of 10MP as falling within some range. When customers look for discrete values in aspect filters, they are most often looking for a specific value—for example, 10MP—that forms a critical part of the information scent. Most people typically think of a camera resolution as a specific value and not as a numeric value within some range.

When users try to look for the value 10MP within a range, usability problems arise because the resolutions 9.9MP and 11.9MP simply do not exist as discrete values. While mathematically it's correct to state that 10MP lies within a 9.9MP–11.9MP range, this range has poor information scent and requires additional thinking and interpretation on the part of the customer, tasks which do not make for intuitive and efficient finding.

Note—Having to think hard about finding something causes problems. In my practice, I have often observed that people who are in a rush, distracted, or simply not adept at working with fractions in math often select the wrong range of discrete values, wonder why they are not getting the results they expected, get frustrated, and quickly leave a site to navigate to a more usable one.

Instead of a range, it is more effective to present lists of discrete values, showing all the possible values for an aspect filter. If doing this results in a filter with too many options, simply rounding off the value to **10MP** works well, as shown in Figure 8.2.

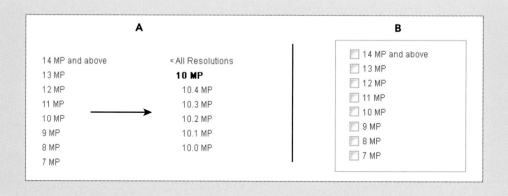

FIGURE 8.2

Recommended redesign of camera-resolution filter

Note that the word *around* is usually implied—though it sometimes shows up in a short form such as **~10MP** or **10+MP**. However, this extra precision is often unnecessary. If a customer clicks a link representing a discrete value, one option is to expand a list of subvalues—for example, clicking the **10MP** link would show all the available subvalues: **10.0MP, 10.2MP, 10.3MP, 10.4MP**, as shown in Figure 8.2A. Should you bother designing and implementing this? Usually not. Unless your customer is a professional who is looking for a particular value, he would not typically drill down past the **10MP** link. Is there that much difference between digital-camera resolutions of 10.2 and 10.3MP to a typical consumer? So, unless your inventory is extremely large or you have specialized clientele, it is often much more useful to present an approximate value like 10MP and leave it at that.

Should you support single or multiple selection for displaying discrete filter values? It depends. The simplicity of single-selection links for discrete values was generally recommended up until a few years ago. Today, I highly recommend that my clients implement multiple selection for discrete filter values— provided the finding user interface supports multiple selection. Mark Burrell of Endeca echoed this sentiment in his 2010 UIE webinar, "Leveraging Search & Discovery Patterns for Great Online Experiences" emphasizing that most ecommerce customers no longer find multiple selection hard to use and prefer the flexibility it offers.

NUMERIC SLIDERS

Numeric sliders have recently become a popular approach to implement faceted search. Sliders can add a touch of interactivity to what many people might otherwise refer to as a "boring" finding interface. Boring user interfaces usually work extremely well because they are intuitive and easy to use, and UX powerhouses like Amazon.com and Netflix do quite well without any sliders whatsoever.

That said, sliders can be helpful in some applications, because they give people tremendous filtering power when implemented correctly. With great power, however, comes great responsibility: Sliders deserve special consideration from designers precisely because they make it so easy for your customers to screw up and over-constrain their queries, leading to search results that are either incorrect or of poor quality. This, in turn, results in frustrated customers who leave your Web site without buying anything. The two issues I see most often with sliders follow:

- :: Inadvertently emphasizing over-constrained filter states
- :: Being parsimonious with inventory information

Now take a closer look at each of these issues and what you can do to resolve them.

Inadvertently Emphasizing Over-constrained Filter States

To examine the issue of over-constrained filter states, take a look at an example of a ratings filter. Ratings filters are deceptively simple, yet raise a host of issues if implemented incorrectly. Figure 8.3 shows the slider ratings control used on TripAdvisor.

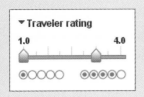

FIGURE 8.3

Slider ratings filter control on TripAdvisor

TripAdvisor implemented ratings filter as a double slider control, which presents a perfect example of inadvertently emphasizing over-constrained filter states. This double slider control enables a wide variety of ranges—some of which are much more useful than others when it comes to finding items or content of interest. For example, ratings ranges spanning only a single star—such as 0–1 stars, 1–2 stars, or 2–3 stars—are simply not useful because short ranges do not match the mental model of the person using the system. Most of the time, people click a ratings filter to filter out all the merchandise below a certain rating—that is, as a way to find higher-rated, higher-quality items in their search results. However, a double slider control makes it easy to get this wrong and over-constrain the query by overemphasizing the ability to constrain the range from both sides.

A much more useful way to approach this design problem is to use a single slider or a set of links like those in Figure 8.4, which shows ratings filter as it is implemented in a much more useful and intuitive fashion on Amazon.com.

FIGURE 8.4

Amazon.com's implementation of ratings as links

Avg. Customer Review
Any Avg. Customer Review
★★★★☆ & Up (316)
★★★☆☆ & Up (425)
★★☆☆☆ & Up (437)
★☆☆☆☆ & Up (449)

You could further improve the control shown in Figure 8.4. Because the goal of people using the ratings control is to get better-quality items, it is not actually that useful to show only a single star—the lowest possible rating. Instead, it might be more intuitive to replace the single star with the word **Any** and make that the default filter state. (Remember that "Any" is an important faceted search concept discussed in Chapter 7.) The filter shown in Figure 8.4 also has the important added advantage of providing vital information about the number of reviews available for each star rating, shown in parentheses. This information helps people using the ratings filter to clearly understand the consequences of their actions and builds appropriate expectations. Understanding what to expect from their actions lets people be more efficient and effective, leading to higher customer satisfaction and better usability.

Being Parsimonious with Inventory Information

Do all dual sliders emphasize over-constrained filter states? Not necessarily. For some filters such as price range, dual sliders are entirely appropriate.

Note—Whenever dual sliders are used, the problem of over-constraining queries and, as a result, providing inadequate information described earlier never actually goes away.

As Figure 8.5 shows, TripAdvisor's dual slider control for the price range filter shows no inventory information. In other words, prior to manipulating the slider, customers would have no idea what the effect of their action might be.

FIGURE 8.5

Dual-slider filter for price range on TripAdvisor

Any action customers take might be a hit or a miss, but it is never clear in advance which it will be because the system simply does not provide the necessary information. As an example of the positive impact the inventory information might provide, compare the dual slider for price range on TripAdvisor to the price control on Staples.com, pictured in Figure 8.6.

FIGURE 8.6

Price control on Staples.com with multiple check boxes

As covered in more detail in Chapter 10, "The Mystery of Filtering by Sorting," over-constraining search results by price is one of the most common human errors you see in usability testing for search user interfaces. Which control would you expect to cause more over-constrained queries: a dual slider or a set of check boxes? The control that causes more issues with query over-constraining is the dual slider because it gives no clue as to what to expect from a particular action. On the other hand, the dual slider provides the bling many business people crave as a means to differentiate their user interface from the competition. In this age of highly interactive Ajax interfaces, clicking links or typing in numbers to specify a price range seems so old-fashioned. Is there a control that would provide the interactivity and fun of the slider, yet offer the inventory information so necessary to helping customers make informed decisions?

One approach would be to use a dual slider for the price range, with a sparkline graphically representing the available inventory information for every price in the range. Figure 8.7 shows my suggested redesign of the TripAdvisor price filter, which uses a dual slider with a sparkline showing the available inventory for each price in the range.

FIGURE 8.7

Suggested redesign of the price range filter on TripAdvisor

Edward Tufte's book *Beautiful Evidence* describes sparklines as "data-intense, design-simple, word-sized graphics." Although I have no idea who first thought of combining a slider with a sparkline, I have been recommending this solution to my clients for more than six years, and I can claim to have arrived at this idea independently. Unfortunately, most of the people I have worked with have remained cold to this idea, stating that a slider with a sparkline would be "above and beyond what an average user could understand." However, my own experience as a user researcher backs the opposite conclusion. All usability test participants who saw the user interface shown in Figure 8.7 confidently stated they understood that the sparkline represented the number of items available, eloquently proving once again that "clarity and simplicity are completely opposite of simple-mindedness," as Tufte said in his book *Envisioning Information*.

Recently, I was supremely gratified to hear Mark Burrell of Endeca recommend dual sliders with histograms as one of the best ways of showing price ranges during his 2010 UIE webinar, "Leveraging Search & Discovery Patterns for Great Online Experiences." Mr. Burrell's experience with dual sliders was similar to mine: He said that most people have no trouble understanding that histogram bars—a step-wise variant of a sparkline—represent item inventory for each part of a slider's range and that histograms clearly help people to avoid over-constraining their queries.

One excellent implementation of a dual slider with a histogram is found on the Swedish site Prisjakt.nu, shown in Figure 8.8.

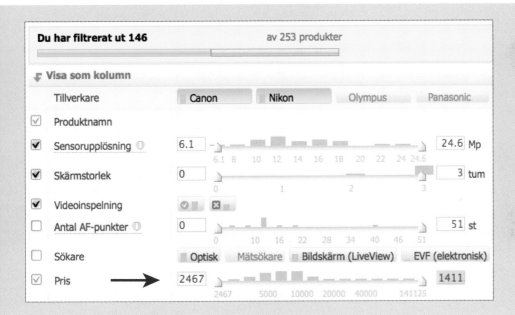

FIGURE 8.8

Intuitive price filter on Prisjakt.nu implemented as a dual slider with a histogram

In an age of rapid development, new ideas and new controls hit the Web almost every day. No matter which control you ultimately decide to use to implement your numeric filters, there is simply no substitute for empathy and solid qualitative user research. Understanding why customers do certain things is extremely important in designing effective user interfaces. You cannot improve the way your system communicates with your customers unless you understand what your customers' goals are and why people fail to reach them. With every new filtering innovation, it becomes ever more important to stay focused on your customers, with patience, empathy, and understanding.

DATE FILTERS:
Successful Calendar Design Patterns

In contrast with the decimal Hindu-Arabic numeral system that was invented in India around 1,500 years ago, the Gregorian calendar has only been in use for approximately 428 years. As a consequence, humanity as a whole has had a bit less practice with calendars and dates than with numbers. Thus, date filters often cause even more usability issues than the numeric filters mentioned in the previous chapter, especially when they neglect basic design best practices. Dates are also among the most complex and time-consuming controls to manipulate: When asked to enter date values during usability tests, people often literally groan in pain. Yet many user interfaces stubbornly fail to safeguard customers from inadvertent errors and simply refuse to retain the calendar information customers so painstakingly provided. Sloppy or indifferent design of date filters can lead to unhappy customers. This chapter focuses specifically on date filters to show you how to design date filters that are as intuitive and pain free as possible.

PROVIDE GOOD DEFAULTS

For user interfaces, the initial impression is usually the most telling. Look at this government search interface from California's Department of Corporations Web site, pictured in Figure 9.1. Not only are there no useful date defaults, but also there is absolutely no indication of what date range input might be acceptable. Can the customer perhaps search as far back as 1913? Unfortunately, from the looks of this page, we have not gone far in making dates easier to handle since the invention of the Gregorian calendar in 1582.

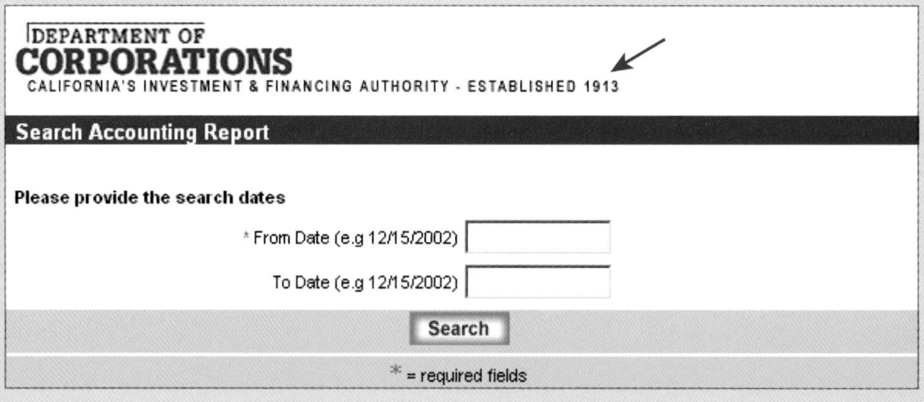

FIGURE 9.1

No date defaults in California Department of Corporations' Web search

DEPARTMENT OF
CORPORATIONS
CALIFORNIA'S INVESTMENT & FINANCING AUTHORITY - ESTABLISHED 1913

Search Accounting Report

Please provide the search dates

* From Date (e.g 12/15/2002) [   ]

To Date (e.g 12/15/2002) [   ]

[Search]

* = required fields

Failure to provide good defaults extends far beyond government Web sites. Figure 9.2 shows a Web site of an upscale Iron Horse hotel in Milwaukee.

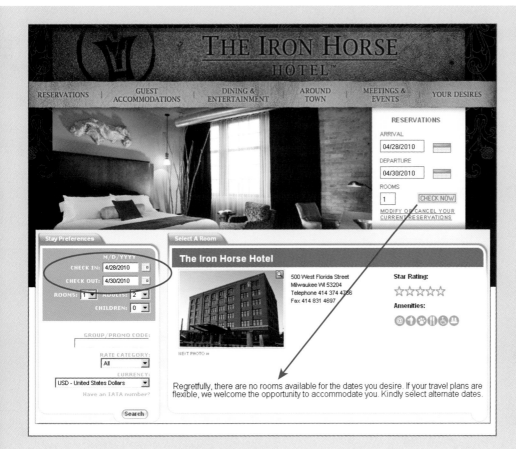

FIGURE 9.2

Default dates at the IronHorseHotel .com produce zero results

As you can see, default date filter settings produced zero search results—not exactly what you would expect from a hotel claiming to be "catering to your every desire." The resulting no search results page commits several of the sins covered previously in Chapter 1. The biggest frustration is that the zero search results page just reuses the same date values originally used to get the zero results, so now the customer is no wiser than before about what might be the soonest date available for a romantic getaway. At this point, the best outcome is that the frustrated customer might pick up the phone and call the company, whereas the worst outcome is that he will simply give up and book their travel on a competing hotel site.

SHOW ONLY VALID DATE VALUES

Providing reasonable defaults is just the beginning of the search process. Successful calendar designs must also prevent customers from picking invalid dates by graying-out or disabling date values that are disallowed or return zero results. Unfortunately, even otherwise top-notch sites often choose not to do this. For example, Figure 9.3 shows the KAYAK site that enables customers to pick dates too far into the future, causing an error.

FIGURE 9.3

KAYAK.com enables customers to select dates too far in the future

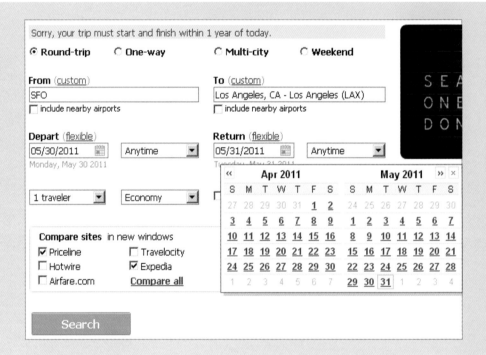

But the difficulties with selecting valid date values do not stop there. Take for example, TripAdvisor.com, shown in Figure 9.4.

When the customer picks a departure date (6/19/2010) and then launches the return date picker, the Web site does not indicate the departure date the customer just selected, nor does the system in any way indicate which return dates occur before the departure date and are therefore unavailable. If the person happens to be unlucky enough to pick the "wrong" departure date that occurs *after* the return date (6/13/2010), TripAdvisor "helpfully" moves the *return* date to 1 day following the departure—an action that is both arbitrary and destructive. Worse, the system never notifies the customer of this action.

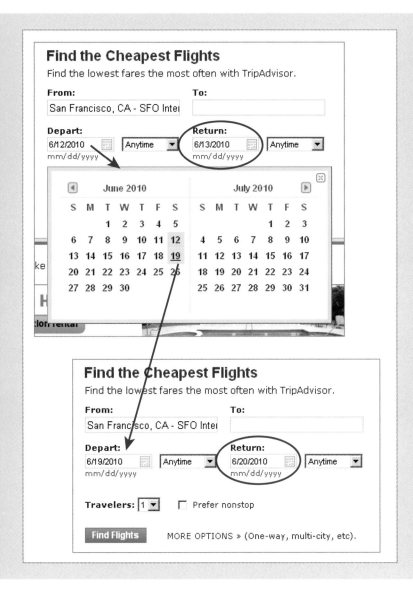

FIGURE 9.4

TripAdvisor arbitrarily moves the return date to 1 day following departure

Note—Most people assume they entered the information correctly unless the system clearly tells them otherwise, so when they discover that the system arbitrarily changed the information they entered, they lose trust in the site.

A much better approach is to indicate the departure date on the return calendar and clearly indicate the dates that occur before the departure date, so the customer does not pick them accidentally. This prevents potential errors and

confusion even before the customer has a chance to enter anything. If the customer still chooses to select a return date that occurs before the departure date, the system can then move the departure date or leave it blank, but in either case it should indicate the action it is taking on behalf of the customer. As shown in Figure 9.5, a similar approach is successfully implemented on Orbitz.com, which disables bad choices and makes it clear which dates to select.

FIGURE 9.5

Orbitz.com makes it obvious which dates to select

Less thinking equals fewer errors and surprises, and fewer errors mean more happy customers. Any design that makes it obvious what to do with the calendar is a big win for your user experience.

MINIMIZE CLICKS

TripAdvisor also demonstrates why, when it comes to dates, it is important to usability test and actually take the time to count the number of clicks needed to enter a date a few months in the future. As can be seen in Figure 9.4, the TripAdvisor calendar shows two months worth of dates at the same time. Unfortunately, fancy JavaScript code enables the calendar to scroll only a *single* month at a time. This design effectively doubles the time it would take to book a flight because in addition to clicking once for every month, the customer now has to wait for the fancy calendar scrolling to come to a complete stop before they can navigate to the next month. I hope you are beginning to see why people groan during date filter usability testing.

UX design expert Alan Cooper proposed a much better calendar design that scrolls continuously in his exceptional book *About Face*. This scrolling calendar design pattern was successfully implemented by the KAYAK iPhone app, shown on the right side of Figure 9.6.

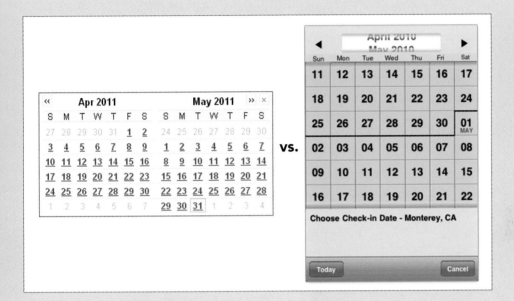

FIGURE 9.6

KAYAK date picker versus scrolling calendar in the iPhone app

Contrast the elegant scrolling calendar design of the KAYAK iPhone app with the Web form calendar picker shown on the left. Note that the KAYAK Web application actually duplicates (and grays out, which adds to the confusion) the flanking and trailing dates for each month. In my opinion, it is features such as this that make KAYAK's mobile interface much more intuitive than its Web application.

Note—Luke Wroblewski explores the topic of mobile search Web forms in more detail in his perspective at the end of this chapter.

Regardless of how fancy your calendar picker is, make sure your form is accessible and allows people to simply type in the dates they want by tabbing around the form fields. I once consulted for a client that proudly showed me his enterprise search date entry interface that disabled the manual entry and instead popped up the date picker "in order to avoid errors."

Note—It is critical to always allow for keyboard date entry, particularly in the enterprise environment, because people are often much faster and more accurate at typing in dates or cutting and pasting into the form field than they are reaching for a mouse.

RETAIN CUSTOMER-ENTERED VALUES

Date values are hard to enter, therefore it makes a lot of sense to retain any customer-entered date information for as long as possible. Unfortunately, many sites do not take the trouble to do so. Figure 9.7 shows the search form that results from being transferred from KAYAK to Southwest Airlines' Web site. Dates are not included as part of the search query transfer, defaulting instead to today's departure date and a return date one day in the future.

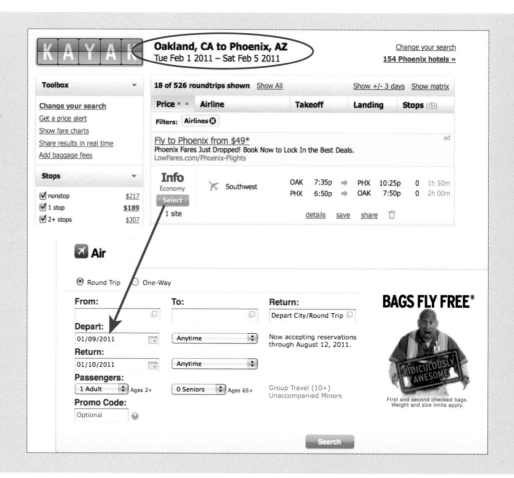

FIGURE 9.7

KAYAK.com drops date selections when transferring the search to Southwest Airlines

Recently, Southwest Airlines implemented a "sticky" date design that retains the dates even when the customer starts the search process over. That is a great improvement. However, what if the customer is considering multiple travel dates or trying to compare several different travel dates to find the best price?

Because dates are so tedious to enter, at the very least, retaining date information entered in the same session usually makes the interface much more consumer-friendly and enables people to be a lot more efficient.

Note—Retaining date information is practically a necessity in some consumer and enterprise applications, like Web analytics, where people often use several date periods over and over in various queries throughout the site.

In cases in which the customer interface needs to display several previously entered dates or date ranges, a drop-down selector showing several previous entries is an effective option. Two possible designs, with the select preceding and following the date entry field, are shown in Figure 9.8.

FIGURE 9.8

Date drop-down selectors enable customers to select from dates used in the past

The drop-down selector is an excellent design pattern that borrows freely from the design of the Internet browsers' URL entry fields that have similar functionality. In my usability testing, a wide range of people understood and used date drop-down selectors effectively. Drop-down date selectors are versatile, used to recall individual dates or date ranges, and help minimize clicks for repetitive date entry tasks. They are the perfect kind of partially hidden "Easter Egg" functionality, that creates sheer delight when discovered unexpectedly.

Note—Only provide the active drop-down selector when past dates are available to populate it. When the drop-down list is empty, the selector arrow should be removed or shown in a grayed-out disabled state.

CONSIDER IF YOU NEED YOUR CUSTOMERS TO ENTER DATES

A lot of times, particularly in an enterprise system, the date range is the default "knee jerk" control the designers reach for when creating simple object management screens and reports. Many times this interface control is a complete overkill. One of the alternative design patterns I call *Presets with Custom Date Range* is shown in Figure 9.9.

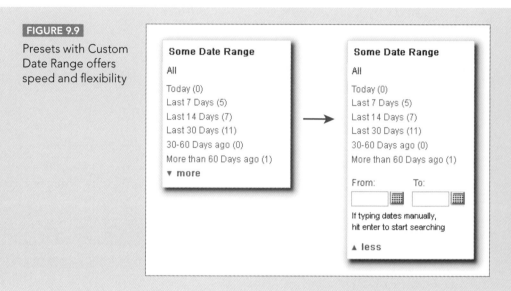

FIGURE 9.9

Presets with Custom Date Range offers speed and flexibility

Presets with Custom Date Range is a simple yet effective design pattern. This pattern presents several preset date ranges (for example, Today, Last 7 Days, and so on) that are frequently used by customers. If a custom date range is desired, the customer can click the **More** link that opens a section with standard date boxes and calendar pickers allowing the customer to enter a custom date range instead. In many cases using this design pattern instead of a simple date range picker can save time and cognitive load on the person using the interface, while still allowing complete input flexibility with only a single extra click.

In many cases, date ranges are orthogonal to the task at hand, yet many designers and engineers reach for the date picker as a kind of knee-jerk reaction. Instead, challenge yourself on your next project. Consider if your customers will not be better served by an interface that, instead of forcing people to search through several different date ranges, helpfully suggests the best time to travel to Thailand? Or the user interface that helps people find the dates that offer the best price on a dream Alaskan cruise? When booking a summer vacation, do most people care if they travel in July versus August? Don't make your customers choose a date range. Instead invent pages that invite browsing and searching to allow people to leave the dreaded date boxes blank. Your customers (and your clients) will both thank you.

BETTER MOBILE FORM DESIGN

The following excerpt is taken from Lukew.com (www.lukew.com/ff/entry.asp?1014), by Luke Wroblewski

Trust me, no one likes filling in forms—especially on mobile devices where one-handed, on-the-go data input and slow connections are common place. As a result, designing forms that make mobile input faster, easier, and less error-prone is crucial. Here's a few ways it can be done.

To illustrate, let's look at two mobile forms for booking a hotel: one from the Expedia mobile Web site, the other from the KAYAK iPhone application.

Expedia's mobile Web site has made several modifications to the desktop version of [its] hotel booking form: The layout has been optimized for slender mobile screens; the "search near" set of options has been listed out; and the room count input uses a set of "+" and "–" buttons instead of a drop-down menu for input. Yet, there's still room for improvement.

1. The form uses a free-form text input field that requires users to provide clarifying information on another screen if a mistake is made. And in many mobile contexts (fat fingers, one-handed typing, on the go)— mistakes do happen.

2. The date selection field makes use of a calendar pop-up that requires people to tap a small ">>" target to advance to the previous or next month.

3. The set of inputs for guest count uses (up to) three drop-down select menus for input, which require manipulating a list of options in a pop-up list.

Depending on guest count, there can be 3 seperate drop-downs required

1. Free-form text field for location

If the location entered has multiple matches, an additional set of inputs is required

2. Pop-up dialog for date selection

3. Drop-down select menus for guest count which use mobile OS controls for item selection

continues

BETTER MOBILE FORM DESIGN (continued)

KAYAK's mobile iPhone application also allows people to book hotels, but it features a few additional mobile optimizations.

1. Current location is available as a single-click input in addition to a free-form text input. This allows people to search for hotels where they are now without typing.

2. The free-form text entry field provides inline suggestions as you type. This not only reduces the amount of typing required (it only took me three characters to see Monterrey, Mexico), but it reduces errors as well. On the KAYAK form, there's little need for the clarification screen Expedia requires.

3. The date selection calendar allows people to use a simple scroll gesture to move between months instead of tapping a small target to change months. Users can just flick the calendar itself up or down through direct manipulation instead of having to use the ">>" control Expedia requires.

4. The KAYAK form doesn't use any drop-down menus, opting instead for "+" and "−" buttons that are easily tapped on a touch screen. (I'm not sure why Expedia uses these for room count but not guest count as both inputs only need to support a small number of possible values.)

In aggregate, these small enhancements go a long way to making forms on mobile devices faster and easier for people to complete. For more on form design, check out Luke's book about Web form usability, visual design, and interaction design considerations: *Web Form Design: Filling in the Blanks*.

1. Current location available as input

2. Type-ahead control for entering location

3. Scrolling calendar for date selection

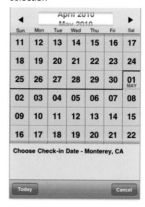

4. Button controls for guest count instead of drop-down menus

REFERENCES

Cooper, Alan, Robert Reimann, and David Cronin. *About Face: The Essentials of Interaction Design*. Indianapolis: John Wiley & Sons, 1995.

Nudelman, Greg. "Starting from Zero: Winning Strategies for No Search Results Pages." *UXmatters*, February 9, 2009. Retrieved May 17, 2010.

Wroblewski, Luke. "Better Mobile Form Design." *LukeW Ideation + Design*, March 9, 2010. Retrieved May 17, 2010.

THE MYSTERY OF FILTERING BY SORTING

What is the difference between filtering and sorting for a search query? Any SQL developer would tell you that sort translates to a SQL ORDER BY statement, whereas a SQL WHERE clause performs a filter. However, the practical distinction between sorting and filtering in the minds of typical ecommerce customers becomes more vague as the number of search results increases beyond a few pages. I've called this phenomenon "filtering by sorting", and it calls into question much of the conventional wisdom around the design of sort and filtering controls.

FILTERING BY SORTING: IT WAS COLONEL MUSTARD IN THE STUDY

During one particularly memorable usability study involving filtering and sorting, my first participant—who I immediately dubbed Colonel Mustard because of his resemblance to the character in Milton Brothers' Classic Game of *Clue*— kept referring to the sort control as a "filter". During the think-aloud portion of the usability test, he repeatedly said, "I am filtering by price," while manipulating an HTML drop-down list that we'd clearly labeled **Sort By: Price: Low to High**. Despite his confusion, this participant was getting exactly what he was expecting—that is, lower-priced items—using the **Sort By** control, so sorting was working fine in helping him reach the task's goal. At the time, I attributed this confusion about filtering and sorting to the participant's lack of technical vocabulary and dismissed the finding as inconsequential.

Much to my surprise, many of the participants who followed Colonel Mustard in subsequent test sessions—many of whom hailed from different professions, educational backgrounds, and levels of site familiarity—also said, "I am filtering by price," while manipulating that same **Sort By** control. After observing this phenomenon numerous times, it became clear that this was not merely a matter of simple confusion of terms between filtering and sorting. Instead, it revealed a strong mental model of "filtering by sorting" that blurred the difference between these two modes of search results refinement.

THE MYSTERY OF FILTERING BY SORTING

As children, we learned to understand sorting by ordering small numbers of items. As adults, we now often sort search results that include hundreds of thousands or even millions of items. At first glance, we might not see any difference between the two tasks. Regardless of the sample size, we think our childhood training should apply perfectly to sorting 100,000 items by price, even without our understanding what's going on technically. Why then this strange confusion between filtering and sorting?

To understand this phenomenon, you need to take into account how people *look* at those 100,000 items after they are sorted. Research clearly demonstrates that, despite there being a virtual cornucopia of data, people usually see only a small number of items in each search result set. As Jakob Nielsen wrote in *Prioritizing Web Usability*:

"Obviously all users saw the first screenful (the one above the fold). But viewing frequency dropped off rapidly after that. More than half the users didn't scroll at all, so only 42% of users saw any information on the second screenful. Only the most persistent one percent of users viewed more than seven screens worth of information."

Although it's generally hard to measure how much people scroll, my own experience studying pagination on ecommerce sites supports this finding. For a result set of 100 items per page, most people do not view even the second page of results, and almost nobody goes past the third page of results. Thus, from a customer's point of view, for a result set of 100,000 items, sorting by price actually *filters* the result set by selecting at most 300 items with the lowest prices and effectively removing the remaining 99,700 higher-priced items from consideration. This is what Colonel Mustard and other participants referred to as "filtering by lowest price," when changing the sort order. Thus, I decided to call this phenomenon "filtering by sorting."

FIVE MYTHS OF SORTING

Usability expert Dan Norman famously said, "There are no secrets of usability, no more than there are secrets of astronomy." Anyone using the correct usability testing methodology would observe the same behavior in their own studies. The catch is using the right methodology. Most companies build prototypes for testing their software in a lab. Prototypes are expensive to build and populate with data, so most usability tasks include as few preset items as possible—usually on the order of a couple of hundred—to test the discoverability and usability of various filtering and sorting controls. For my study, I lucked out and got a large test database, which allowed me to observe this filtering by sorting mental model.

Note—This example demonstrates the importance of doing frequent field studies, observing real systems, so you can decipher people's search behaviors and mental models.

When you accept the mental model of filtering by sorting, you can see all kinds of interesting implications for search user interfaces. It becomes necessary, for example, to debunk some myths about sorting that Web development professionals have long accepted as truths. Hopefully, looking at these myths will inspire you to think about killing a few of your own sacred search user interface cows, in the interest of improving the search experience on your site.

Myth #1: Sort Should Be Visually Separate from Search Filters

Typically, sorting controls are outcasts among search controls. Not wanting users to confuse sorts with filters, most designers place sorting options in a drop-down list that is as far removed as possible from the search box and filters on the left. This outcast placement results in users not using sorting controls as much because it sends a clear signal that these controls are not as important as the others. I recall a project in which the marketing lead suggested we remove the sort control altogether and replace it with an ad. Apparently this sentiment isn't particularly rare. As Figure 10.1 shows, on Amazon.com, sorting is not even available until a customer chooses a category.

FIGURE 10.1

Amazon.com makes customers choose a category before sorting

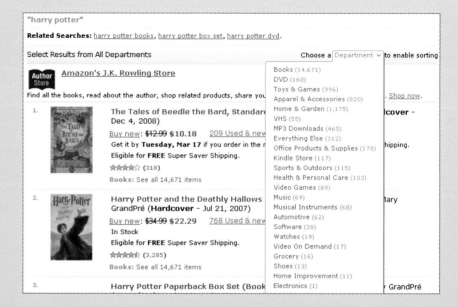

The ostensible need to visually separate sorting and filtering controls is a myth. As discussed earlier, for search result sets that exceed a few pages, which covers most queries on the majority of ecommerce sites, filtering by sorting phenomenon kicks in, making the distinction between sorting and filtering less distinct. Thus, for most consumer-facing applications, articulating what such controls do in general terms is enough. Understanding in detail how sort is different from filtering is not critical to a customers' ability to find what they are looking for. There is simply no value in placing sorting controls far away from filtering controls.

In his book *Don't Make Me Think*, Steve Krug proposed that you should place search controls in such a way that users can read their settings as an English sentence. This provides a perfect way to position sorting controls. In Figure 10.2, you can see my proposed redesign of a typical ecommerce user interface, using an English sentence structure for better placement of the sort control.

FIGURE 10.2

Incorporating filtering and sorting controls in a sentence

Although, at first glance, the proposed search user interface appears to be slightly more complex than the Amazon user interface shown in Figure 10.1, this redesign ensures that the **Sort By** control is in a more noticeable position and would be considerably easier for most people to understand and use. This is important because according to my field and lab study observations, sorting is much more successful than filtering in some cases.

Myth #2: Sorting Is Less Successful Than Filtering in Helping Customers Find Content

Anyone who's ever observed a usability study that involved filtering search results by setting a price range can readily attest that shoppers tend to over-constrain their queries. A good example would be a task such as "find a digital camera that fits in your pocket and costs around $100". Most people respond to this simple task by setting the price range to—you guessed it—**Price: from $100 to $100**. A typical search user interface would invariably respond to this query by returning no results. This outcome is the result of a basic mismatch between a human's understanding of what "around $100" means and the machine logic that delivers *precisely* what the user asked for—no more, no less.

As it turned out, in the study in which we asked participants to shop for a digital camera, there were about 50 camera models for sale under $99.99 and about the same number for sale over $100.99. The mean price for cameras on the site happened to be $100, so this price should have been a perfect starting point for exploring the site's inventory. Instead, the nature of the search user interface caused users to manipulate the filters in a way that was detrimental to their success in finding a camera.

As Neal Stephenson said in his book, *In the Beginning... Was the Command Line*:

"Giving clear instructions, to anyone or anything, is difficult. We cannot do it without thinking, and depending on the complexity of the situation, we may have to think hard about abstract things and consider any number of ramifications, in order to do a good job of it. For most of us, this is hard work. We want things to be easier."

To use range filtering controls effectively, you must give instructions to the system that are sufficiently precise—but not *too* precise.

Note—Most filtering controls that ask users to type a range from a number to another number are detrimental to the goal of producing useful search results.

The same goes for price sliders that do not show the price range for the available inventory and make it too easy to over-constrain the query to a single price point or to too small a range. (Chapter 8 covers sliders.) And, although most people would not care whether they spent $99 or $109 on a camera, those same people would care deeply about spending $99,000 versus $109,000 for a house. In the latter case, rather than a price range, the upper limit of the user's price range would be a more appropriate filter for a query. However, for most ecommerce applications, price is at best a fairly vague parameter such as "around $100."

Additionally, most people do not have a clear idea of a price they would expect to pay for most items and are easily swayed by other factors such as features, brand recognition, ratings, and social pressures. Thus, in many cases, a well-placed **Sort By Price** control is often much more successful in producing a useful set of search results than a filtering control.

In contrast to filtering, sorting controls never produce zero search results. So, sorting eliminates many of the common search misunderstandings that people encounter with filtering and help people to be more successful, while applying considerably less thought. Sort displays the result set in the right configuration for efficient exploration. If, when sorting by price, a customer chooses the **Lowest Price** sort, budget models appear first, enabling customers to reach their target price point via scrolling. If a user chooses **Highest Price** sort, the search results present a useful entry point to the higher-end models. For finding mid-range cameras, the most appropriate interaction model would be a combination of sort and filter. We'll get to that in a moment. For now, let's just say that, in many cases, sort is a great way to entice your customers to explore the site inventory so that they'll find something interesting. Search success leads to more satisfied customers who come back more often.

Based on my research for consumer applications, I can state with confidence that sorting by price—**high-to-low** and **low-to-high**—is quite intuitive and quickly understood by diverse audiences. So, unless we are talking about the larger sums of money customers might spend on cars, real estate—and political donations—a simple bidirectional **Sort By Price** control is sufficient, even without using a price filter.

Myth #3: Sort Should Be Hidden in a Drop-Down List

ırlier, various sorting options offer superb starting points for
entory on an ecommerce site, so there is no reason to hide
lown list. The Apple iPhone App Store shown in Figure 10.3 pro-
mple of an alternative sorting user interface. The two buttons
screen and all the tabs at the bottom are actually—you guessed
ort-by controls that have been liberated from a drop-down list.

his user interface successful? For this screen, a typical use case might be something like this: "Find a new to-do list application for your iPhone that is easy to use." The best way to accomplish this task is actually through browsing because searching by keywords like *to do easy to use* is not likely to be productive. As we all know, these days, most manufacturers tout their applications as "easy to use" when they are nothing of the sort, and with thousands of iPhone apps in the app store, the application's name is unlikely to match its function closely. Therefore, a better finding strategy might be to browse **Productivity Apps**, sorting by **Most Popular** or **Highest Rated**. The strength of using a tabs-based sorting mechanism as the App Store's primary navigation is the ability to offer inventory in a format that is optimized for a specific entry point, thus forming a series of parallel views of their inventory. These tabs-based sorting controls are extremely usable and intuitive, and readily contribute to a customer's success.

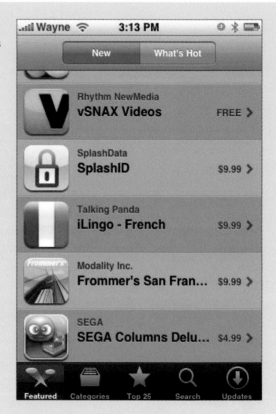

FIGURE 10.3

The iPhone App Store's sort-by controls facilitate browsing

Myth #4: Sorting and Filtering Cannot Be Combined in One Control

As the amount of information retrieved increases, sorting search results becomes less and less about reordering the results and more about providing a convenient way to massage the results into a manageable form that more closely matches the person's goals. This is especially important for user interfaces with limited screen real estate—like those on the mobile platforms.

However, even on the Web, the demarcation between filtering and sorting is not necessarily a rigid one. For example, as Figure 10.4 shows, the Facebook applications inventory screen conveniently combines sorting and filtering in the same drop-down list.

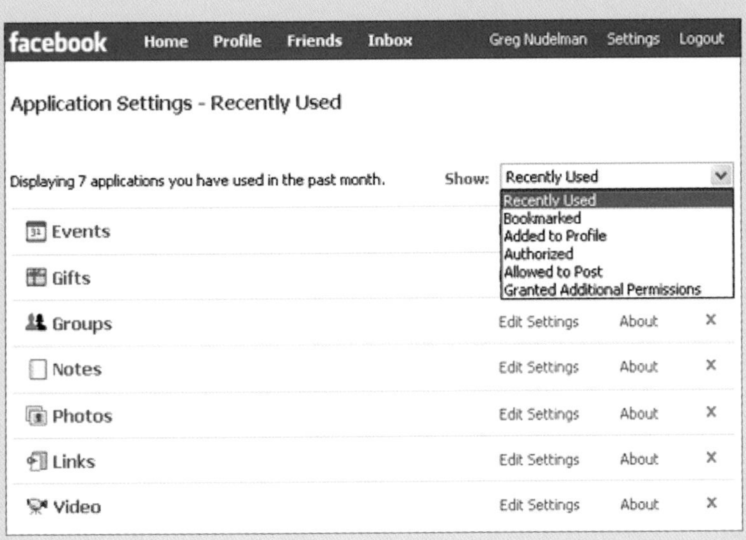

FIGURE 10.4

Facebook combines sorting and filtering options in one drop-down list

For example, the **Recently Used** setting sorts the entire applications inventory by date of use, whereas **Bookmarked** or **Authorized** are basically filtering controls based on flags.

Of course, there are some disadvantages to simply throwing a bunch of sorting and filtering options into the same drop-down list. For example, in the case of the **Bookmarked** or **Authorized** filters, the order in which items in the inventory appear is not clear. In the case of Facebook applications, filtering by bookmarked apps may be the primary intent, and sort order might not matter much. However, in some cases, you can apply the principle of filtering by sorting to combination sorting and filtering controls to create a more graceful user interface (see "Case Study: Redesigning Hotmail Sorting" at the end of this chapter).

The best sites use a creative combination of sorting and filtering to help customers reach their goals faster and easier. For example, Netflix combines **Top 50** and **New Arrivals** sorts with a **Genres** filter on the navigation bar under **Watch Instantly**, as Figure 10.5 shows.

FIGURE 10.5

Netflix navigation offers a combination of sorting and filtering controls for exploring their inventory

Clicking **New Arrivals** sorts the Netflix inventory by date of entry. In contrast, the **Genres** drop-down menu filters the inventory by category, sorted by relevance. These two controls coexist on the same navigation bar without causing any confusion and reflect the most efficient and popular ways to drill down into the Netflix inventory.

Top 50 is an interesting variation that combines a popularity sort with a count filter that cuts off the list of results at 50 items. There is no technical reason for cutting off the popularity sort at 50 items. However, people who use such features might feel that a **Top 50** or **Top 100** list represents a manageable number of items they can explore effectively, whereas a list of 100,000 movie titles sorted by popularity could be quite intimidating.

In your own search user interfaces, look for opportunities to address your customers' goals by providing appropriate combinations of controls. If it is appropriate for a task, do not hesitate to place sorting and filtering controls side-by-side—or even to combine them in creative ways that help people meet their goals.

Myth #5: Sorting Implemented Using Column Headers Is Superior to Other Sorting Methods

Clickable column headers are an excellent way to implement sort user interface—they save screen real estate and look slick. Is header-based sorting superior to other methods, like tabs and drop-down? The answer is, as always: It depends. At least when it comes to ecommerce, the header sort has the following serious drawbacks:

- Some people do not realize that the column headers are clickable.

- It's hard to tell a sort direction on a column at a glance. (Up/down arrows do not always translate into tangible sort direction, like price low to high, for example.) Most people click a column header several times to figure out the sort direction.

- Default sort direction (for example, always descending, the down arrow) does not always translate correctly to the primary use case, so some headers always need to be clicked twice. To accommodate the most common use cases, some columns like **Date**, need to start with sort arrow *up* (for example, **Most Recent First**), whereas the others such as **Price** start with the sort arrow *down* (for example, **Cheapest First**). This mismatch between the initial sort directions for different primary use cases introduces additional elements of confusion and cognitive friction to the interface.

- It is difficult to clearly indicate common "combined sorting" conditions, for example, Sorting emails by **Sender** and **Date**, **Newest First**.

- It's impossible to allow sorting by an attribute that is not shown in the columns, for example, the primary Amazon use cases of sorting via **Bestselling** and **Most Popular** can't be implemented via header sort unless you display a **Sales Rank** and **Popularity** columns, neither one of which carry any useful information.

- Column headers do not readily translate into mobile UIs due to a lack of horizontal screen real estate.

In most common ecommerce applications, tabs and drop-downs generally work better as **Sort By** user interface controls than column headers. Drop-downs (and to the lesser extend tabs) enable the designers to specify precisely what items will appear first using natural language that maps best to a user's mental model. Drop-downs are by far the most common because they are more flexible and completely independent from the format and nature of the data in the search results and are more frugal than tabs with screen real estate. For example, the **Price: Cheapest First** drop-down option and a **Most Popular** tab both offer clear, unambiguous, and goal-oriented sort controls. It is difficult to achieve this level of clarity with a sort implemented via a column-header.

CASE STUDY: REDESIGNING HOTMAIL SORTING

Often a well-chosen combination of sorting and filtering controls, creatively recombined to allow the customer to apply both controls together, creates a more useful and intuitive experience. For example, the **Sort by** drop-down list in Hotmail, shown in Figure 10.6, combines various **Sort by** options—including **Date**, **From**, **Subject**, and **Size**—with just a single filtering option: **Show only messages with attachments**.

FIGURE 10.6

Hotmail combines many sorting options with a single filtering option

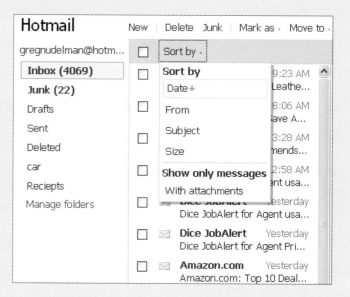

Although there is nothing wrong with combining sorting and filtering, in this case, the filtering task is the odd one out. It is separated visually from the sorting options, and it appears that the text of the filtering option wraps. You are left wondering how email messages with attachments will be sorted. In this case, their sort order is not a trivial matter. Will messages be sorted by date or by attachment size? If by attachment size, in what order—ascending or descending? How does this differ from the **Sort by Size** option?

If you use the filtering by sorting paradigm, you can avoid all this confusion by adding a fifth sorting option, **Sort by Size of Attachment**, as shown in Figure 10.7. In this case, messages without attachments would follow those with attachments. (Logically, messages without the attachment have an attachment size of 0.)

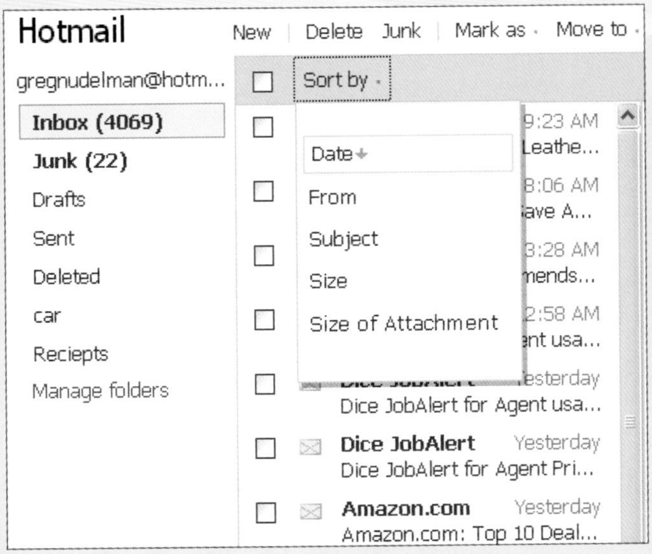

FIGURE 10.7

Proposed use of the filtering by sorting paradigm in Hotmail

By adding this sorting option, you avoid splitting options in the drop-down list into two groups and create a much more minimalist and graceful user interface. This option even follows the existing paradigm that enables two-way sorting by attachment size—ascending and descending (the choice that is missing from the option **Show only messages with attachments** that enables only filtering).

CHAPTER 11

DESIGNING QUERY DISAMBIGUATION SOLUTIONS FOR ONLINE SHOPPING

Our language is limited and imperfect. Typical search queries executed quickly and with little forethought are even more so. When a customer constructs a query that can have more than one meaning, a quality search interface must provide the tools to help the customer define the query in less ambiguous terms, so the search results more closely match the person's intended topic. This process is known as *disambiguation*, and best practices for doing this effectively are the subject of this chapter.

WHICH CANON?

Recently, I came across Kosmix.com—a new search engine promising a combined search and browse approach. I was curious, so I put this new search app through its paces by typing a query *Canon*. As shown in Figure 11.1, Kosmix

FIGURE 11.1

Original Kosmix.com results for the query "Canon"

returned a great variety of search results. In addition to images of cameras, the new search engine displayed results for the company profile typed in for investment purposes, Pachelbel's "Canon" (which is a famous piece of music) and (to my great surprise) a Canon mattress pad and a Canon ottoman, both of which were prominently featured in the products section. Unfortunately, these results represented a fairly typical situation that results when the system does not correctly understand the meaning of the query.

Interestingly, the Kosmix search results were recently redesigned as shown in Figure 11.2. At first glance, the search results seem somewhat improved because both the mysterious Canon mattress pad and ottoman are now thankfully gone.

FIGURE 11.2

Improved Kosmix.com results for the query "Canon" needs more improvement

However, you soon realize that the problem is far from solved. The search results page is a confusing mishmash of unrelated links and product links that lacks any semantic structure and meaning. The redesigned *Canon* search results are now graced by tweets in Spanish and German, discussions about Canon Paper and Linear Regression Calculators, news from blogs such as IdiotInc and

TheUseless, and even what looks like a mysterious Web analytics graph. Not much of the page is dedicated to more mainstream Canon products such as cameras and related electronic accessories.

What's going on here? The fundamental problem is that Kosmix segments the search results by content *type* (for example, Video, Articles, News, and so on) and not according to the more useful content *category* (for example, cameras, electronics, music, investment ideas, and so on). In other words, Kosmix does not attempt to refine the meaning of the query to deliver search results more in line with the customer's goals. The user interface does not provide any tools whatsoever to help customers define their query better. The only way to improve the search results is by typing more keywords into the search box, which requires both thought and work, two things any busy, distracted Internet user can do without. As human-computer interaction expert Jef Raskin famously quipped in his book *The Humane Interface*:

"A computer shall not waste your time or require you to do more work than is strictly necessary."

—JEF RASKIN

What can be done to improve communication between customer and the system to better convey the meaning of the customer's query? The three strategies for query disambiguation used most often follow:

- **Show Related Searches:** a module that shows how people modified queries similar to the one the customer typed in.
- **Default to a category:** Apply a category filter automatically if disproportionate number of items falls in the same category.
- **Present a prominent category selector:** Call the customer's attention to selecting a category before proceeding.

The following sections discuss the advantages and limitations of each approach.

SHOW RELATED SEARCHES

Related Searches is a fairly standard module that you can find on many mainstream ecommerce sites and search engines. You can see one example of this in the Amazon.com interface shown in Figure 11.3.

Most Web sites use some way to track how people modified their original query. The related searches module applies some algorithm to this tracking data to show the most common ways that people modify their queries. As shown in Figure 11.3, people who typed in *Canon* augmented their queries by typing in **Canon camera**, **Canon lens**, and others.

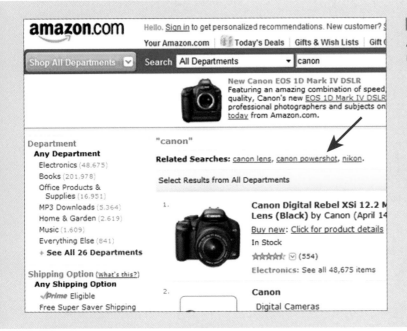

FIGURE 11.3

Amazon.com's related searches module in the results for "Canon"

In her recent book, *Search User Interfaces*, search interface expert Marti Hearst discusses the related searches algorithm in detail and quotes several impressive studies that document the effectiveness of this approach. Indeed, in my experience, people mostly found related searches module relevant and used it to find more of what they wanted, mainly due to the good information scent presented by this module. The related searches often seem to represent the keyword combinations that the people unconsciously wanted, yet could not quite formulate themselves without some thought. Essentially, related searches eliminates the thinking and effort required to create a good query, making the user interface more intuitive and enjoyable, without using a great deal of the precious screen real estate. The back-end algorithm does require a fair bit of the infrastructure to implement the query tracking; although, some third-party APIs such as Yahoo BOSS are now available to make the job of created related searches easier.

In my studies, I discovered that the majority of suggestions that revolved around modifications of the original query were positively received due to a strong user perception that these recommended queries represent the combined "wisdom of the crowds" similar to the concept of folksonomies and tagging.

Note—On the other hand, many people I observed were highly suspicious of any orthogonal queries that recommended competing brands or products.

For example, a related query shown in Figure 11.3 that recommends "Nikon" when the person typed in *Canon* would quickly cause some people to become mistrustful and question the value of the other suggestions shown in the related searches module. For this reason, I generally recommend that finding interfaces concentrate on showing only the original query modifications in the related searches module and show competing products and brands in a different module. Showing only the queries that contain the original keyword can easily be achieved via a simple **grep** command. Despite these minor drawbacks, Related Searches is a useful device for helping people disambiguate their queries and improve the quality of their search results to create a better finding experience.

DEFAULT TO CATEGORY

Automatically defaulting all the search results to a specific category or topic is also a common strategy for disambiguation. Determining a category or topic automatically can be accomplished using supply data, demand data, or some combination of the two.

To make the automatic category determination using supply data, the system might measure the number of items in the inventory that match the specific keyword query. For example, if 70% of the items that match the query *Canon* are of the **Digital Gadgets** category, the search algorithm might place the customer into the **Digital Gadgets** category automatically, omitting the results in **Music** and **Other** categories. A more sophisticated way to do this might be to use supply data instead, by answering the question "how many customers proceeded to visit (or buy) items in the **Digital Gadgets** category after typing in *Canon* versus all other categories? If that number exceeds a certain threshold, the **Digital Gadgets** category might be automatically selected.

What might be some of the advantages of selecting a category automatically? Interpreting the query *Canon* as a request for **Digital Gadgets** and automatically showing a Canon brand catalog interface (and not Pachelbel's music piece) allows Best Buy to create a compelling visual browse experience, complete with custom subcategories, aspects, and so on, as shown in Figure 11.4.

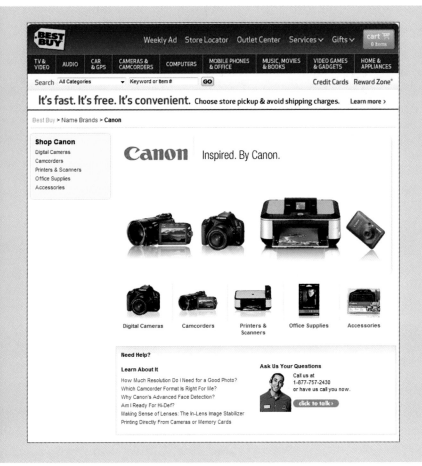

FIGURE 11.4

BestBuy.com results for Canon automatically understand Canon as a brand of digital gadgets

Notice how extremely committed Best Buy's category selection is as compared with the Amazon.com search results for the same query shown in Figure 11.3. Not only is the Canon brand selected automatically, there is no trace of any other *Canon* results also present on the site. This is a great experience for someone looking for Canon electronic gadgets, but it could be confusing for someone looking for Pachelbel's music masterpiece.

Note—Selecting a category or topic automatically is a strong action, and evidence shows that half-hearted measures to indicate the presence of other categories of results on the site do not work particularly well.

Here is an example. As part of doing some user research for one of the top Internet retailers, I tested a memorable interface that automatically selected a category **Shoes** when the user typed in a query *Nike*. However, unlike BestBuy.com shown in Figure 11.4, the interface also provided a prominent link to undo the category selection shown as **Not looking for Nike Shoes?** The test involved finding Nike bags. A significant finding was that the vast majority of the participants did not discover or click the link **Not looking for Nike Shoes?** This might have occurred because the link did not contain any information scent of the category **Bags** that the participants were searching for. Additionally, processing a negative statement "Not looking" turned out to be fairly difficult by quickly scanning the page, as most people tend to do. The link might have been more successful if instead it dynamically provided other available Nike categories and started with strong keyword scent words. For example: **Nike Bags, Shirts, Pants, Jackets & more...**

The moral? If you do commit to a topic or category as part of the disambiguation strategy, make sure it is for the right reason and based on the metrics that can help you meet your business goals. Decrease your risk by providing a clear, actionable way out of the automatically selected category that starts with prominent keywords providing a strong information scent of other popular categories or topics that match the same keyword.

PRESENT A PROMINENT CATEGORY SELECTOR

In addition to the Related Queries widget, most ecommerce sites also provide a category selector widget. In Figure 11.3, Amazon.com presented the available categories in the left nav bar. Although this strategy is standard and widely accepted, some sites go further to emphasize the categories as a strategy for disambiguation. Compare, for example, Amazon.com results shown in Figure 11.3 with the HomeDepot.com search results search for the query *drill*, which display the categories prominently above the search results, as shown in Figure 11.5.

There are many good reasons to emphasize the categories as part of your disambiguation strategy. Prominent categories above the search results clearly signal to the customer that the site is confused about the meaning of the query. Prominent categories also enable the customer to correctly customize the interface following the category selection to provide the aspects and finding tools that match a specific category. For example, the next screen following the **Drills** category selection might feature **Power** aspect, instead of **Size** or **Hardness** aspects that might be surfaced following the selection of the **Drill Bits** category. Showing categories above the search results instead of to the left nav bar often also enables displaying longer category names without wrapping, improving the information scent without compromising readability.

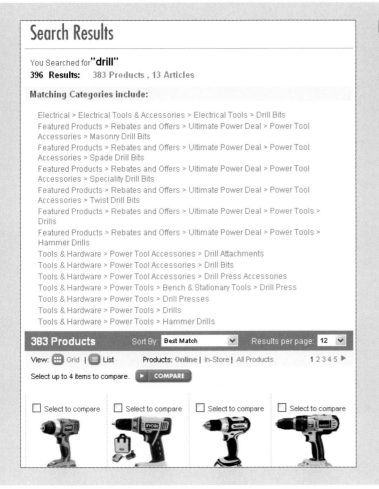

FIGURE 11.5

HomeDepot.com results for thr query "drill" feature prominent categories above the search results

Unfortunately, nothing is free. Anything you place above the search results, including category links, detracts from the actual shopping, so use this disambiguation solution with care. Showing prominent categories above the search results is best suited for cases when the system is actually confused about the meaning of the query. One solution worth considering is the *Expanding Category Widget* design pattern described in the *Case Study: Home Depot Query Disambiguation Redesign* at the end of this chapter.

Note—For many high-value queries, approaches based on modifying the standard search results pages discussed here do not go far enough. For those cases it is often worth creating a separate page specifically dedicated to query disambiguation. This design pattern, known as *More Like This* is discussed in the next chapter.

CASE STUDY: HOME DEPOT QUERY DISAMBIGUATION REDESIGN USING THE EXPANDING CATEGORY WIDGET DESIGN PATTERN

Although showing prominent categories above the search results is an effective query disambiguation strategy, it can also have some pitfalls when incorrectly implemented. If you look carefully at Figure 11.6, you can notice that HomeDepot.com search results actually feature *two* separate category selectors: one in the left nav and the other above the search results, which can be confusing.

FIGURE 11.6

HomeDepot.com has two different category selectors that cause confusion

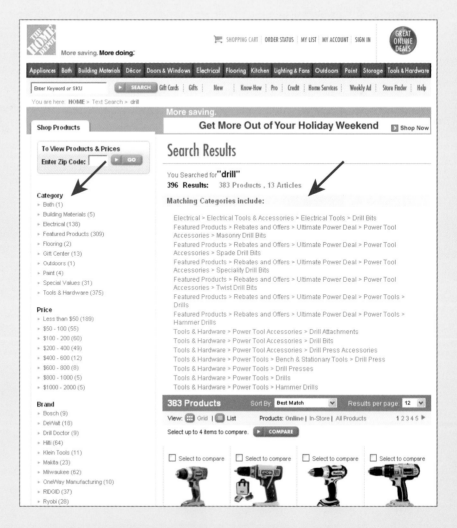

Though similar, the two sets of categories are not exactly the same, leading the customers to wonder where they should click and why. The links in the left nav are sorted alphabetically (not in the order of popularity) which is suboptimal, whereas it is entirely not clear how the categories on top of search results are selected and sorted and why they are displayed in such a prominent location. As a result, the categories displayed above the search results feel a bit like a band-aid for jumping directly to the popular areas of the site—the job that is better served by providing an additional information scent for the main categories. You might expect each of the subcategories to be a separate link (for example, clicking the **Power Tools** to bring up a level-two subcategory) but this is not the case. Instead, each of the links is a complete selection that navigates 3–4 levels deep into the hierarchy, forcing the customers to make a committed category choice before they had a chance to see a wider inventory. This also exposes the subset of a detailed hierarchy, forcing the users to make an effort early on to understand the category structure to make an informed decision. Last but not least, hierarchical category layout causes a huge readability problem: Many categories start with the same keywords; for example, seven of the available categories start with the keywords **Tools & Hardware > Power Tool** that makes it hard to distinguish the tools and the accessories categories from one another to make the right choice.

The screen displays too many categories (14) that appear above the search results, and even despite the generous amount of available real estate, the category names wrap several lines. Together, these two factors push the "real" search results down on the screen, actually placing any product's search results below the fold on many screen resolutions. The author's research indicates that many customers are confused by this system behavior. Instead of scrolling down to the search results, many people feel that the site forces them to click a category before they can see any actual search results.

A better choice might be to commit to showing the detailed level 1 categories only once, above the search results. These level 1 categories might be augmented with additional keywords to help the customers make the right decision as the space allows to avoid wrapping. As Daniel Tunkelang notes in his book *Faceted Search*, showing 4–7 values for each aspect seems like a sweet spot. That finding is well supported by the author's experience, who would stick to Daniel's recommendation and reduce the number of Home Depot categories at least by half. The resulting interface might look something like what is shown in Figure 11.7.

FIGURE 11.7

Recommended redesign of the HomeDepot.com interface using the expanding category widget design pattern

Figure 11.7 shows a new Expanding Category Widget design pattern, similar to a search interface the author recently designed for an enterprise client that had long category names, forcing the categories to wrap 3–4 times if they were placed in the left nav. Placing categories above the search results solved the problem of effectively handling long category names and provided a great way to disambiguate complex queries.

Note—However, be aware that even this improved user interface basically distracts the customer from actual shopping. Showing a prominent category practically forces your customers to deal with the complexities of your interface and category hierarchy on your site instead of doing the actual shopping.

If the query is less ambiguous, a good middle ground may be to experiment with an Expanding Category Widget pattern. In this pattern, the wide category widget collapses to a standard size in the left nav, while retaining the handle to expand the category hierarchy control (as shown in the lower half of Figure 11.7). For queries where the system is confused, the widget first loads in the expanded state. In all other instances, the category widget loads in the collapsed state but can be opened by the user to allow for a better information scent and shortcuts to allow drill-down into popular subcategories. The Expanding Category Widget is a useful design pattern that might be worth exploring as part of the category-driven disambiguation strategy.

Judicious use of simple animation to show expand-collapse transition is helpful to make the most of this design. For example, when the search results page loads for the first time, the widget can be shown fully expanded; then it can smoothly collapse into a normal size in the left nav using transition animation to demonstrate the expanding functionality. Typically this demonstration needs to be done only once per customer when the site first loads.

CLARIFY, THEN REFINE

Once the province of library scientists, facets have become a staple of on-line shopping sites. Faceted classification overcomes the rigidity of using a single hierarchical taxonomy through a more flexible scheme that uses multiple, independent facets. For example, the facets for a wine catalog would include varietal, region, vintage, etc. In a more heterogeneous collection, such as a department store, there could be dozens of facets, some of which only apply to a small subset of the collection (e.g., screen size).

Shopping sites that employ faceted classification allow users to refine their search results based on facets. Typically, the user performs a text search and then progressively narrows the search results by selecting facet values. For example, a user might search for "digital cameras" and then refine by brand, price, and number of megapixels.

Faceted refinement can address two scenarios: clarification of ambiguous queries and refinement for general ones. While both of these scenarios involve narrowing down large result sets, they are quite distinct from one another. You can think of an ambiguous query as dropping you someplace at random on a map: Before you start trying to find nearby towns and attractions, your first task is to find a road (see Figure 11.8). In contrast, refinement leverages the network of relationships in your content (i.e., the network of roads) to enable navigation and exploration.

Ambiguous queries call for a simple and immediate clarification dialog to establish the user's information need. For example, the search query "intelligence" on a library or bookstore might retrieve books about mental ability or information gathering; until the system has established the user's intended meaning, presenting results is a guessing game. As discussed in this chapter, a site can support users by offering users a prominent category selector—typically using a single facet—in response to ambiguous queries. Such a category selector is much more useful than a collection of facets that may not even be applicable to the user's query intent.

For unambiguous queries, there is less urgency around offering a refinement dialog because the results will at least make sense to the user, even if they are not optimally relevant. But it is here that facets shine, since they organize the set of relevant results and allow users to navigate and explore that set.

FIGURE 11.8

Query Disambiguation
vs. Faceted Refinement

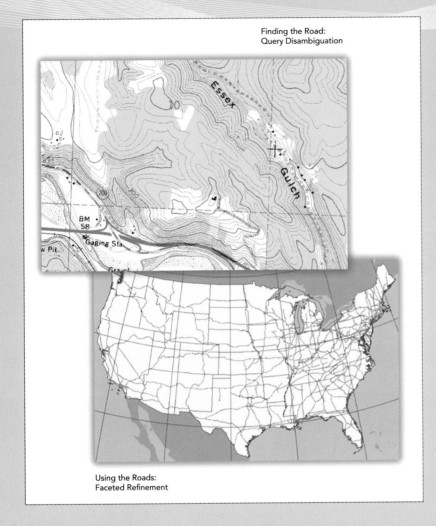

Finding the Road:
Query Disambiguation

Using the Roads:
Faceted Refinement

In summary, faceted search can help users clarify ambiguous queries and refine general ones. But these tasks are distinct and have a clear order: Clarify, then refine.

—DANIEL TUNKELANG

REFERENCES

Hearst, Marti. *Search User Interfaces.* Cambridge University Press, 2009.

Raskin, Jef. *The Humane Interface: New Directions for Designing Interactive Systems*, Addison-Wesley Professional, New York, 2000.

Tunkelang, Daniel. *Faceted Search.* Morgan & Claypool Publishers, 2009.

INTRODUCING THE MORE LIKE THIS DESIGN PATTERN

The previous chapter presented several design strategies for query disambiguation. This chapter continues the discussion of query disambiguation by exploring a simple but powerful design pattern, *More Like This*, which is a versatile design pattern that provides the information scent and structure that enables customers to make quick, easy, and intuitive navigational decisions. Unfortunately, most sites do not make sufficient use of this pattern, and others that do use it, often implement it incorrectly.

SHOW ME MORE

The idea behind the More Like This pattern is deceptively simple: Within each group of items representing a particular category from a catalog or accompanying each item in search results, provide a prominent link or button with a label that is some variation of **More Like This >** or **See All X >**. Of course, the devil, as they say, is in the details. Figure 12.1 shows one of the more successful implementations of this pattern, the Amazon.com home page.

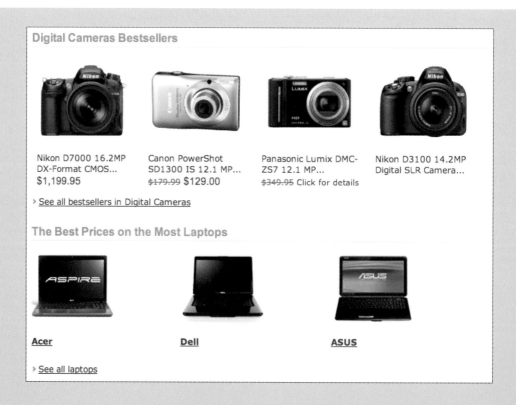

FIGURE 12.1

Amazon.com's successful implementation of More Like This

On close examination, Amazon.com's implementation of this design pattern yields a few important guidelines:

:: **Make group organization simple and obvious.** Each group title should be prominent and simple, not inviting deep thought or much examination. The words and the color treatment of group titles should flow in a way that allows customers to easily skim them.

:: **Focus on helping customers make decisions.** Although the items in each group are fairly relevant, the subtle focus of the whole page is not on finding exactly the right item on the current page, but instead on displaying some relevant entry points to an unfathomably large list of relevant choices on Amazon.com as each group of items exemplifies.

:: **Format groups differently from search results.** The items in each group have a horizontal layout, in a gallery format. This layout makes it easy to differentiate More Like This groups from the search results, which typically appear in a vertical list.

The most important thing to keep in mind is that all these design features support a single key goal: to help customers find what they want by providing the information scent and motivation that makes their navigational decisions easy and intuitive. Now examine what happens when sites ignore these simple guidelines.

MAKE GROUP ORGANIZATION SIMPLE AND OBVIOUS

Any cognitive friction around the organization and format of different groups makes navigational decisions more difficult. Instead of diving directly into making decisions mainly on the basis of the information scent embedded in each group's content, customers frequently try to understand why certain groups have a different format—a confusing and usually futile endeavor. Figure 12.2 shows one example of such an over-designed More Like This page, displaying search results for the query *Thai Restaurant San Francisco* on Yelp.com.

FIGURE 12.2

Yelp's over-designed More Like This page

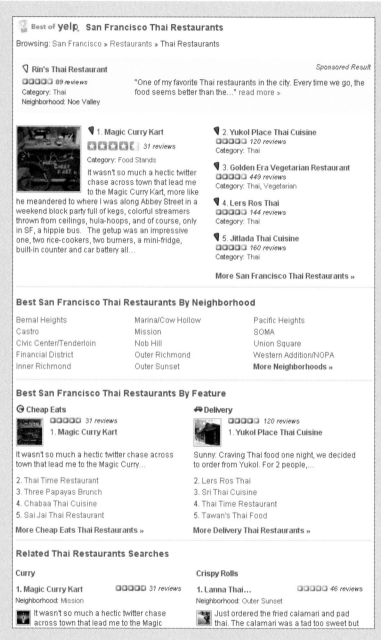

The purpose of this landing page is not to present all possible choices but to help customers chose a method that would best let them explore a selection of Thai-food restaurant recommendations. Unfortunately, this purpose does not appear to guide the design. Observe that the page has no fewer than seven different groups, each with its own branding and formatting, in an overly complex, nonstandard layout. Together, all these differences create a cacophony of results, making it hard to compare the different groups without studying them in detail. Fancy formatting and noticeably different layouts of various groups of results on the page greatly hinder customers from making navigational decisions quickly, which should be the page's primary aim.

Contrast this page with the Amazon.com home page in Figure 12.1, in which each group has the same simple format, drawing the eye to the content. This page design enables customers to scan various groups of items and make navigational decisions to further explore a particular group of items quickly and easily.

Last, but not least, the first section, **Best of Yelp**, does not look like the other groups because it is the only one that contains breadcrumbs. As a rule of thumb, on More Like This pages, breadcrumbs should appear above all the More Like This groups, not within any of them.

FOCUS ON HELPING CUSTOMERS MAKE DECISIONS

In helping customers make navigational decisions in More Like This groups, is more content better? The answer is it depends. Amazon.com's More Like This pattern includes one subtle but powerful feature, as shown in Figure 12.3: When a customer increases the page width, the number of items in each horizontal group in this liquid layout automatically expands, so higher resolution screens and wider windows show more items in a group.

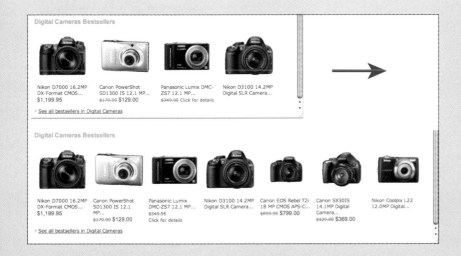

FIGURE 12.3

Expanding page width on Amazon.com increases the number of items in the group

The benefits of liquid screen layouts are discussed in Chapter 3, "Choosing the Right Search Results Page Layout," so this topic is not covered in detail here. However, this kind of horizontal expansion is no simple trick, so don't expect it to work out-of-the-box. Though, if you can afford the time that developing the right CSS style sheet involves, this is one feature well worth implementing.

On Amazon.com, more content is better. Partly, this is because the presentation of additional items increases the likelihood of one catching the interest of a prospective buyer. But most important, showing a greater number of items presumably creates a better information scent for each group, helping to motivate customers to explore a group in more detail.

 What if there was a way to show even more content in each horizontal group on a page? One way to do that would be with a carousel widget that scrolls from side to side, like the one shown in Figure 12.4, on a category page on Netflix.com.

FIGURE 12.4

Netflix's Show More Like This carousel pattern

In many ways, the Netflix More Like This implementation is similar to that of Amazon.com. The page organization is simple and obvious, and the groups look different from the search results. There is, however, one important difference: Clicking an arrow at either side of each group scrolls the contents of a group to the right or left, displaying an additional four items. Does the addition of this carousel widget help or hinder the primary goal of the page?

Well, the jury is still out on that. However, one thing is clear: The carousel takes the focus away from a customer's ability to make a decision about which group to explore and instead invites the customer to linger on the page longer to explore each of the groups. This is not necessarily a bad thing. But keep in mind that, even though a carousel can show customers twice as many items in a group, it still shows only 8 to 10 items in total. This is in contrast to the hundreds, if not thousands of items a customer could see in the complete search results by clicking the **See all** link for a group. Providing larger secondary targets—the left- or right-pointing arrows—also makes people think they should click them. If customers do click the arrows, there is a good chance they might become mesmerized by the fancy scrolling interaction and miss that the page is supposed to help them choose a subcategory to explore.

Note—A customer might look at the eight items the widget presents, find none of them relevant, and leave the site, thinking those eight items are all there were to see in a particular subcategory.

A carousel might seem like a fun, beneficial feature, but remember that the main purpose of the More Like This design pattern is to direct customers to explore the entire selection of items under each category—that is, to select a category to explore—not to find exactly the item they want among the 8 to 10 items each carousel displays. To drive people to explore, the overall design of each group must be fairly Spartan, so customers can make their decisions quickly and move on to exploring the main body of the search results. If fancy group formatting or Ajax carousels make customers disregard the more important More Like This buttons, such a page fails to meet its primary objective.

Note—If you are still thinking about using a carousel for your More Like This groups, consider that Netflix has one of the best recommendation engines in the world and can usually select very relevant items to include among its 8 to 10 options. Amazon.com, which also has an exceptional recommendation engine, tried incorporating carousels for all its groups in the past, but has since dropped the feature. Amazon.com now uses the carousel feature sparingly, if at all, presumably, because the results underperformed the Spartan group design, which is optimized for quick scanning.

Although a typical More Like This page does not warrant the use of carousels, in some circumstances they can be appropriate. One place in which a carousel widget might come in handy is in the *Two-Dimensional More Like This* design pattern discussed in the case study at the end of this chapter. But first, take a quick look at what happens when groups look just like the actual search results.

FORMAT GROUPS DIFFERENTLY FROM SEARCH RESULTS

So far, this chapter covered More Like This pages that, for the most part, look quite different from search results pages. What happens if you apply the More Like This pattern to subgroups containing vertical lists of results? One page that does a particularly poor job of helping customers choose a category of items to explore is the query disambiguation page on TripAdvisor.com, as shown in Figure 12.5.

This is clearly a page that does not invite further exploration. There is much that does not work on this page, including the bevy of no less that ten generic, monochrome icons; intermixed, ungrouped results that seemingly show up in random order; the small number and poor quality of results; and the absence of any pictures. However, as bad as all these problems are, customers might actually overlook them if the page did not also commit the cardinal sin of any grouping presentation: making the groups on the page look like actual search results.

Note—In all my user research, nothing was more confusing to participants or generated more sheer exasperation in customers than dealing with a page that looked and felt like a search results page that was actually some kind of fancy, special-purpose page containing groups, whose aim was to take customers to actual search results.

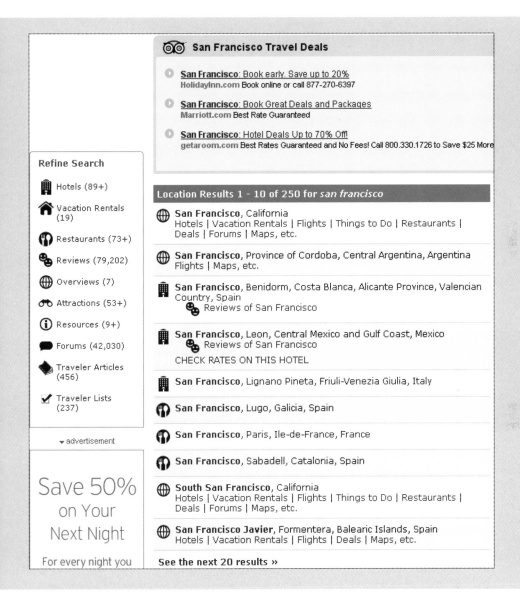

FIGURE 12.5

Search results
for the query
San Francisco on
TripAdvisor

TripAdvisor's query disambiguation page for San Francisco, shown in
Figure 12.5, is exactly such a page. I strongly recommend avoiding this approach
in your designs.

CASE STUDY: TRIPADVISOR REDESIGN USING THE TWO-DIMENSIONAL MORE LIKE THIS PATTERN

How could you improve TripAdvisor's query disambiguation page for San Francisco? One excellent approach is to use the Two Dimensional More Like This design pattern to provide an improved information scent and sophisticated information architecture that enables customers to make quick, easy, and intuitive navigational decisions.

In my user research, I've discovered that precisely because it's possible to show only a small number of items—typically 4–5—for each topic, customers' expectations are not to discover specific items of interest on this disambiguation page, but instead to see a *representative* set of items in each specific subcategory. What if, instead of showing a fairly random sample of 4–5 generic hotels, attractions, or restaurants, you instead showed 4–5 specific items that represent a more granular subdivision, or *aspect*, of each category? In other words, instead of getting item details for 4–5 random hotels, customers could use each of the hotels shown in a group to drill down to one of the most popular representative hotel *types*—for example, **Family**, **Business**, **Boutique**, or **Bed and Breakfast**. Clicking one of these 4–5 generic hotel stubs in the **Hotels** group would take customers to a search results page whose content was filtered by *both* the category **Hotels** and a type of popular hotel, making it possible for them to perform a rapid, visual, two-dimensional drill-down into their area of interest. This is the idea behind the Two-Dimensional More Like This pattern. Figure 12.6 provides an example, showing a suggested redesign for the TripAdvisor query disambiguation page for San Francisco.

This Two-Dimensional More Like This pattern is particularly appropriate for cases in which the content includes thumbnail images and both the category and aspect are clearly defined. In many cases, **Brand** is another popular search facet that provides an easily recognizable secondary aspect you can apply across a row.

Interestingly, there is little need for secondary aspects to be consistent across categories. Here's an example. The last chapter showed how Home Depot search results for the query *drill* fell into three categories: **Drills**, **Drill Bits**, and **Hammer Drills**. If you were to apply the Two-Dimensional More Like This pattern to that example, it would be highly appropriate to use **Brand**—**Black & Decker**, **Dewalt**, and **Makita**—as a secondary segmentation for the **Drills** category. On the other hand, it would be best to segment the **Drill Bits** category by types of drill bits— for example, **Sets**, **Drill Bits**, **Philips Screwdrivers**, and **Flat Screwdrivers**.

Typically, there are no issues with applying different secondary aspects to different More Like This groups on a page, so long as they make some intuitive sense. This might be because the customers using a search results page usually quickly narrow the results down to a specific category, following its information scent. So, customers need to figure out only the organizational pattern behind a single subcategory in which they are interested, and not spend any time or effort comparing different subcategories to one another.

FIGURE 12.6

Suggested redesign for the TripAdvisor query disambiguation page for San Francisco

As mentioned earlier, the Two-Dimensional More Like This pattern is an excellent use case for using a carousel widget. As Figure 12.6 shows, if there are more aspects—such as brands or hotel types—than can fit in the 4–5 thumbnails that can appear on a page at once, you can safely hide the less popular aspect values on the carousel. In this case, the expectation would be for customers to first narrow down their search to a specific category, and only then invest more attention in selecting the appropriate secondary aspect using the carousel. If customers cannot find the secondary aspect value they want by scrolling from side-to-side using the carousel, they can still click the more prominent **See All »** link to view all the search results for an entire category.

The Two-Dimensional More Like This pattern works wonders for resolving ambiguous queries and creating category pages on which customers can clearly express their desired search refinements by clicking a single label or image. However, this pattern would be less appropriate for information categories that are somewhat arbitrary and less clearly defined. In the Netflix example shown in Figure 12.4, is there actually that much difference between the categories **Anime Action** and **Anime Fantasy**? What movies would you choose to represent the subcategory aspects of **New Arrivals**?

One difficulty in designing a Two-Dimensional More Like This page is selecting which specific items to show as representatives of each aspect. You should select the first thumbnail in the set of search results that would appear if a customer clicked a subcategory plus an aspect. Selecting the first thumbnail in a list of search results as the representative aspect performs particularly well when sorting a search result set by **Best Selling** or **Best Match** because the first item usually provides an excellent representation of a constrained results set.

Note—Sometimes customers click a specific item not to select a subcategory and aspect, but simply because they liked the item in a thumbnail for some reason. Placing the item selected to represent a subcategory and an aspect first in a set of search results satisfies both the display criteria and the I-want-this-specific-item mental model perfectly.

What if a specific criterion such as price is important to decision making when selecting an item on a Two-Dimensional More Like This page? In this case, as Figure 12.6 shows, it is perfectly appropriate to use a list format—for example, **Priced from $XX.XX**, which shows the lowest-priced item in a given search results set—even if the results set that customers see when they click a link is sorted by **Bestselling** or **Most Popular**.

DESIGNING EFFECTIVE BREADCRUMBS

In a 2007 *Alertbox* entry titled "Breadcrumb Navigation Increasingly Useful," Web-design expert Jakob Nielsen states: "Breadcrumbs show people their current location relative to higher-level concepts, helping them understand where they are in relation to the rest of the site. Breadcrumbs afford one-click access to higher site levels and thus, rescue users who parachute into very specific, but inappropriate, destinations through search or deep links. Breadcrumbs never cause problems in [usability] testing. People might overlook this small design element, but they never misinterpret breadcrumb trails or have trouble operating them."

Based on his statement, you might conclude that breadcrumbs have attained the status of an essential finding user interface element; however, the prominent usability expert Jared Spool disagrees. In his blog post *Design Cop-out #2: Breadcrumbs,* Jared Spool states that, although breadcrumbs themselves aren't bad, many sites implement breadcrumbs poorly and use them as a design hack to compensate for a poorly designed finding experience. According to Jared, the biggest problem with many breadcrumb implementations is "the lack of [information] scent for the other areas of the site. If a user is in need of breadcrumbs because they are in the wrong part of the information tree, what they need most is a good [information] scent to the right part of the tree. However, the breadcrumbs only communicate the branch they're on—not the branch they need to be on."

Both Jakob Nielsen and Jared Spool raise valid points. The effectiveness of breadcrumbs—or any other interface element for that matter—depends on their implementation and the particular finding scenario. In 2002, information architect Keith Instone presented a poster titled "Location, Path, & Attribute Breadcrumbs" at the 3rd Annual IA Summit. It described three different types of breadcrumbs. The main distinction between them is the *Hierarchical* versus *Historical* order of breadcrumb elements. Now examine this distinction in depth.

HISTORICAL BREADCRUMBS

Historical, or *path,* breadcrumbs display the path a person took traversing a Web site's information-architecture space to arrive at the current page. The role of this type of breadcrumb is equivalent to the one that breadcrumbs played in the original tale of *Hansel and Gretel.* In modern ecommerce user interfaces, historical breadcrumbs most often contain a combination of both categories and faceted search attributes, as shown in Figure 13.1.

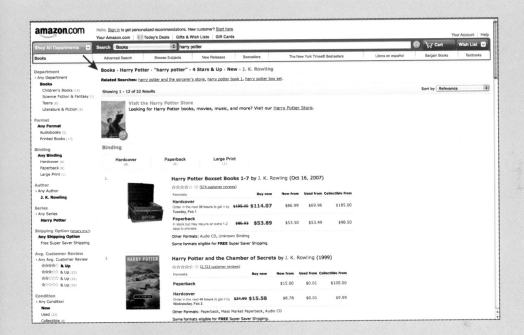

FIGURE 13.1

Amazon.com's historical breadcrumbs contain both categories and attributes

The combination of categories and attributes in breadcrumbs reflects the nature of the Web search process, in which people move fluidly between searching and browsing. These combined breadcrumbs show the entire path a customer has taken to get to the current page or state and support an effective and engaging finding flow.

Note—This strength of historical breadcrumbs is also their greatest limitation: Historical path/attribute breadcrumbs are not helpful from the standpoint of integrating search and browse activities with helping people find related content.

As shown in Figure 13.2, the path/attribute breadcrumbs on the Ariba Discovery Network demonstrate that historical breadcrumbs cannot show customers where they *could* go next. They show only where they've already *been*.

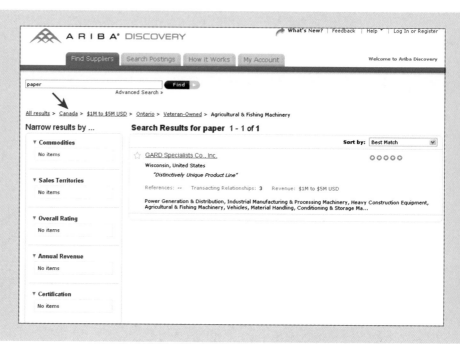

FIGURE 13.2

Path/attribute breadcrumbs
on the Ariba Discovery
Network

Note—Historical, or temporal, breadcrumbs cannot provide links to anchor categories, landing pages, brand catalogs, and other browsable pages, precisely because they carry the entire path/attribute history instead.

Often, customers wander through Web sites, leaving a trail that goes in circles or backtracks from deadends—when they find themselves in an unwanted part of a site. If a customer modifies a query, temporal breadcrumbs must also change, making query attributes appear to randomly jump around in the breadcrumbs and adding confusion.

Carrying a customer's entire navigational history in the breadcrumbs means a content page might look somewhat different, depending on the path the customer has taken to reach it and the selected attributes . Therefore, temporal breadcrumbs offer no help to people who go directly to a page buried deep within a site's information architecture by clicking a link on a Web search results page. In fact, Web search engines cannot reliably index pages whose content reflects a customer's navigational history—including historical breadcrumbs—because the site generates a different URL each time a customer accesses the page. (See the perspective *Usability, SEO, and Faceted Navigation* by Jaimie Sirovich at the end of this chapter).

An important variation of the historical breadcrumb is the *Breadbox* design pattern that Endeca perfected. The breadbox is an effective and popular interface device for showing name-value pairs of the facets in the order in which they were applied to the search results, as shown in Figure 13.3, from Endeca pattern library.

FIGURE 13.3

Breadbox design pattern

Many sites use the breadbox to present applied search facets vertically, in a visual treatment distinctly separate from the category hierarchy, or omit the category breadcrumbs altogether. There is an important reason for this. As the Endeca Design Pattern library cautions, the temporal breadbox might confuse the user if it is mixed with "you are here" hierarchical breadcrumbs. Problems arise because of the mental model mismatch between the two distinct, yet similar controls used for searching and browsing—customers cannot figure out the order in which various categories and filters are presented and fail to operate all the various moving parts of the finding interface effectively.

HIERARCHICAL BREADCRUMBS

In contrast, location breadcrumbs are hierarchical. They don't indicate where a customer has been, but instead, reflect the customer's current location within a site's information architecture. Hierarchies are helpful for a wide range of organization, finding, and navigating tasks and provide a simple way to manage complexity and easy access to the resources on a site.

As Figure 13.4 shows, on Edmunds.com, a unique, specific URL anchors the location of each page—so search engines can index its pages—and the site's hierarchical breadcrumbs provide a unique and consistent breadcrumb trail for each page on the site.

FIGURE 13.4

Hierarchical breadcrumbs on Edmunds.com anchor each page for search engines

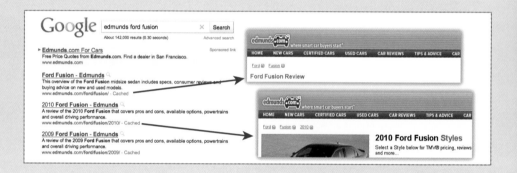

Note—Hierarchical breadcrumbs show customers where they are *right now* within the site's hierarchy, which makes it easier for people to orient themselves when they land on a page deep within a site.

Hierarchical breadcrumbs are also well suited to show customers where they *can* navigate, enabling them to discover related content by navigating up the hierarchy toward a category hub. Thus, for helping customers navigate, hierarchical breadcrumbs are more effective than the historical breadcrumbs. Jakob Nielsen's research findings support this view: "Breadcrumbs should show the site hierarchy, not the user's history."

Can applied faceted search aspects be also ordered hierarchically? My research indicates that most people find it intuitive when the Attribute-Location breadcrumb simply replicates the order in which *unselected* facets are presented (most typically in the left nav bar). Replicating the order in which unselected facets appear also provides an effective way to integrate search and browse by treating the Category as just another Attribute in the breadcrumb. In the vast majority of finding interfaces, Category appears first in the left nav bar, which automatically places any applied "browse" Category Attributes in front of the applied faceted search values. A recommended redesign of the Amazon.com search using hierarchical combined breadcrumb is shown in Figure 13.5.

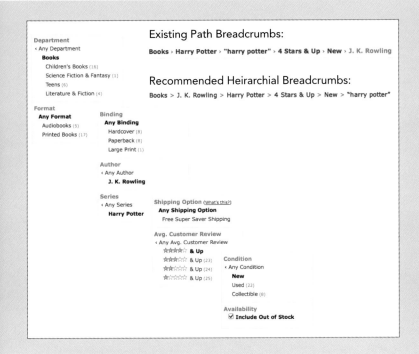

FIGURE 13.5

Recommended hierarchical breadcrumb matching the order of unselected facets in the left nav bar on Amazon.com

Based on my research, I can confidently state that most people we've observed and interviewed over the years found this faceted hierarchy scheme straightforward and intuitive and could confidently and accurately predict the expected system behavior for complex filtering tasks that involved applying, removing, and changing aspect values. The idea of showing both the categories and aspects in a single control opens the door to many innovative breadcrumb designs that integrate search and browse.

EMERGENT BREADCRUMB DESIGNS THAT INTEGRATE SEARCH AND BROWSE

In a recent UIE Virtual Seminar, "Search & Discovery Patterns," Peter Morville lauded the advantages of integrated finding: "Browse and search work best in tandem…. The best finding interfaces achieve a balance, letting users move fluidly between browsing and searching." Although user interfaces made giant strides in the last few years, combined finding controls that gracefully integrate search and browse remain an elusive goal.

Although, traditionally, people have used breadcrumbs mainly for browsing, a modified breadcrumb holds a promise to become the solution that integrates both searching and browsing, including faceted search and category navigation. Although no overarching trend has yet emerged, some of the more forward-looking solutions discussed in this section offer innovative, interesting ways to use breadcrumbs to combine searching and browsing:

:: Overstock.com's Set-Remove-Set Breadcrumb

:: Edmunds' breadcrumb with mega-menus

:: The Guardian.co.uk Web site's bidirectional breadcrumb

:: Microsoft Services' bidirectional breadcrumb with mega-menus

:: Yahoo! TV's tabbed breadcrumb

Finally, I discuss my own experimental design pattern called Integrated Faceted Breadcrumb (IFB) introduced in a *Boxes and Arrows* article. The case study, "Integrated Faceted Breadcrumbs on Walmart," at the end of the chapter describes the IFB design pattern in detail.

Note—Although none of the creative solutions discussed in this section have been universally adopted, and the combined breadcrumb control is certainly not ideal for every situation, the discussion of the merits of these designs can prove instructive. Ultimately, you will use the material in this section as a jumping off point for your experimentation.

Overstock.com's Set-Remove-Set Breadcrumb

Overstock.com uses a historical breadcrumb control that enables customers to remove applied aspects by unchecking a check box. Although this approach adds useful functionality, it is far from being intuitive and efficient. Another issue with the Overstock.com approach arises from lack of integration of the keyword query with the breadcrumb: After the query is run, keywords cannot be changed, only removed.

Antipattern: Changing Attributes with Set-Remove-Set

Traditional breadcrumbs afforded only a single mode of interaction, clicking on a link. As usability expert Jakob Nielsen so eloquently stated:

"Breadcrumbs are almost always implemented the same way, with a horizontal line that

- progresses from the highest level to the lowest, one step at a time;
- starts with the homepage and ends with the current page;
- has a simple text link for each level (except for the current page, because you should never have a link that does nothing); and
- has a simple, one-character separator between the levels (usually >).

... There aren't too many ways to mess up breadcrumbs in a design. No fancy stuff, just a line of textual links."

However, the relatively recent trend of integrating aspects within the breadcrumb created a way to remove individual breadcrumb elements, leaving the rest of the breadcrumb intact. This is the interaction I dubbed *Set-Remove-Set*: A customer removes one aspect of the query only to replace it with a different aspect value. A good example of that interaction mode is Overstock.com, shown in Figure 13.6.

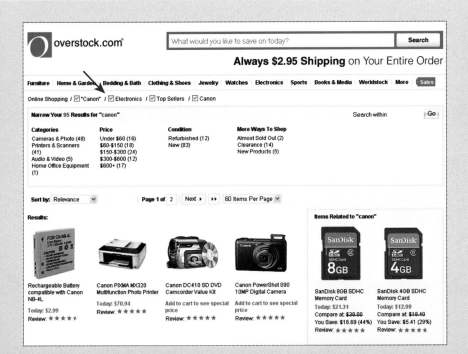

FIGURE 13.6

Overstock.com Set-Remove-Set implemented via check boxes

Applied aspects are removed from the breadcrumb by unchecking the check box next to the applied aspect in the breadcrumb. Set-Remove-Set can also be implemented via a close or cancel button located on each of the aspects.

Enhancing the functionality of the breadcrumb with the ability to remove individual elements or applied aspects is a great idea.

Note—Unfortunately, by far the most common use case is not *removing* an applied aspect but *changing* its value, such as changing the value of Brand aspect from Canon to Nikon.

To change the aspect value on Overstock.com, the customer has to remove the aspect entirely and then re-apply the same aspect, now with a different aspect value. For most people, this Set-Remove-Set interaction conflicts with their mental model and can therefore be considered an antipattern. As one of my evaluators stated: "This feels like having to turn off the radio every time I want to change the station." Breadcrumb-based interfaces such as Edmunds. com, that enable their customers to *change* the value directly without first removing it, appear to be easier to use and more efficient.

Antipattern: Lack of Direct Keyword Query Manipulation

Another issue with the Overstock.com breadcrumb interface is the way it handles keyword queries. Overstock.com pictured in Figure 13.7, has two search boxes: one to "search within" the existing query, and the other to start over with a new keyword-only search. Having two search boxes takes up precious screen real estate and increases the potential for confusion. Worse yet, the customer cannot directly modify their keyword query after the search is executed because the system converts all the keywords into a single monolithic aspect that cannot be modified, only removed in its entirety. People tend to change their keywords several times throughout the search process.

Note—Given that an average ecommerce query tends to be 2–3 keywords long, having to retype the *entire* query each time a customer wants to change one of the keywords is awkward.

Thus, the lack of direct query manipulation can be considered an antipattern.

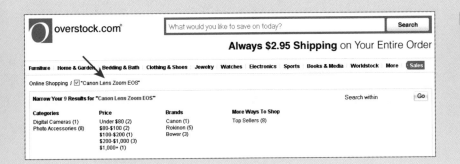

FIGURE 13.7

Overstock.com does not enable direct manipulation of the keyword query

Note—Not fully integrating keyword queries into the finding process is a serious drawback that is the Achilles heel of many breadcrumb-based interfaces that attempt to combine searching and browsing. Experimental IFB offers one solution that appears to be fairly effective in preliminary usability studies. The case study, "Integrated Faceted Breadcrumbs on Walmart," at the end of the chapter describes in detail how IFB integrates keyword queries while retaining direct manipulation of the text.

Edmunds' Breadcrumb with Mega-Menus

Edmunds is a fine example of a hierarchical enhanced breadcrumb control that takes up little space while offering a tremendous amount of useful functionality. Edmunds' breadcrumb uses mega-menus to enable its customers to easily change the attribute values. Unfortunately, Edmunds does not retain relevant query attributes when the customer changes one of the values in the breadcrumb. Edmunds also does not enable its customers to drop one of the attributes in the middle of the query while keeping the rest of the query intact.

Recommended Pattern: Changing Attribute Values Using Mega-Menus

Rather than removing an attribute to set a different attribute value—for example, removing the attribute Brand to change the value from Canon to Nikon as Overstock.com does—most people think in terms of simply *changing* the Brand from Canon to Nikon. A customer can most easily accomplish such a change using a drop-down list box or menu. This approach is more comprehensible than the typical remove mechanisms previously described because it enables a user to see all the value options available for an attribute or category. Luke Wroblewski first introduced the idea of using drop-downs on the breadcrumb elements to quickly jump between different areas of the site in his excellent book *Site Seeing: a Visual Approach to Web Usability* (Wiley, 2002). Edmunds.com implements the same idea using mega-menus in its multifunctional breadcrumb control, as shown in Figure 13.8.

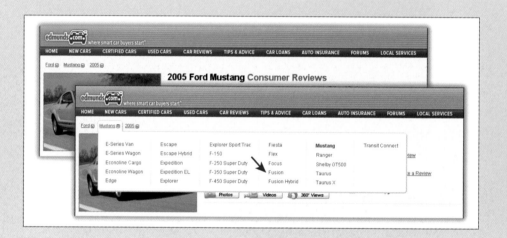

FIGURE 13.8

Edmunds' breadcrumbs with mega-menus

In my user research, the vast majority of people preferred this design to the more common Set-Remove-Set antipattern and found it effective and easy to use.

Recommended Pattern: Retaining Relevant Query Information

In my research, people seldom want to start the query over completely from scratch, unless they specifically indicated this action. Instead, a vast majority of the people interviewed wanted to retain as much of the query as possible with every change of the facet values and desired the system to help them construct a query that "makes sense," gracefully dropping facet selections that no longer applied to their modified query.

Unfortunately, although the Edmunds' interface design supports the *ability* to retain useful query information, this function is not implemented well on the back-end. For example, the person searching for a car might reasonably expect that changing the model from Mustang to Fusion can retain the previously selected year, 2005. Instead, as Figure 13.9 shows, the Web site resets the model year to the current year, and the year quietly disappears from the breadcrumb.

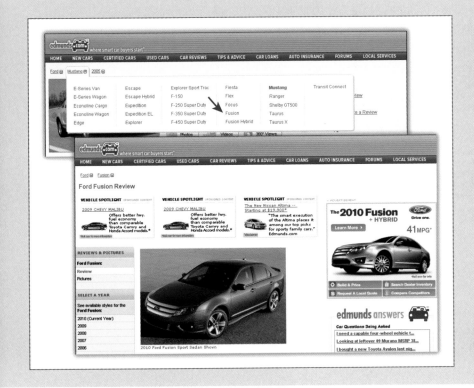

FIGURE 13.9

Changing attribute values drops useful parts of a query on Edmunds.com

A more useful system behavior would be to retain any relevant attribute values that apply to a new query—preferably in ways that always produce some search results. For example, suppose a customer has landed on a page with these breadcrumbs: **Home > Camera & Photo > ProductType:Digital Camera > Brand:Canon > Resolution:12mp > CameraType:EOS**

If the customer decides to change the **Product Type** from **Digital Camera** to **Lens**, it would make sense for the system to retain the **Brand** and **Camera Type** attributes, while dropping the **Camera Resolution** attribute because it doesn't apply to lenses, producing the following breadcrumbs: **Home > Camera & Photo > ProductType:Lens > Brand:Canon > CameraType:EOS**.

Note—Retaining aspects of a query that still apply to an updated query is a powerful user interface mechanism that enables customers to concentrate on their finding goals while the system takes care of the details.

With all these fancy new interactions added to the breadcrumbs element, you might be wondering: Would people still be able to browse just the **Home > Camera & Photo > ProductType:Lens**? My research has shown that despite the addition of the mega-menus to the breadcrumbs, most people still found it easy and intuitive to navigate up the hierarchy by using the traditional breadcrumb interaction of simply clicking the **ProductType:Lens** link in the breadcrumbs control. Providing the ability to change attributes while automatically retaining all relevant query information turns the breadcrumbs into a powerful and flexible finding mechanism, without making the resulting interface overly complicated or difficult to use.

Recommended Pattern: Removing Individual Aspects Using *See All*

In contrast to the Overstock.com example, where the breadcrumb enabled customers to only remove aspects, not change them, Edmunds.com only enables customers to change aspect values but does not enable aspect removal. This is a shame because for certain types of targeted broadening tasks (see Chapter 2), people often find it useful to remove aspects from the middle of the hierarchical breadcrumb while keeping the rest of the applied aspects intact.

For example, while browsing **Ford > Mustang > 2005**, people might want to remove the **Mustang** attribute to browse the page showing the entire **Ford > 2005** lineup of vehicles.

Can this type of navigation be enabled through the existing Edmunds interface? One way to do this would be to add a popular **Remove Filter** option in the aspect mega-menu. This is a viable option, but my research shows that people have a hard time understanding what this control actually does. There are two reason for this. First, most people do not generally think of applied aspects as filters. Second, it is difficult for most busy, distracted Internet users to think through the logical problem of seeing *more* stuff by *removing* something—this is contrary to most people's mental model of search and requires additional thinking.

Fortunately, there is an easy, effective solution: a *See All* design pattern. My considerable usability research on the topic has shown that rather than having to think in terms of removing a filter, most people find it easier to grasp the need to select a **See All** option, as in **See All Models** (and the corresponding **See All Brands**, **See All Body Styles**, and so on). The resulting interface matches most people's mental model well and translates perfectly into an English sentence: **Ford > See All Models > 2005**, which the system translates into **Ford > 2005**. I recommend placing the **See All** option first in the list in the mega-menu as, shown in Figure 13.10, that depicts the recommended redesign of Edmunds' breadcrumb interface.

FIGURE 13.10

Upgrading Edmunds.com to allow aspect removal using a See All design pattern

Guardian.co.uk's Bidirectional Breadcrumb

Although, according to Jakob Nielsen, breadcrumbs have traditionally occupied "only a single line of text," some sites have chosen to buck this trend and make a variation on breadcrumbs the central feature of a site's navigation strategy. One such site is Guardian.co.uk, shown in Figure 13.11, which employs what I'd call a *bidirectional breadcrumb*.

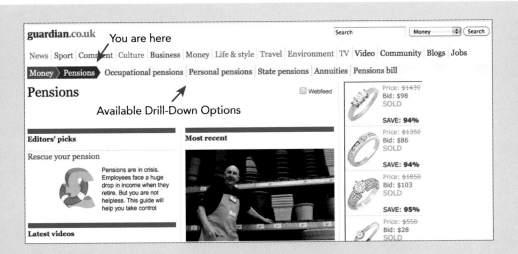

FIGURE 13.11

Navigation using bidirectional, color-coded breadcrumbs on Guardian.co.uk

As you can see, the prominent, colorful breadcrumbs on Guardian.co.uk borrow the Apple's chevron breadcrumb visual design. In the example shown in Figure 13.11, a user navigated from the parent topic **Money** to **Pensions**. In this case, the twist on traditional breadcrumbs is that when a user clicks the topic **Pensions**, its suptopics—**Occupational Pensions**, **Personal Pensions**, **State Pensions**, **Annuities**, and so on—appear immediately to the right, inviting exploration of the various subtopics. The bidirectional breadcrumbs on this site display *both* the parent and child elements of the current node. This is an interesting enhancement to traditional breadcrumb user interfaces, which enable users to navigate only back up a hierarchy or back in a search flow.

Microsoft Services' Bidirectional Breadcrumb with Mega-Menus

The Microsoft Services Web site took the bidirectional breadcrumb approach even further, making its breadcrumbs the site's primary navigation system. The addition of drop-down menus enables users to quickly traverse the entire information architecture by changing any of the parent elements to their siblings or navigate directly to the landing page for a parent topic by clicking it, as shown in Figure 13.12.

FIGURE 13.12

Bidirectional breadcrumbs with mega-menus on Microsoft Services

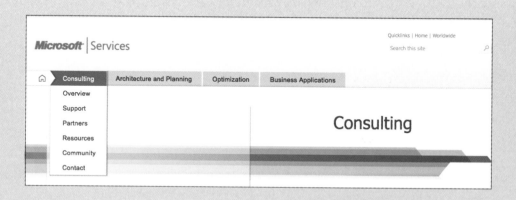

The mega-menus enable users to change attributes in a way that is similar to Edmunds.com previously described and is subject to some of the same limitations.

Yahoo! TV's Tabbed Breadcrumb

Another interesting breadcrumb navigation design comes from Yahoo! TV. Geoff Teehan of Teehan+Lax dubbed this design, shown in Figure 13.13, *Tabbed Breadcrumbs.*

FIGURE 13.13

Tabbed breadcrumb navigation on Yahoo! TV

As Geoff said in his blog (www.teehanlax.com):

"The navigation becomes focused on whatever section you're in, and all of the parent sections become part of an integrated breadcrumb. The first level of navigation is held within a drop-down [menu] on the home tab…. We were immediately intrigued by how natural this navigation system felt. It just seemed to get out of the way and provide a high level of focus on the section we were in. No matter how deep we dove, we never felt lost [or] abstracted from the top-most navigation tier."

In my opinion, adding a mega-menu to each of the top-level tabs—while automatically retaining relevant query information whenever a user changed any of the parent topics, as suggested earlier—would improve the Yahoo! TV navigation model even further.

CASE STUDY: INTEGRATED FACETED BREADCRUMBS ON WALMART

An emerging design issue for modern search user interfaces is the integration of faceted search and browsing. Unfortunately, most of today's ecommerce sites have not implemented effective solutions for this problem. For example, as shown in Figure 13.14, Walmart.com approaches searching and browsing through two completely separate user interfaces, creating a jumble of duplicated controls that overwhelm customers and make the site more difficult to use.

FIGURE 13.14

Disjointed mechanisms for faceted search and browsing on Walmart.com

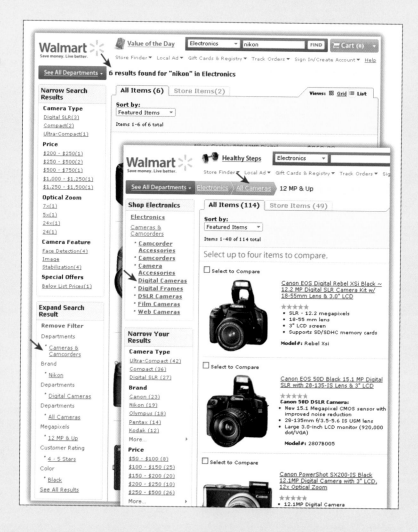

 The veritable cornucopia of filters, links, and options on Walmart.com makes it unlikely that customers can successfully duplicate a search or efficiently discover related products or content. Duplicate methods of finding also create a

problem for natural search because each search results page exists only within the context of a specific session.

As Marti Hearst says in Chapter 8 of her book *Search User Interfaces*, "The overarching design goals...[are] to support flexible navigation, seamless integration of browsing with directed (keyword) search, fluid alternation between refining and expanding, avoidance of empty results sets, and at all times allowing the user to retain a feeling of control and understanding." To meet the challenges the integration of searching and browsing presents, you can use an IFB design pattern, first published on *Boxes and Arrows* April 5, 2010. To illustrate this design pattern, I've created the wireframe of my proposed solution for a Walmart.com user interface redesign, as shown in Figure 13.15.

FIGURE 13.15

Wireframe of Walmart.com redesign with IFB

Preliminary usability testing has shown the IFB pattern to be useful, flexible, and usable. This pattern takes advantage of many of the best practices discussed in this chapter and takes breadcrumb design one step further by integrating the best of the breadcrumb solutions with search keywords, creating a unified user interface for searching and browsing.

The IFB pattern combines hierarchical Location and Attribute breadcrumbs by treating categories as just another attribute. The breadcrumbs' hierarchical organization ensures that the user interface creates a unique breadcrumb trail for every search results page on the site. This, in turn, enables easy indexing and navigation.

The IFB pattern incorporates the Change Attribute pattern—avoiding the Set-Remove-Set antipattern—by adding mega-menus to each of the breadcrumb elements. Furthermore, as shown in Figure 13.16, the IFB pattern automatically retains relevant query information, which makes jumping to any desired pages easy.

FIGURE 13.16

IFB retains relevant query information

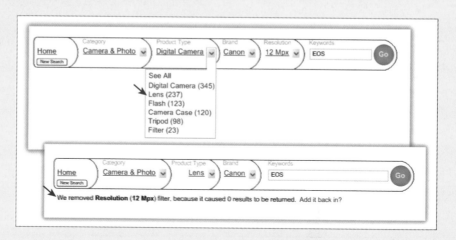

When considering various breadcrumb enhancements, it is important not to neglect information scent. In "Design Cop-out #2: Breadcrumbs," Jared Spool mentions that the biggest problem with breadcrumbs is their "lack of scent" and "the wording of the individual trail elements becomes very important."

Although most sites simply display selected categories and applied attributes in breadcrumbs, my research has shown that providing a clear attribute name label for each of the applied attributes adds a great deal of information scent. An important feature of the IFB is clear labeling of the individual breadcrumb elements I called *Breadcrumb Tiles*. The use of Breadcrumb Tiles greatly improves the page's information scent and enables any customers who were catapulted deep into the site's information architecture to easily find their way out using the appropriate drop-down menus and links.

Last, but not least, the IFB pattern enhances the traditional breadcrumb pattern by treating keywords as attributes and enabling users to directly edit them. As previously discussed, many faceted search user interfaces—like that on Overstock.com shown in Figure 13.17—have two search boxes: one that enables users to search within an existing query and another to start over by creating a new, keyword-only search string. Having two search boxes takes up precious screen real estate and increases the potential for customer confusion. Worse, customers cannot directly modify their keyword queries after they've executed a search because the system converts all keywords into attributes customers can remove completely but cannot modify.

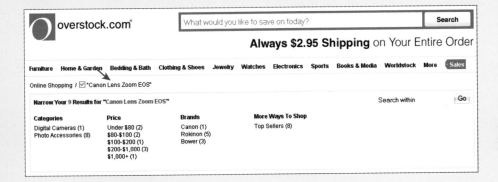

FIGURE 13.17

Overstock.com does not enable direct manipulation of a keyword query

In contrast, the IFB pattern provides direct keyword query manipulation through the editable *Keyword Attribute*, the integrated query search box that always appears last in the breadcrumb trail, as shown in Figure 13.18.

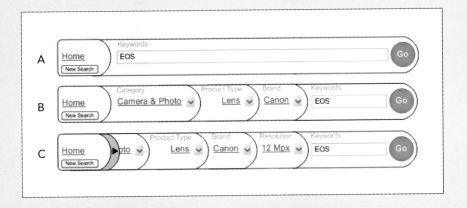

FIGURE 13.18

Direct keyword query manipulation with a Keyword Attribute

At the beginning of a finding session, the search box occupies the full width of the faceted search user interface, as shown in Figure 13.18 (A). This Google-like initial keyword search simplicity of the IFB design and clear, logical progression to a more complex finding state makes the interface both inviting and usable, and helps people to quickly become familiar and comfortable with using the IFB interface. After a customer types some keywords and submits a search, the search box retains the keywords to enable the customer to easily edit or add keywords. Any facets and categories applied during the course of the search appear to the left of the search box. As more facets are applied, the search box becomes progressively smaller, until it reaches its minimum size, as shown in Figure 13.18 (B). If the customer applies still more facets at this point, a carousel control arrow appears immediately to the right of the **Home** link, enabling customers to view all the applied attributes, without ever hiding either the **Home** link or the search box, as shown in Figure 13.18 (C). The IFB pattern, with directly editable keywords and attributes, proved to be successful with my user research participants, who found it useful and easy to use.

USABILITY, SEO, AND FACETED NAVIGATION

Search engine optimization (SEO) and marketing is a rich area that is replete with research—and even a bit of snake oil. Fortunately, usability professionals are among the best equipped to grasp the responsibilities of SEO. In fact, the challenges of these two fields are similar in nature. Start by viewing search engines as another demographic—one that you surely want to please.

The goals of search engine optimization and marketing parallel those of usability. Both aim to ensure a Web site's audience is able to view and understand the content. Both go hand-in-hand with marketing as a whole, aiming to connect with users and ensure they tell their friends, sharing via a hyperlink.

In turn, these goals influence the various signals search engines are designed to follow, and improve a Web site's rankings on search engine results pages. The search engines are perhaps the most important users your site can connect with.

Although many organizations painstakingly test for usability in all Web browsers and for all demographics, almost as many fall short by neglecting to design and test for search engine robots.

SEO and Usability

There are many topics to discuss in search engine optimization and marketing that speak to usability professionals. One of most relevant is internal link architecture. A user must be able to navigate a Web site intuitively, and too many choices may overwhelm users.

Sometimes, in designing a user interface, it is necessary to design for different audiences. As a typical example, some users may prefer advanced options. However, these may confuse or intimidate novice users. By way of compromise, the advanced options often appear only after some prodding.

Search engines are another audience, and you should be mindful that search engines also see the Web site features you implement. Oftentimes, designing for search engines entails avoiding intimidating or confusing them—usually as a result of duplicate content and spider traps.

Unfortunately, you don't have Googlebots or Bingbots at your disposal—and you can't interview them to ask what they think of your usability. Web server logs and the tools purveyors of Web search engines have provided for Webmasters may reveal some errors or indicate pages that are unreachable, but often fail to shed light on problematic Web site architectures.

There are well-understood solutions for problems with category-based navigation schemes. However, faceted navigation presents a more complex set of problems.

Faceted Navigation

UX professionals have said much about the benefits of faceted navigation. Users don't enjoy navigating through hierarchies of pages on large Web sites—where they run the risk of clicking a wrong link. Marketers have said less about the search marketing ramifications.

Faceted navigation seems to be a universally positive user experience. Four of the most important benefits for users include the following:

- Facets permit users to combine selections variously to narrow results.
- Facets prevent users from navigating to pages with zero results.
- Facets permit users to make selections in any order.
- Facets assist in removing noise from categories and keyword search.

Without faceted navigation, a Web site eventually abandons users in their decision-making process: Category trees work well for high-level decisions—whether a shopper wants a camera or a cable. However, since a tree structure presumes the exact process by which consumers make their decisions, at any point when navigating such a structure, users may not see a way forward or may begin to experience click fatigue. The problems with keyword search are similar.

Keyword searches do not know user intent and do nothing to aid users in their decision-making process. Users may not know how to use or want to be bothered with using Boolean operators to narrow search results or remove irrelevant results.

Facets rise to the task. The synthesis of a shallow category tree with a series of facets may be the best analog of a knowledgeable consultant we've yet discovered. He doesn't even take lunch. Unfortunately, he's also potentially a giant spider trap. Pay attention to two of the benefits of facets in particular—that they may be selected in any order and combined variously. Only some pages should be indexed by search engines.

Problems with Faceted Navigation

Without having taken some precautions, faceted navigation can create spider traps with seemingly infinite combinations of the same content. Some implementations of faceted navigation attempt to address this problem simply by excluding all of their facet-based pages from search engines. This is clearly not ideal, because that dismisses many organic opportunities. It's desirable to let facets assist with some organic search marketing.

Facets and Duplicate Content Problems

Having consulted on various facet-related duplicate content problems, it is clear that much duplicate content derives when robots apply facets in ways that are not useful. This might occur both because:

:: Facets permit robots to combine selections variously to narrow results.

:: Facets permit robots to make selections in any order.

If those points look familiar, it is because they are. I should also add another admonition:

:: The permutation space is rather large to begin with—even without accounting for duplication—and not all permutations are particularly useful to search engines. Unlike humans, search engines do not intentionally enter a Web site with a particular question, and then stop applying facet filters when they achieve the answer.

Most combinations of more than two selections are not interesting to search engines, and they cannot possibly spider all of them. For example, most Google users would not search using the query sale red leather boots. Even most long-tail queries have fewer than three modifiers.

Search engines are not interested in the order in which facets are selected, and it would be wise not to depend even on the intelligence of Google engineers to infer sameness among such URLs. Just like presenting users with too many choices can be overwhelming to them, search engines do not always cope well with large amounts of duplicate content.

The most straightforward solution may seem to be employing that ever-popular rel="canonical" link tag. However, on a multi-thousand product site, that is not feasible. The raw number of pages that would yield the same result would still frustrate a robot. Instead, the solution is eliminating duplicate content entirely by doing the following:

:: Present the facet parameters in a predictable order within URLs, regardless of selection order—for example, color, then brand, then price.

:: If a Web site needs breadcrumbs showing the facet values in the order in which a user selected them, use a session-based method of storing the selection order. You can also use this approach to show breadcrumbs on product pages, as you will see.

Then, reduce the scope of the problem by excluding some of the unimportant content and highlighting the important content.

:: By default, allow search engines to spider the combination of only a limited number of facet dimensions within each section—or entirely block faceted navigation from search engines, with the exception of those combinations you determine to be useful to them.

:: Lastly, list your Web site's most important pages in a sitemap, which provides a means of advising a search engine which pages on your site are most important—either through a weight field in the sitemap's XML or, implicitly, via omission of some pages.

Bots will no longer get dizzy, while the human user experience remains equivalent. Those who pay attention to these concerns will receive rewards accordingly—yet another example of leveraging data in search marketing.

Facets and Landing Pages

Faceted navigation provides relevant landing pages for long-tail keywords, just as category-based navigation always has—albeit in contrived ways. For example, you might combine a Color or Brand facet with the category Cameras, providing a high-quality relevant page for shoppers looking for a camera in a certain color or from a particular company, while assisting search engines in providing users with relevant information.

Additionally, you can use such pages as landing pages for highly targeted Pay Per Click (PPC) campaigns. Users can use other facets to further refine search results, making this approach much more effective than static pages or keyword search pages, for the aforementioned reasons. However, you should not ignore the precautions I outlined in the previous section.

Facets and Problems with Breadcrumb Navigation

The canonical link tag can often solve the duplicate-content problems resulting from multiple categorization. For example, some products on an ecommerce Web site might reasonably belong in two or three different categories. Even if a page's URL itself indicates a particular category—that is, http://example.com/footwear/boots/steel-toe-leather-boot-sku1234.html versus http://example.com/footwear/work-boots/steel-toe-leather-boot-sku1234.html), you can reconcile the small amount of duplicate content that results with this tag.

However, faceted navigation presents a more difficult challenge. Because combinations of facets can yield a great deal of duplicate content, it is no longer feasible to use the canonical link tag if you want to show a breadcrumb in this manner. Don't expect robots to wade through a morass of hundreds of thousands of product pages just to be rudely told that what they are spidering is essentially useless.

Therefore, you must devise other methods of creating a persistent taxonomy for product pages. For example, J&R uses a session-based technique to avoid this problem, while presenting a taxonomy comprising both categories and facets in their product-page breadcrumbs, as shown in Figure 13.19.

FIGURE 13.19

J&R product-page breadcrumbs

Note—The page's URL includes neither category nor facet information, in this case. J&R has chosen to avoid the duplicate content that results from categorization as well.

Facets and Speed: Be Quick!

Faceted navigation presents an occupational hazard for any business relying on commodity databases or Web hosting. Its implementation is difficult, and few software platforms—which typically rely on commodity components—currently offer an adequate faceted-navigation feature.

Without attention to technology, faceted navigation might succeed with a few hundred products. However, facets really shine with product databases comprising many thousands of products. The problem becomes more complex when you must seamlessly integrate keyword search with categorization and facets. (In technology parlance, this requires the use of an inverted index in coordination with traditional database indexes such as btrees or hashtables.) The result can be extremely expensive, slow queries. In this case, you may need specialized database or search-engine modules such as Solr, Sphinx, or Groonga. Paid search-engine modules include Endeca's Information Access Platform and Microsoft Enterprise Search. Various hosted or SAAS solutions are available for monthly fees.

Lastly, even when you use the proper components, the raw computational power that faceted navigation requires may outstrip a single server's ability to answer queries. At that point, you must use advanced traffic-scaling techniques such as replication and sharding.

When a Web page takes more than a second to load, it degrades the user experience. We all know what we do when a Web site makes us wait—even with a polite admonition. We leave. The revelation that site speed is now itself a factor search engines use to rank pages further underscores this as a problem.

Site speed absolutely should be a ranking factor. The robots likely do not mind waiting for the data, but search engines must rank the quality of the Web sites to which they refer people, and a Web site's speed contributes to its overall user experience.

Google, Yahoo!, and Bing are in the business of providing users with a great user experience in exchange for eyes on their advertisements. While site speed may not be the most important ranking factor, it makes sense to incorporate it.

So Where Does This Leave You?

Facets present a great opportunity. Even as the various content management and ecommerce platforms scramble to adopt some form of faceted navigation, they require more computational power than ever before just to provide it.

Users may not be able to identify navigation as faceted navigation, but they certainly do bounce away from your Web site when they cannot find something as easily as on another site.

The barriers to entry and competitiveness in the Web space are increasingly fierce. Paying careful attention to the proper implementation of faceted naviga-tion helps users find what they want. If you also address the search marketing angle, this contributes to a greater competitive edge in your industry.

—Jaimie Sirovich

ON THE FUTURE OF BREADCRUMBS

Although there are still debates about the value and effectiveness of breadcrumbs on Web sites—as there should be—that does not mean you should stop researching them or trying out new ideas with them. The idea of breadcrumbs as a navigation aid is old, but we are actually just beginning to get a sense of how people use them. What are some possible futures for breadcrumbs?

Breadcrumbs may become ingrained into the fabric of the Web—instead of being only a site design element that is often just different enough from site to site to discourage use. Perhaps browsers might pick up the slack on path breadcrumbs, improving their history function. Or maybe some browser plug-in could start showing path breadcrumbs above the page, within the browser frame, so users know where to find breadcrumbs regardless of the site.

More likely there will be different Web-based services using breadcrumbs to display meta-information about pages across the Web. Here's one example: Google search results that extract location breadcrumbs from Web sites and display them on results pages to help users select relevant pages from among the many possibilities. Perhaps a breadcrumb-sharing service will evolve, making it easier to share meta-information—such as a location within a hierarchy and other attributes—across Web sites. I am sure someone at some startup is working on something like this now, perhaps under the semantic Web banner.

Breadcrumbs may evolve to become an integral part of key navigational structures—instead of their being a last-resort mechanism, as is common today. This is what this chapter focuses on. Breadcrumbs have started out as a simple way to show a single location or a single path—which reflects constraints from the physical world—but a powerful aspect of the virtual world is that an object can live in many places, and you can find it in many different ways at the same time. In a faceted world, will breadcrumbs evolve to help users accomplish their goals?

Perhaps only the formatting of breadcrumbs—that is, a list of items separated by a symbol such as > will stand the test of time. I often use that format as a form of shorthand outside the context of Web navigation to show things such as positions within a corporate org chart or major milestones in a timeline.

Of course, the future of navigation breadcrumbs could mimic the fate of the original physical breadcrumbs from the story *Hansel and Gretel*—something we hoped would be useful early on in our journey, only to have them eaten up, so never providing lasting value.

Breadcrumbs are just a small design element, so lowly it has *crumb* in its name. Still, the research and innovation around this element are fascinating—at least to me!

—KEITH INSTONE

REFERENCES

Cooper, Alan, Robert Reimann, and David Cronin. *About Face 3: The Essentials of Interaction Design*. 3rd ed. Indianapolis, IN: John Wiley & Sons, Inc., 2007.

Hearst, Marti. *Search User Interfaces*, Chapter 8, "Integrating Navigation with Search." Cambridge, UK: Cambridge University Press, 2009.

Instone, Keith. "Location, Path, & Attribute Breadcrumbs." 3rd Annual IA Summit, March 15–17, 2002.

Morville, Peter. "Search & Discovery Patterns." User Interface Engineering, January 12, 2010.

Nielsen, Jakob. "Breadcrumb Navigation Increasingly Useful." *Alertbox*, April 10, 2007.

Nudelman, Greg. "Choosing the Right Search Results Page Layout: Make the Most of Your Width." *UXmatters*, March 9, 2009.

Nudelman, Greg. "Experience Design for a Viral Mobile Community." Net Squared Conference, San Jose, CA, May April 26–28, 2009.

Nudelman, Greg. "Design Patterns for Mobile Faceted Search, Part I." *UXmatters*, March 8, 2010.

Nudelman, Greg. "Design Patterns for Mobile Faceted Search, Part II." *UXmatters*, March 8, 2010.

Nudelman, Greg. "Faceted Finding with Super-Powered Breadcrumbs." *Boxes and Arrows*, April 9, 2010.

Nudelman, Greg. "Design Caffeine for Search and Browse UI." Information Architecture Summit 2010, Phoenix, Arizona, April 9–11, 2010.

Spool, Jared. "Design Cop-out #2: Breadcrumbs." *User Interface Engineering*, August 21, 2008.

"Breadbox." Endeca Design Pattern Library. Retrieved January 1st, 2011.

THE FUTURE OF ECOMMERCE SEARCH

Building mobile first allows teams to utilize this full palette of capabilities to create rich context-aware applications... When a team designs mobile first, the end result is an experience focused on the key tasks users want to accomplish without the extraneous detours and general interface debris that litter today's desktop-accessed Web sites. That's good user experience and good for business.

—LUKE WROBLEWSKI

CHAPTER 14

THE BRAVE NEW WORLD OF VISUAL BROWSING

COAUTHORED BY AHMED RIAZ

When the Web first came into existence, pages were mostly text. Over time, thanks in part to improving layout standards and the ubiquity of digital cameras and mobile phones, images have become central to the browsing experience. This shift toward content that is primarily visual introduces new challenges and opportunities for developing intuitive and powerful user interfaces for browsing, searching, and filtering visual content.

INTRODUCING VISUAL BROWSING

Visual browsing refers to all the ways we find and consume digital image content, such as:

- Browsing images or photos using text attributes or tags—for example, on Google Images and Flickr
- Using images in queries to describe attributes that are hard to describe with text—as on Like.com
- Using images to facilitate wayfinding and navigation in the real world— such as on Google Maps and Photosynth
- Reading barcode images on mobile devices—like on RedLaser and NeoReader
- Augmented reality and near field computing–such as Yelp Monocle

Each of these approaches to visual browsing supports different goals for searchers and introduces its own unique challenges, design directions, and best practices, which are explored next.

BROWSING IMAGES USING TEXT ATTRIBUTES OR TAGS

No discussion of visual browsing would be complete without mentioning Google Images and Flickr. For finding images published somewhere on the Web, Google Images is the site most people go to first. Google uses a proprietary algorithm to assign keywords that describe each image and then indexes and ranks all the images in its enormous database. It captures a thumbnail of each image and stores it with the source URL.

Although Google Images is undeniably a useful site, it exemplifies several visual browsing challenges. The primary mechanism for finding images is a text-only query, which perfectly demonstrates the impendence mismatch that exists between text and image content. Because no single keyword can adequately describe all the pixels that make up an image—and, most of the time, the keywords that surround an image on a page are incomplete at best—Google Images tends to loosely interpret search queries. Typically, it interprets multiple keywords using an OR instead of the usual and expected AND operator used in most text search engines. As a consequence, Google Images omits some keywords from the query without letting the searcher know explicitly what is happening.

On the one hand, because Google Images interprets search queries in a such a loose fashion, it rarely returns zero search results. On the other hand, image searches sometimes give you strange and unpredictable results, while making it challenging to understand what went wrong with your queries and how to adjust them to find the images you actually are looking for. Figure 14.1 shows an example—the search results for *Africa Thailand elbow Indian*.

FIGURE 14.1

Google Images search results for *Africa Thailand elbow Indian*

The results for the query seem to omit words randomly, without indicating to the searcher it has done so. Of course, you could argue that getting such poor results to a query is an example of garbage in/garbage out. But this example demonstrates that the keywords Google takes from the surrounding content on a Web page—and possibly some Web pages that link to it—do not always match an image. Although an image may *technically* be located at the intersection of *Africa, Thailand, elbow,* and *Indian,* this by no means guarantees that the image would actually contain a picture showing Indian warriors demonstrating the perfect Muay Thai elbow strike technique on the plains of the Serengeti.

Note—A computer-generated index usually makes no distinction between the different possible meanings of an image's surrounding keywords—for example, a search engine can't tell when an image appears in juxtaposition to text to illustrate a counterpoint or simply to add humor. Automated indexing engines also poorly handle images that have purposes other than providing content—such as images that add visual appeal or bling or those used for marketing or advertising. Such image content is, at best, orthogonal to its surrounding text.

Image search filters based on text are, at the moment, not particularly robust. For example, Figure 14.2 shows Google Images search results for *iPhone* with filters **Large**, **Clipart**, and **Green** applied. As you can see, the resulting images have little to do with the iPhone.

As a photo-hosting site, Flickr enjoys the distinct advantage of having *people* rather than computers look at, interpret, and tag the images they create and view. Thus, Flickr customers search for images by looking at the title and description of the image the author has originally provided, and by searching for tags applied by users who later viewed the image.

Although Flickr is not a perfect image-searching system, it provides an entirely subjective, human-driven method of interpreting and describing images. Why is that valuable?

According to Jung's conception of the *collective unconscious,* we can assume *all* individuals inherit the same universal archetypes at their births. These archetypes dictate their innate psychic predispositions and aptitudes, which condition their responses to life experience and basic patterns of human behavior. At the root of all folksonomies (see sidebar) is the inherent assumption that people—looked at collectively—tend to respond in similar ways when presented with the same stimuli. Simply put, people looking for images of cats would be quite happy to find the images that many other people have taken the time to tag with the word *cat*.

FIGURE 14.2

Google Images search results for *iPhone* with filters Large, Clipart and Green applied

FOLKSONOMY

Folksonomy is a term coined by Thomas Vander Wal in 2004 using a combination of two words, *folks* and *taxonomy*. Folksonomy refers to a system of classification based on the practice of collaboratively creating and managing tags to annotate digital content. It has also been called *collaborative tagging*, *social indexing*, or *social tagging*.

As Gene Smith describes in his book, *Tagging: People-Powered Metadata for the Social Web,* folksonomies and tagging usually work well—in most cases adequately resolving the auto-indexing issues that occur in the context of Google Images, as described earlier. Unfortunately, the human element also introduces its own quirks along the way. Take a look at the example of a Flickr image shown in Figure 14.3.

FIGURE 14.3

One of the Most Interesting Flickr images tagged with iPhone

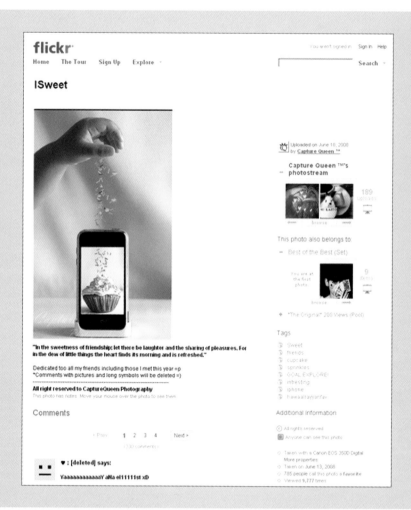

Among almost 2 million Flickr images tagged **iPhone**, this image is considered by Flickr as one of the most interesting, with 785 favorites and 37 comments. As you can see at the bottom of the image, one of the problems with

having a community-driven popularity algorithm is some people will post non-sense comments just to say they've added a comment to a popular item.

Another problem occurs when strictly personal tags are added. For example, tags such as **GOAL:EXPLORE!** and **hawaalrayyanfav** have meaning only to the one person who actually tagged the item—and little or nothing to the population at large. On the other hand, adding tags such as **funny** and **humor** is actually quite useful because computers are currently incapable of recognizing humor, which is one aspect of an image description in which algorithm-based search results fail most spectacularly.

Note—The subject of social search and personalization is an active area of research and innovation (see the Conversation Search excerpt below). Pabini Gabriel-Petit and Brynn Evans explore some important personalization challenges and social search concepts in their excellent perspectives found at the end of this chapter.

For now, just say that *neither* way of finding images—through text tags or associated surrounding text—is perfect, and there is a great deal of room for improvement, perhaps through combining both search approaches using a single algorithm and a user interface that has yet to be developed.

CONVERSATION SEARCH

The following excerpt is taken from the book *Designing Social Interfaces* by Christian Crumlish and Erin Malone (O'Reilly Media/Yahoo Press, 2009)

People sometimes want information or advice that can't be found in a neutral, objective reference guide, and they would ask another human being directly if they could find someone interested in or knowledgeable about the topic of their question (Figure 14.4).

This pattern fosters communication and cooperation among people using your social application. Start by providing a large, inviting text-entry box to encourage questioners to write full sentences (like a human being) instead of query strings or Boolean operators, and label the form button with a word such as "Ask." At the same time, expose open questions to people as a way of inviting them to answer (or route questions to likely, willing answerers based on affinities you derive from the meta-data in your social graph).

continues

CONVERSATION SEARCH (continued)

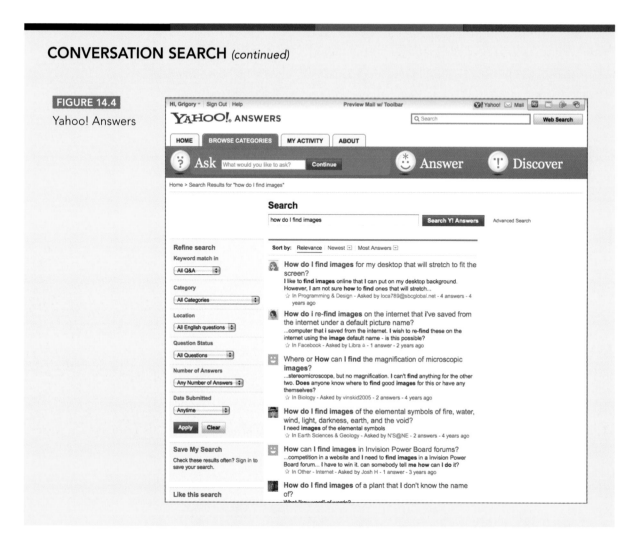

FIGURE 14.4

Yahoo! Answers

USING IMAGES IN QUERIES

One of the most intriguing aspects of visual browsing has to do with the mis-match between images and the text used by both algorithms and people to describe the images. This text-image mismatch highlights the inherent limita-tion of finding and managing images through text-based queries. Typically, peo-ple see an object, determine what to call it, and then try a few keyword searches based on their interpretation. Using an image as part of the query lets a searcher bypass the interpretation step and just have the computer *see* the query directly.

One of the more successful examples of image-based search is the shopping site Like.com, which uses images as parts of queries to describe the attributes of an item that are difficult, if not impossible, to describe precisely using text alone.

Although Like.com has some issues about presenting efficient entry points into its enormous inventory, after you find an item you're interested in, the search engine is absolutely phenomenal at picking up visually similar items. For example, Figure 14.5 shows the results for an image-based search based on a picture of a striped shirt. The algorithm is smart enough to explore useful and popular degrees of freedom, enabling for deviation from the original image, while keeping the meaning of the original image intact.

FIGURE 14.5
Like.com image-based search results

In addition to doing a great job of exploring the possible degrees of freedom from the original image, the system enables shoppers to fine-tune their queries to match a specific part of an image by zooming in on the part they're interested in. This is similar to selecting part of an image on Flickr and tagging only that part of the image. For example, a user could tag a person in an image as **friend** and a snake in the image as **giant anaconda**, while naming the entire image **The last-known picture of Billy**—hopefully adding the tag **humor**, while he is at it. As images become more ubiquitous on the Web—and generate more layers of meaning—selecting and annotating only *part* of an image will become more and more important in a visual browsing user interface.

The Like.com search algorithm can relax different attributes, including color, pattern, and shape, and combine image searching with text attributes, demonstrating the enormous potential and flexibility of image-based searching and browsing. Although government sources can neither confirm nor deny this, image-based searching is a rapid, well-funded research and development effort, fueled in part by the Department of Homeland Security's desire to have a working facial recognition system. As of the date of this writing, commercial-grade facial recognition technology appears to still be a work in progress. Search algorithms can generally recognize *which* part of an image is a human face and venture a fairly accurate guess at a person's gender, but recognizing a specific face requires matching the precise expression and angle of the face in a photograph with the sample, which can often be difficult. Despite these limitations, the potential of image-based search technology is enormous.

Note—Does a user interface need to have a true visual-search algorithm to perform image-based search? Although technology helps, it does not afford the only way of performing a visual browse. One alternative is to have a human being tag items, using abstract visual attributes—such as a range of icons or outlines of shapes, using limited screen real estate—that, in turn, would enable customers to describe their visual queries. This kind of a pseudo-image-based search could, for example, successfully complement the existing *people who shopped for X, also shopped for Y* metrics-based algorithm.

USING IMAGES FOR NAVIGATING IN THE REAL WORLD

By now, most people are familiar with Google Maps' street view, pictured in Figure 14.6.

FIGURE 14.6

Google Maps street view

This phenomenal technology provides users with a sense of almost "being there," providing virtual-reality controls for navigating through a series of interconnected photos that realistically depict the actual location. Visual browsing controls enable users to walk, turn around, and jump through real space, using virtual projection. However, as everyone who has looked up their street and their house can tell you, these pictures are frozen in time. Some people can even tell you when the Google Maps' picture of their house was taken because a friend's car was captured in the satellite photo.

In contrast—or perhaps as a complement to Google Maps—Photosynth, Microsoft's recent acquisition, uses crowd-sourced photographs to construct and let users navigate through 3D street-level space. It can also add the fourth dimension of navigating through time, enabling users cross-reference multiple images. The feel of the interaction evokes looking into vignettes and shifting your point of view through space and time. One of the best examples available of this new capability is the CNN Photosynth of President Obama's inauguration, as shown in Figure 14.7.

FIGURE 14.7

Photosynth of President Obama's inauguration

What's interesting about this emerging technology is that it sidesteps—quite literally—the issue of a finite density of information within a single photograph. With systems like this, you are moving into a world where, rather than relying on just keywords and tags, a deep image analysis can sort and restructure sets of images to make sense of what you are looking at. The computer can truly *see* the real 3D space.

READING BARCODE IMAGES ON MOBILE DEVICES

Using images as input for searches on a hand-held device is reminiscent of using barcode readers to enter inventory counts into a computer. Historically, barcode recognition required the use of a specialized device available only to governments and businesses. However, recent developments in mobile technology are rapidly challenging this paradigm, changing the nature of near-field computing. An increasing number of mobile phone applications such as NeoReader, LifeScan, and RedLaser, the latter of which is depicted in Figure 14.8, now enables customers to snap photos of barcodes, using their mobile phones and then to immediately use the photo as input for a search algorithm.

FIGURE 14.8

RedLaser iPhone application

A Semapedia tool offers an interesting way to use mobile barcode recognition. Semapedia makes it possible to tag any item in the physical world with a QR ("Quick Response") two-dimensional matrix barcode that contains a link to the appropriate Wikipedia Web page. A person can use a mobile phone with the free mobile QR code reader app (such as NeoReader or RedLaser) to read the link's URL and navigate to the Web page providing Wikipedia content about the object or place that a person is looking at.

Other historic landmarks are developing their own solutions. As reported by an on-line magazine *2d code*, the Italian city of Senigallia has declared itself a "QRCity" by tagging all the historic buildings with QR codes. When scanned with a mobile phone, these QR codes transfer the user to the city's mobile site with extensive tourist information in Italian and English. Figure 14.9 shows a QR Code in the plaque on the Senigallia's Palazzo Comunale.

FIGURE 14.9

Senigallia's Palazzo Comunale historical site tagged with a Semapedia barcode

Another example of the capability of mobile barcode-recognition technology comes from the Suntory Company in Japan, which tagged its beer cans with a QR code. Scanning this barcode with a QR code reader app navigates consumers to a mobile Web site where visitors can register to offset 100g of CO_2 emissions once per day and get tips for mitigating their own greenhouse gas emissions.

Both of these examples demonstrate that we are moving ever faster toward a world populated by smart objects, which Bruce Sterling dubbed *spimes*—a word made up by combining *space* and *time*. We can track spimes' history of use and interact with them through a mesh of real and virtual worlds created by pervasive RFID and GPS tracking. Mobile picture search is certainly emerging as the input device of choice for connecting the real and the virtual worlds to create the *Internet of Things* (see sidebar).

INTERNET OF THINGS

Internet of Things, also known as *Internet of Objects*, refers to a self-configuring wireless network connecting regular everyday objects to one another. Internet of things is a term attributed to Auto-ID Center, originally based at Massachusetts Institute of Technology (MIT). Eventually, Internet of things will connect 50-100 trillion of objects and be able to track their movement and state through the use of computers. Companies like Arrayent, Inc. have already developed practical, low-cost solutions that connect everyday things like thermostats to mobile phones and tablets.

AUGMENTED REALITY AND MOBILE NEAR-FIELD COMPUTING

Mobile devices with the on-board camera introduce another interesting possibility for navigating real space in real time: augmented reality. Figure 14.10 shows Yelp Monocle's view of the San Francisco's financial district.

FIGURE 14.10

Augmented Reality using Yelp iPhone Application Monocle feature

The Monocle projects the real-time image captured by the iPhone's camera overlaid with the tiles showing nearby restaurants and points of interest that correspond to the particular GPS location and orientation as determined by the iPhone's compass direction. Initially released as an experiment, a hidden "Easter Egg" that customers had to do some work to find, Yelp Monocle has emerged as a force of its own. According to a recent Design4Mobile 2010 report from mobile form guru Luke Wroblewski, users of the Yelp Monocle feature tend to use Yelp 40% more than people not using Monocle.

Although Monocle is still somewhat limited because of the tiny iPhone screen, you can't help but get excited by the enormous potential of near-field computing. With the augmented reality industry working on adding facial recognition and RFID tagging, you will soon be able to obtain near-instant information about people, landmarks, objects, and just about anything else of interest. However, to fully exploit augmented reality, you might need a screen that is slightly larger than that of a typical smart phone.

Note—It is hard to see all the richness of the real world additionally augmented with enormous amounts of information already available, all on a tiny screen that severely limits your filtering options. Additionally, in our society it is not yet socially acceptable, and downright dangerous, to hold your phone in front of you when meeting someone for the first time or walking down a busy city street.

On the other hand, a large tablet device such as iPad with an on-board camera or a pair of augmented reality glasses (coming soon to the gadget store near you) might be just the catalyst that will propel mobile near-field computing to the next level. Chapter 17, "Search on Tablet Devices: The Flight of Discovery" discusses some intriguing possibilities offered by the next generation of the tablet devices.

In his book *Ambient Findability*, Peter Morville talks about the sensory overload, trust issues, and bad decisions that are sure to result from interactions with the Internet of things. However, it is hard to elude the siren's call of such technology. It is now *almost* possible to use technology similar to that of Like.com to analyze every image and frame of video a mobile phone captures and tag it with text, GPS coordinates, time, and author, while at the same time cross-referencing this image with other images of the same place or similar things along with all the text tags, content, and links the entire world has added to this collection of images. The technology to collect all these images in a massive 3D collage that users can navigate along a time axis, Photosynth-style, is also just around the corner.

Interactions of this kind make it possible to establish a unique and natural connection between the real world and the Internet computing cloud. The key is the added meaning the computer provides, based on its understanding and interpretation of the content of an image, combined with other device inputs such as camera, GPS location, RFID reader, and compass direction. Imagine, for example, taking a picture of a CD (or simply picking up a CD and bringing it near to your mobile device to read the RFID tag) to instantly share it with your friends to learn what they think about the music; using the same RFID or picture data to get more information about the artist on the Web—pictures, videos of recent concerts, and a biography; finding out where you can download the songs on this CD at the best price online, or using GPS to find coupons to purchase a physical CD from a local merchant. Imagine doing all this with only a few screen taps, without typing a single character, all the while listening to a sampling of the CD tracks playing through headphones connected to your mobile device.

This future is not that far off. The next chapter covers Amazon Remembers, an experimental feature that enables near real-time recognition of a wide variety of products simply based on their picture. After the product has been identified, the customer has full access to a rich and complex variety of data Amazon collected about the product, which includes samples, reviews, and social networking features.

We are just starting to scratch the surface of these types of massively distributed "human-mobile-world" interactions. Although image-processing speeds are improving—witness the smooth, fast scrolling of iPhone photo album images versus the slow shuffle of images on an "old" Palm Treo—the time it takes to process images on a mobile device and send them back and forth from a server is still the biggest barrier to this type of technology. After the image feedback loop becomes nearly instantaneous, the augmented reality and near field computing will truly come into its own, bringing the digital world ever closer to the real world and ushering in the arrival of a brave new world of visual browsing.

SOCIAL SEARCH CAN'T BE SOLVED BY AN ALGORITHM

A lot of fact finding and information discovery already comes from people turning to friends, colleagues, and even acquaintances. Online social networks facilitate this by organizing our personal relationships and reducing barriers to information exchange. However, social networking sites weren't designed with search in mind. It's still possible to post a status message or a Facebook Question asking for your friends' opinions, but the results are usually limited in scope (in the case of Facebook where results contain only users' public-facing content) or are untrustworthy (in the case of Twitter where results contain noise and spam). An example of such "social search" questions come from people post-ing "lazy tweets" on Twitter, asking for information about something they're pretty sure someone in their Twitter network will know the answer to:

- "Wondering where Bowtie saves it's themes… Anyone? #LazyTweet" –@iphone360
- "Looking for social media trends in the healthcare industry. Anyone out there have resources they can share? #lazytweet #healthcare" –@chrismevans
- "Anyone know if there are Brocade SAN and Cisco MDS simulators? #lazytweet #healthcare" –@sloane

The real value for social search is in making the search experience more per-sonalized. If a search tool can integrate the data coming from my social networks (relationships, strong ties, weak ties), they can bubble up results that come from friends I already trust or distant acquaintances who've had experiences that might be relevant to me right now. At the same time, our personal networks are narrow and not every search you perform may have counterpart results from social networks. The dream of personalization comes with a risk of null results, which is why traditional search algorithms (like Google's and Bing's) will con-tinue to play a large role in search, regardless of how "social" it gets.

Thus, the benefits to "social search" come from using social network infor-mation in conjunction with search algorithms. Services can begin to "learn" which of your friends have expertise or knowledge about certain topics. Then when you search for those topics, people from your network who may have relevant knowledge could be made available to you. It's still unknown how users will want to interact with people in the search interface. People may appear only as a search result listing, linking to their profile or email address; or they could appear as a direct contact, like through an instant messaging window on the same page as the search results. Either way, person-to-person interactions can greatly supplement the search process (as I discussed in the paper "Do your friends make you smarter?" (http://brynnevans.com/papers/Do-your-friends-make-you-smarter.pdf).

Another area where social networks can support during search is during search difficulties—or when people are struggling to find certain information. Anytime you can't find what you're looking for on the first try, or you rework your query over and over again, these are use cases that could benefit from asking a friend a question, pinging your social network, or finding a colleague/acquaintance who may have experience with this particular problem.

"Social Search" Engines

There aren't "social search" engines per se, but a number of services have cropped up in the last few years that are trying to provide human answering. These mostly do not include a search algorithm component (Facebook Questions and Google's social search integration are exceptions), meaning that results are driven only by a direct human contribution. *Wired* recently published a diagram (Figure 14.11) titled *"Which Social Search Site Should I Use?"* that presents a fairly current list of the social search services available today.

FIGURE 14.11

A Social Search Service Diagram

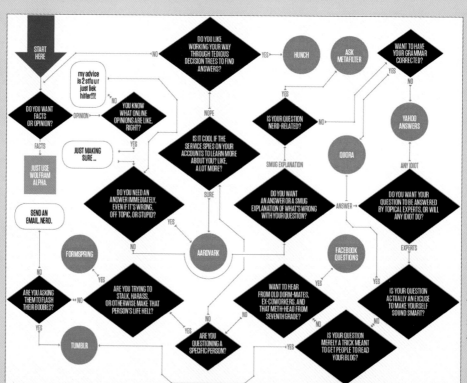

(Image credit: *Wired*, November 2010): http://www.wired.com/magazine/2010/11/st_flowchart_social/.

Yet, there's another class of social search services that makes use of aggregated social data from large networks. I call this "collective social search" since it's like the wisdom of crowds effect, in that you can see trends from the collective that might be useful in guiding your search. Google Search Suggest is an example of this—it shows you the common search phrases for a given few words. Twitter's Trending Topics and OneRiot are similar. I think the popularity of this approach is that it's algorithmic, meaning you can throw more programmers at it and hopefully improve the results. But it's lacking in the trust factor since trends across an entire network have no intrinsic relationship to the searcher. Such results may help in the early stages of search when you're still trying to formulate an ill-formed query but won't be as useful when you want to narrow down to a specific answer to your question.

Thus, the "social" component I want to see in search engines of the future will require combining human answering with smart algorithms. This is not trivial, and many unknowns exist about how people will respond to a service that does this. How will people react if their search history is shared with their social network? Will it be different when we see the value of having our networks' search results shared with us (the reverse case)? How will reputation and obligation come into play? How will reactions differ by personalities? By location? By past history? By the political climate?

If Facebook's nearly forgotten Beacon experiment taught us anything, it's that "social" can't be solved by an algorithm. We're still a distance from solving social search.

—BRYNN EVANS

References

Enterprise Social Search slides: www.slideshare.net/bmevans/designing-for-sociality-in-enterprise-search

Wired article (*Wired*, November 2010): www.wired.com/magazine/2010/11/st_flowchart_social/

"Do your friends make you smarter" paper: http://brynnevans.com/papers/Do-your-friends-make-you-smarter.pdf

PERSONALIZED SEARCH AND RECOMMENDER SYSTEMS

Machine learning lets search engines draw reliable inferences and deliver improved search results by leveraging customers' data. In the ecommerce realm, personalized search lets an online vendor use a customer's past purchasing history—and possibly other data like product ratings, search history, the customer's user profile, and even social networking activity—to interpret search strings, predict what products might be of interest to that customer, and deliver more relevant search results.

On ecommerce sites, *recommender systems*—which are sometimes called *implicit collaborative filtering systems,* a bit of a misnomer—often use the past purchasing history of *other* customers who are similar in some way to a particular customer to predict what products might be of interest to that customer. To generate a set of recommendations for a customer, such recommender systems typically do the following:

- Identify a set of customers whose purchasing history and product ratings overlap those of the current customer.
- Aggregate a list of items those similar customers have purchased.
- Eliminate any items the current customer has already purchased.
- Recommend the remaining items to the customer. [1]

According to an article by Greg Linden, Brent Smith, and Jeremy York, titled "Amazon.com Recommendations: Item-to-Item Collaborative Filtering," Amazon .com takes a somewhat different approach, using what it calls *item-to-item collaborative filtering*. This approach also takes a customer's purchasing history and product ratings into account but focuses on finding other similar items for sale on Amazon rather than similar customers. "Item-to-item collaborative filtering matches each of the user's purchased and rated items to similar items and then combines those similar items into a recommendation list. To determine the most similar match for a given item, the algorithm builds a similar-items table by finding items that customers tend to purchase together…, iteratively calculating the similarity between a single product and all related products. … Given a similar-items table, the algorithm finds items similar to each of the user's purchases and ratings, aggregates those items, and then recommends the most popular or correlated items." [1]

Amazon employs its recommender system to great effect—delivering product recommendations that encourage customers to browse additional products and, thus, helping users to find similar products of interest. Recommendations are particularly effective on product pages, where Amazon uses them in cross-selling additional products to customers. Amazon also personalizes the content on its home page extensively by providing many different types of recommendations. The recommender system Amazon has innovated helps customers find what they need and, because its recommendations actually provide a valuable service to customers, increases customer loyalty—and ultimately enhances Amazon's bottom line. However, Amazon has *not* yet embraced personalized search. How might Amazon personalize search, primarily using its recommender system and, therefore, deliver more relevant search results to customers?

Searching for Products on Amazon

First consider the current Amazon search experience—and a possible, personalized search experience—from my perspective, as a frequent and loyal customer of Amazon. What ecommerce site currently holds the greatest amount of my personal data? Amazon. How does Amazon use that data to provide a superior search experience? As far as I can tell, Amazon doesn't do anything to personalize my search experience. I wish they would.

Personalizing Search

When I search for products on Amazon, I'm usually searching for books—probably about 18 times out of 20. But every time I start a new session on Amazon, the search user interface appears in its default state, with **All Departments** selected in the **Search** drop-down list, as shown in Figure 14.12, rather than **Books**, which is likely where I last left it. Why not retain my last setting across sessions? Or use my most common setting by default?

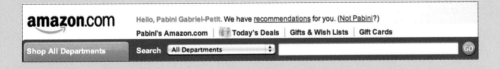

FIGURE 14.12

All Departments is always selected by default

Being able to sort search results on Amazon requires customers to select a department *before* searching—though unless they have already discovered this the hard way, customers have no way of knowing this when searching. Thus, retaining the department setting would both add convenience and ensure customers could avoid landing on an unsortable search results page like that shown in Figure 14.13.

FIGURE 14.13

Unsortable
Amazon search
results page with
All Departments
selected

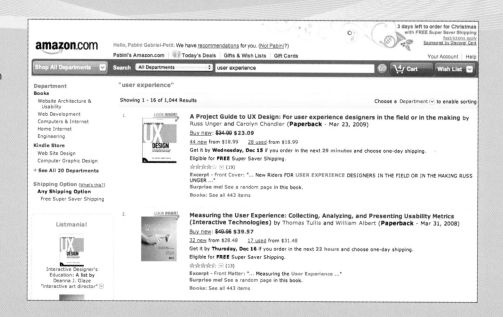

Now, you might ask: What if customers don't notice which department is selected by default and end up with search results that aren't what they expected? Here's how I would handle this problem:

- If there *are* search results for the selected department:

  - Display those results first.

  - Also display the top search results for the other departments for which there are matching items.

  - Allow the customer to filter the search results by selecting a different department, *without* reloading the search results page.

- If there are *no* search results for the selected department, first display the top search results for the departments for which there *are* results—using the customer's purchasing and ratings histories to determine which departments to display first. Then, allow the customer to view more results for whatever department is currently of interest.

- In other words, *always* provide search results for *all* departments, but display results grouped by department and let the customer expand department groupings or drill down to view more results in a particular department.

Personalizing Autocomplete

In all the years I've been searching for products on Amazon, I don't think I've ever started a search string with the word *used*. However, I frequently search for *user experience*. So, wouldn't it make sense for autocomplete to present *user experience* as an option when I type *use* in the search box? It doesn't, as you can see in Figure 14.14. Autocomplete doesn't use customers' search or purchasing histories to personalize the options it displays. But if it did, it could offer options of greater interest to a particular customer.

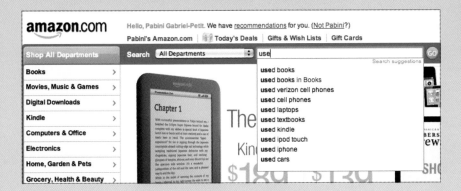

FIGURE 14.14

Autocomplete isn't personalized

Search Results Pages on Amazon

By default, search results pages on Amazon are sorted by **Relevance**, as shown in Figure 14.15. But relevant to whom? For example, when I recently searched for *user experience,* the top result was *A Project Guide to UX Design*—a book I already own *and* purchased on Amazon! So, *not* highly relevant to me at this time, unless I'm shopping for a gift for a friend who's a UX designer. If the search algorithm factored my purchasing history into the relevance rankings, that book would appear further down in the list of results.

The search algorithm could also factor recommendations into the results it displays, but apparently does not. If it did, the **Sort by** drop-down list could offer an option like **Recommended for You**, which would let customers elevate recommended items that match their search string in the list of results. Alternatively, customers could select a **Recommended for You** filter to view *only* recommended items that match their search string in the search results. The existing filtering options on the search results page do not include any that would give a customer a personalized view of the search results.

The only personalization the search results page offers is **Your Recent History**, at the bottom of the page, which displays just a few recently viewed items from a customer's current session, plus some recommendations under **Customers Who Bought Items in Your Recent History Also Bought**, as shown in Figure 14.16. However, this ever-present functionality is completely unrelated to the search results.

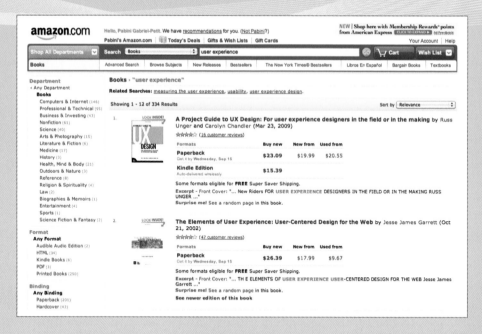

Using Customers' Search Histories to Personalize the Amazon Home Page

In personalizing its home page, Amazon does use its customers' search histories a bit. How is the Amazon home page personalized for me? The recommendations under **Customers with Similar Searches Purchased**, shown in Figure 14.17, leverage collaborative filtering—that is, Amazon uses the purchasing histories of *others* who have done similar searches to make recommendations to me.

Customers with Similar Searches Purchased

Here I Stand
▸ Usher
Audio CD
$9.97

LOOK **INSIDE!**

Measuring the User Experience...
▸ Tom Tullis, Thomas Tullis, William Albert
Paperback
$49.95 $44.51

LOOK **INSIDE!**

An Echo in the Bone: A Novel (Outlander)
▸ Diana Gabaldon
Hardcover
$30.00 $19.80

▸ View or edit your browsing history

FIGURE 14.17

Customers with Similar Searches Purchased on the Amazon home page

In Conclusion

Amazon.com is doing a great job of using collaborative filtering to leverage the purchasing histories of others to help customers find what they need when they're browsing—and thus, influencing customers' purchasing decisions. It's also doing quite a lot of personalization based on a customer's purchasing history and ratings. But, so far, Amazon has done nothing to personalize search.

What if Amazon lets customers sort or filter search results to view recommended results? By combining its superlative recommender system with search, Amazon could provide a personalized view of search results and present recommendations that would improve the relevance of search results. Through personalized search, Amazon could provide an even better and more fruitful shopping experience. Customers could more easily find what they want—especially when they don't know exactly what they want—with the result that they'd likely make more purchases on Amazon.

—PABINI GABRIEL-PETIT

References

[1] Linden, Greg, Brent Smith, and Jeremy York. "Amazon.com Recommendations: Item-to-Item Collaborative Filtering." [http://www.win.tue.nl/~laroyo/2L340/resources/Amazon-Recommendations.pdf] *IEEE Internet Computing*, January-February 2003.

REFERENCES

Dodson, Sean. "The Internet of Things." *The Guardian*, October 9, 2003.

Jung, Carl Gustav. *Man and His Symbols*. New York: Dell, 1968.

Morville, Peter. *Ambient Findability*. Sebastopol, California: O'Reilly, 2005.

Nudelman, Greg. "Making $10,000 a Pixel: Optimizing Thumbnail Images in Search Results." *UXmatters*, May 11, 2009. Retrieved July 26, 2009.

Riflet, Guillaume. "Semapedia, or How to Link the Real World to Wikipedia." *Webtop Mania*, August 26, 2008. Retrieved July 26, 2009.

Smith, Gene. Tagging: *People-Powered Metadata for the Social Web*. Berkeley: Peachpit Press, 2008.

Smolski, Roger. "Beer, Carbon Offset, and a QR Code Campaign." *2d code*, July 27, 2009. Retrieved July 26, 2010.

Smolski, Roger. "QRCity Claimed by Senigallia." *2d code*, July 29, 2010. Retrieved March 12, 2011.

Sterling, Bruce. *Shaping Things*. Cambridge, Massachusetts: MIT Press, 2005.

Photosynth of the Obama inauguration, CNN, 2009.

Vander Wal, Thomas. "Folksonomy: coinage and definition." Vanderwal.net, February 2, 2007. Retrieved March 11, 2009.

Wroblewski, Luke. "Mobile Forms Workshop," *Design4Mobile* 2010.

CHAPTER 15

DESIGNING MOBILE SEARCH:
Turning Limitations into Opportunities

If you are thinking about porting your store site to iPhone-, Android-, or Windows Mobile-based devices, it would be shortsighted to treat these devices as simply computers with tiny screens. Designing a great mobile search experience requires a way of thinking quite different from that employed when designing search for Web or desktop applications. To put it simply, designing a mobile search experience requires treating limitations as opportunities. This chapter discusses some of the limitations of mobile platforms, and the opportunities they afford, and shares a few design ideas that might come in handy when embarking upon your own projects.

UNDERSTANDING MOBILE PLATFORMS

One of the challenges of mobile application design involves understanding both the capabilities and limitations of each platform. Today's mobile device has quite a bit to offer, including a high-resolution screen, multitouch controls, accelerometer, persistent data storage, smooth video transitions, push content delivery, and GPS. On the other hand, these devices present quite a few challenges to application developers, including the following:

- the difficulty of typing
- the small amount of screen real estate
- awkward touch controls
- the so-called fat-finger problem

Few sources discuss these in detail, so this chapter describes the most important challenges of designing for the new generation of smartphones—at least as they pertain to search.

The Difficulty of Typing

Traditionally, searching requires users to enter a search string, and typing on a mobile phone is difficult—partly because of the size of the device. In a July 2009 *Alertbox* entry, usability expert Jakob Nielsen called the mobile experience "miserable," reporting, "Text entry is particularly slow and littered with typos, even on devices with dedicated mini-keyboards."

For many users, touch-screen devices such as the iPhone exacerbate this problem. When text entry is required, touch-screen devices display a virtual keyboard and other buttons. One issue with this keyboard design is poor visibility: A user's finger must, by necessity, cover buttons on the screen when a user is pushing them. Thus, when pushing a button on a virtual keyboard, a user's hand obscures his view of the keyboard.

Another problem of virtual keyboards is the lack of tactile response. Thus, typing on touch devices presents a particular problem when a person is multitasking—whether riding in a taxi, using public transportation, or walking down a busy city street.

Another challenge users encounter when searching on smartphones is that they're likely to lose anything they've laboriously typed into a search box if a device receives an incoming phone call because mobile applications cannot block phone functions.

The Small Amount of Screen Real Estate

Mobile screens are by necessity small because a mobile device has to fit into a person's pocket or purse. This small size logically limits the number of controls and the amount of content that can appear on them. In the previously mentioned *Alertbox* post, Jakob Nielsen reported, "Unsurprisingly, the bigger the screen, the better the user experience."

High-end mobile phones like the Apple iPhone and HTC EVO running Google's Android OS have larger screens and support an extensive set of touch-screen controls and multi-touch gestures that facilitate rich interactions. However, at least at the date of this writing, the bulk of the phones on the market are lower-end smartphones and feature phones with smaller screens, tiny keyboards and considerably fewer capabilities. These lower-end phones are harder to use and more prone to user errors: According to Nielsen, users' success rates with typical search tasks on high-end touch phones such as the iPhone are about double the success rates with feature phones.

Awkward Touch Controls

One of the consequences of mobile devices having smaller screens and controls that users must manipulate through touch interfaces is that some controls no longer look like their Web and desktop counterparts. For example, rather than the usual drop-down list or set of option buttons, the selection control on an iPhone is instead a spinning control called a *picker*, as shown in Figure 15.1.

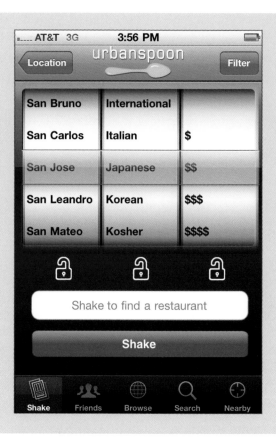

FIGURE 15.1

Three pickers in the Urban Spoon iPhone app

A picker that a user can quickly manipulate with a finger eats up precious real estate, so it's not possible to show users much outside the picker. Large pickers also place limitations on how users can filter search results on mobile devices. Similar size restrictions exist for all of an application's touch controls.

The Fat-Finger Problem

The high-resolution screens on higher-end mobile devices—such as the iPhone, Android, and Palm Pre—can accommodate fairly high information density. Unfortunately, at the same time, touchscreens limit the on-screen density of controls that users can accurately manipulate with a finger. Thus, placing multiple controls close together on a touchscreen mobile device presents difficulties. This challenge is known as the *fat-finger problem*.

Typically, an iPhone touchscreen can comfortably support a maximum of only three to five clickable buttons or tabs across a screen. More than this leads to frequent frustrations due to users inadvertently pressing the wrong control.

Although five controls across a screen is the absolute limit for relatively frustration-free mobile computing for people with relatively small fingers, I highly recommend a limit of four or fewer controls.

Note—Of course, if one control is larger than the others, you'll have to reduce the overall number of controls accordingly.

For example, Figure 15.2 shows the Yelp mobile application, which has only three controls across the search bar at top of the screen, but five controls across the tab bar at the bottom.

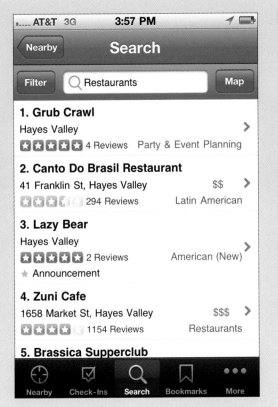

FIGURE 15.2

Yelp iPhone app

Because Yelp's search box takes up a large part of the navigation bar, the designers had to reduce the overall number of controls to three to ensure users wouldn't press the wrong controls with their fingers too often.

OPTIMIZING USER EXPERIENCE FOR MOBILE CONTEXT OF USE

The challenge in designing mobile applications is the need to accommodate the design constraints and usability challenges mobile devices impose, while focusing on users' goals within a mobile context of use.

Note—Simply duplicating the functionality of a Web application—while trying to work around the mobile design challenges described—*always* results in a subpar mobile application.

It's not enough to think: *How can I duplicate our Web application's user experience within the limitations of the mobile platform?* Instead, it's better to start from scratch, focusing on *What experience would work best for mobile users?* Putting users' goals first allows a design team to concentrate on the new opportunities a mobile application presents rather than seeing the challenges of mobile devices simply as barriers to implementing a Web application's existing functionality.

The next section presents some ideas about how to approach the design of search experiences for mobile devices in a way that lends itself to taking full advantage of their capabilities within a mobile context of use. These ideas by no means represent an exhaustive catalog of all possibilities but merely provide a few examples that may inspire further exploration as part of your own search projects.

Preloading Pertinent Search Results

Because of the difficulties involved in entering search queries into a mobile device, saving previous searches is an obvious and simple way of reengaging people in a search task. Previous searches provide useful context and actionable starting points when an application first opens.

Unlike Web applications, native mobile applications are persistent, so it's easy to cache their search results. Cached results load quickly, meaning a customer could conceivably reengage in the search process almost immediately. Some mobile device APIs even enable native applications to detect whether a phone call interrupted the person's previous session or the user exited an application normally and determine how much time has elapsed since a user last opened the application. These capabilities present interesting possibilities in terms of configuring the application in a way that returns users to their previous tasks or instead presents new possibilities for user interaction.

Providing Local Results

On mobile devices that support GPS, Wi-Fi, or other location-tracking mechanisms, you can determine the current location of a person who is using the mobile device, allowing applications to offer location-aware services. Mobile applications with search capabilities can serve highly relevant, fresh results that perfectly match a user's current mobile context. For example, Loopt is just one of a whole cadre of social networking mobile applications that enables people to track the locations of their friends who are currently nearby and exchange messages with them, get coupons from local merchants, and discover neighborhood happenings, as Figure 15.3 shows.

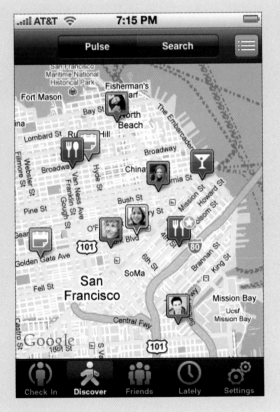

FIGURE 15.3

Local search results in the Loopt iPhone app

Providing Real-Time Search

Mobile devices are always with us, on the go, which makes them ideal for viewing real-time news and social network updates. Often, real-time search is also combined with local search to make it extremely relevant and very useful. Twitter allows people to search Twitter feeds labeled with the unique hash-tag using their mobile device. For example, a search for **#ixd11** tag searches tweets relevant to the Interaction 2011 design conference. People routinely monitor the mobile Twitter feeds while they are attending conference events to find out ultra-local and up-to-the-second event information, like schedule changes and social happenings. With Twitter, a real-time social search pattern has become a big part of the list of mobile device capabilities (see *Real-Time Search* excerpt below).

REAL-TIME SEARCH

Excerpt from *Designing Social Interfaces* By Christian Crumlish and Erin Malone (O'Reilly Media /Yahoo Press, 2009)

People can't always find breaking news and current topics of public conversation with ordinary keyword searches of indexed web resources, and already get frequent pointers to current information by the electronic equivalent of word of mouth (Figure 15.4).

This social search pattern enables people to find concepts in up-to-the-minute status updates and activities. It's important to provide familiar elements of the search interface (a text box and a search button) and make it clear that the results will be ordered by recency (reverse-chronological order) and not by relevancy. Optionally, give hints about the sort of things that can be profitably searched for in a real-time search interface, such as current top trending topics. Another option includes the ability to subscribe to search results, most commonly in the form of an RSS feed, to give people the ability to track a term or phrase and be notified almost immediately whenever it appears.

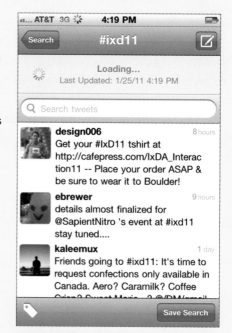

FIGURE 15.4

Twitter mobile offers real-time search of its public feed.

Offering a Value-Added Interpretation of the Real World

As discussed in the previous chapter, using mobile devices for sense-making in the real world offers one of the most intriguing possibilities for mobile applications. When it comes to finding, however, one of the most exciting developments is the **Amazon Remembers** feature offered by the Amazon.com Mobile iPhone app shown in Figure 15.5.

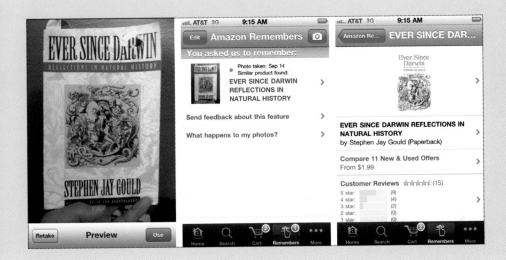

FIGURE 15.5

Amazon Remembers

Amazon Remembers enables customers to take pictures of any real-world items and add them to their lists of things to remember. After a customer uploads a photo, Amazon.com figures out what the item is and, if there is a corresponding item available for sale on Amazon.com, displays that item and sends the customer an email alert, encouraging her to purchase the item. Customers often get a response in a matter of seconds, but the search can take up to 24 hours. This application lays a solid foundation for the idea of a mobile Internet of Things described in the previous chapter.

Providing Various Sorting Options

As previously mentioned in Chapter 10, "The Mystery of Filtering by Sorting," thoughtfully designed sorting options are an excellent way to open up an ecommerce site's inventory for browsing. One of the best ways of doing this is to provide two or more buttons on a search results screen that enable multiple ways of dissecting an inventory, without ever failing to serve some results. By using sorting options together with geolocation, customers can even avoid having to type in any query. As Figure 15.6 shows, the ThirstyPocket iPhone app enables customers simply to press the **Search Nearest** or **Search Newest** button to see a sample of local results without having to type anything in the search box.

FIGURE 15.6

ThirstyPocket iPhone app

Of course, a customer can always type keywords in a search box to narrow down the results. As I explained in my presentation at the Net Squared Conference in May 2009, using this design pattern lets customers engage with an inventory of items or content immediately, and then invest the effort of typing in keywords after they have caught the scent of something that interests them or to refine the search results further.

Note—Given the fat-finger problem and a mobile device's limited screen real estate, you can't provide more than three to five sort options on the screen at one time. However, as the ThirstyPocket example shows, even a couple of sort options is often enough to add value and provide opportunities for customers to begin exploring.

Considering Custom Controls

One consequence of mobile devices having a smaller screen is not having the space to create a navigation bar of filters, facets, or categories on the left, providing a map to the aspects by which a customer can effectively narrow down a result set. Consider, for example, the all-important category filter. If an application were to use the standard iPhone picker, shown in Figure 15.1, it would obscure most of the search results on the screen. Various applications deal with this challenge in different ways. Some mobile applications have created a dedicated category-filter page—such as that in Amazon Mobile, shown in Figure 15.7. Clicking **Refine** takes customers to a different, full-sized screen on which they can select a category.

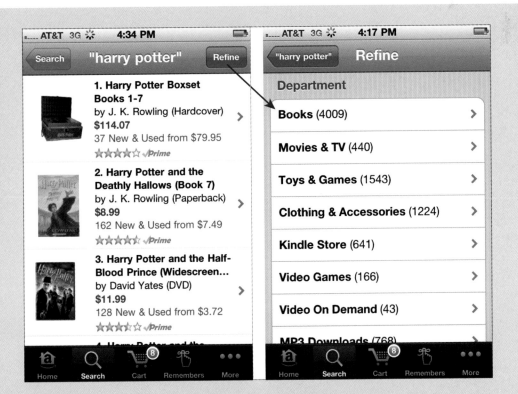

FIGURE 15.7

Dedicated category-filter page in Amazon Mobile

As shown in Figure 15.8, the ThirstyPocket iPhone app uses a different approach for creating a custom picker control. Because the list of sort options is fairly concise, instead of using a standard iPhone picker, ThirstyPocket displays the list using a custom popover. Another interesting twist is that visual design of the button that initiates the popover is reminiscent of the familiar Web and desktop drop-down list control, taking full advantage of customers' existing mental models and helping them understand what behavior to expect.

FIGURE 15.8

Custom sort control implemented via popover in the ThirstyPocket iPhone app

CHANGING SEARCH PARADIGMS

Because of the unique mix of constraints and opportunities that mobile application design presents, this design space is rich with possibilities for changing the existing paradigms for search and finding. Consider speech recognition, for example. Although, on the desktop, speech recognition does not yet enjoy widespread popularity and use, mobile represents an entirely different context—where speech recognition can offer an ideal solution. Not interpreting a spoken word correctly on a mobile device might not be quite as big a deal as it is on the desktop because the accuracy of speech recognition may actually approach, if not exceed, that of typing on a mobile phone's awkward mini-keyboard. For some mobile contexts, like driving, speech recognition may even offer a way to access full-featured search when typing is not available. Combine speech recognition with the use of an accelerometer and magnetometer, enabling gestural input, and you have the Google Mobile search application for the iPhone, shown in Figure 15.9.

FIGURE 15.9

Google Mobile iPhone app

Google's iPhone application recognizes the gesture of a person's swinging the phone up to his ear to know when to record a search command. When the user speaks, the search engine accepts and interprets his voice commands and then serves up search results. This user interface implements what is literally a game-changing design paradigm because its designers have taken the time to truly consider the mobile context of use and map natural interactions such as speech and gestures to mobile device functions. As Peter Morville said in his book *Search Patterns*, "We simply raise our phones to our ears and speak our search, relying on Google Mobile to derive what we want from who we are, where we stand, and what we say.... Like placing your hands under a tap to turn on the water, this is the type of smart design that 'dissolves in behavior.'"

When it comes to designing for a mobile context, we are just starting to scratch the surface. As Tom Chi of *OK/Cancel* famously quipped, "A well-defined and exciting problem (and its associated constraints) is the catalyst that makes design go." When you stop thinking about the limitations of mobile platforms and, instead, truly focus on the user goals you are working to support, you might just find those limitations turning into opportunities for redefining how people find, remember, and discover things in their world.

REFERENCES

Morville, Peter. *Search Patterns*. Sebastopol, CA: O'Reilly, 2010.

Nielsen, Jakob. "Mobile Usability." *Alertbox*, July 20, 2009. Retrieved February 27, 2010.

Nudelman, Greg. "Experience Design for a Viral Mobile Community" Net Squared Conference, May 2009.

Wroblewski, Luke. "Defining the Problem: Q&A with Tom Chi." *Functioning Form*, April 27, 2006. Retrieved February 27, 2010.

Wroblewski, Luke. "Enhancing User Interaction With First Person User Interface." *Smashing Magazine*, September 21, 2009. Retrieved February 27, 2010.

CHAPTER 16

DESIGN PATTERNS FOR MORE EFFECTIVE MOBILE FACETED SEARCH

As covered in Chapter 7, "Best Practices for Designing Faceted Search Filters," faceted search can be extremely helpful for certain kinds of finding—particularly for ecommerce apps. Unfortunately, the designers of mobile applications do not have established user interface paradigms they can follow nor abundant screen real estate for presenting facets and filters in traditional ways. To implement faceted search on mobile devices, you need to be creative because of this inability to follow established design patterns. This chapter examines several patterns that are well suited for mobile devices, including *Four Corners, Status Bar Drop-Down Menu, Modal Overlay, Watermark, Refinement Options, Teasers,* and *Parallel Architecture.* Following these patterns can move you one step closer to making faceted search a usable reality on mobile devices.

Before discussing these patterns, first take a look at several mobile-specific challenges that require designers to look at search in new ways, including: navigational elements that demand precious screen real estate, limited search-refinement options, and the general lack of an iterative refinement flow.

MOBILE FACETED SEARCH CHALLENGES

Recall that one of the mobile applications discussed in the previous chapter was Amazon.com's iPhone app. On the Web, Amazon.com's faceted search is the gold standard, so comparing its Web faceted search experience to that of its iPhone app is instructive. Looking at the Amazon.com iPhone app in Figure 16.1, consider the amount of screen real estate devoted to widgets and content secondary to the search results.

FIGURE 16.1

Amazon.com's iPhone app search results screen devotes 24% of pixels to navigation and chrome

Amazon.com's fairly standard iPhone app page layout consists of an iPhone device bar (battery, network, and signal indicators), navigation bar at the top, and a tab bar at the bottom, which together take up approximately 228 vertical pixels on the 640 × 960 pixel screen.

Note—In all, Amazon.com permanently devotes *almost 24%* of its precious screen real estate to chrome, navigation, and other features.

As a consequence, it can display only three search results at a time. And Amazon.com is actually fairly frugal with its screen real estate—at least in comparison to other mobile ecommerce applications.

Another interesting issue is that the user's keyword query—in this case, *Harry Potter Sorcerers Stone*—does not appear in its entirety in the application's navigation bar—both because the user interface displays the query in a large font and because the query text has to compete with a search refinement button that is also on the navigation bar. With the screen's limited real estate, the query gets cut off, allowing only **Harry Potter So**... to appear there.

Mobile search refinement options are also much more limited. As shown in Figure 16.2A, the only two search refinements Amazon.com presents to customers is by **Shipping Option: Amazon.com Prime Eligible**—which is just a binary on/off switch—and by **Department**—which enables customers to limit the search to a specific category. Although **Amazon.com Prime** is important for business development, and **Department** is definitely one of the most useful and frequently applied facets, offering only two faceted refinements hardly compares to the rich array of search-refinement options available on Amazon.com's Web site, as shown in Figure 16.2B. Conspicuously absent are various sorting options and filtering by price.

However, in these screenshots, you cannot see one of the most important and striking differences between search on the Web and on mobile devices, which can be understood only in terms of the app's search-refinement flow. Figure 16.3 illustrates the differences between Amazon.com's Web and mobile search-refinement flows.

On the Web, Amazon.com's search features promote progressive, faceted search refinement and exploration. As Peter Morville said in his book, *Search Patterns* (O'Reilly Media, 2010), "Faceted navigation ... helps us learn. Search becomes an iterative, interactive experience where what we find changes what we seek." For example, on the Web, a customer who starts with the keyword query *Harry Potter* can narrow down the search results by department (**Movies & TV**), additional keywords (*Harry Potter Sorcerers Stone*), format (**DVD**), and edition (**Widescreen**).

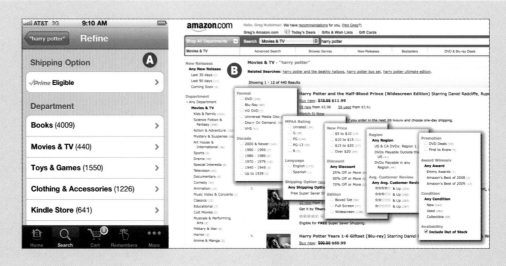

FIGURE 16.2

Search on Amazon.com's Web site presents many more refinement options than Amazon.com iPhone App

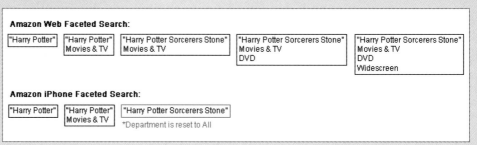

FIGURE 16.3

The differences between the Web and mobile search-refinement flows

In contrast, Amazon.com's iPhone app does not preserve search refinement as part of its finding flow. The customer who starts with the keyword query *Harry Potter* and then refines the results by **Department (Movies & TV)** cannot refine the query further, as shown in Figure 16.4.

FIGURE 16.4

Amazon.com's iPhone app does not preserve search refinement as part of its finding flow

If a customer attempts to refine a query by adding more keywords (*Harry Potter Sorcerers Stone*), the app removes the customer's prior department selection (**Movies & TV**), doing a completely new search for the query *Harry Potter Sorcerers Stone* and searching all departments. This behavior has the unfortunate effect of interrupting the flow of step-wise exploration and discovery that is central to the faceted search experience. Obviously, there is a need for better patterns for the step-wise narrowing, expanding, and refining of faceted search results on mobile devices.

Note—Mobile faceted search needs to balance customers' needs to both refine results and maintain their search-refinement flows against the limited screen real estate and fat-finger issues. You must especially guard against introducing false simple-mindedness in the name of simplicity.

Simplicity is a great goal, but as John Maeda said in his masterful book, *The Laws of Simplicity* (The MIT Press, 2006), "Some things can never be made simple." Using the words of Albert Einstein, we have to strive to make the most of the available tools and make user interfaces "as simple as possible, but not simpler." The design patterns that follow make the most of the available screen real estate, while providing intuitive and useful search-results refinement capabilities and improving the mobile faceted search experience.

FOUR CORNERS AND MODAL OVERLAY PATTERNS

As discussed previously in Chapter 4, "Balancing Pogosticking and Page Relevance," maximizing the number of results on a search results screen is key to improving information scent and overall finding efficiency. One of the most successful design patterns for maximizing the use of screen real estate is the Four Corners pattern, shown in Figure 16.5.

The *Four Corners* pattern devotes almost the entire mobile screen to search results. Users can display particular functions by tapping the semitransparent corners, which provide access to filters, the home page, and two additional menus. This pattern includes a thin, persistent status bar across the top of the screen, which displays an entire search query, *plus* any applied filters, rather than just the few characters Amazon.com Mobile app displays in a large font. Displaying an entire query is highly beneficial, given users' mobile context of use and the frequent interruptions inherent in the mobile finding experience.

FIGURE 16.5

Four Corners and Modal
Overlay patterns

Although the design pattern is called Four Corners and triangles are the most effective shape for the corners, they don't necessarily have to be triangles. Other alternatives include semitransparent buttons or floating icons overlay that retracts into the corners of the phone. However, for transparent buttons, it's best to keep icons simple and minimize text labels.

In addition to freeing up more room to display the search results, Four Corners also solves a common fat-finger problem found with tab bars on the bottom of the touch screens:

Note—When people flick to scroll the search results screen, they "over-swipe" and end up accidentally tapping one of the tabs in the center of the tab bar on the bottom of the screen. Over-swipe is more common when people using the phone are jostled in tight spaces and commute vehicles, so it's hard to observe this behavior in the lab usability studies.

Controls that are relegated into screen corners are moved out of the path of the vertical flick, and any accidental miss-flicks will no longer be interpreted as taps to reach the controls but will simply continue to scroll the search results.

Another pattern that works well with Four Corners is the *Modal Overlay* pattern, shown on the right in Figure 16.5. A modal overlay can display various search-refinement options such as filtering and sorting. As shown in Chapter 10, "The Mystery of Filtering by Sorting," it is not necessary to place filtering and sorting in two different areas of a screen. Most people have, at best, just a vague idea of the differences between the two features. This is particularly true for the mobile experience, where screen real estate is at a premium and minimizing the number of taps necessary to achieving a goal is key.

The Four Corners and Modal Overlay patterns work particularly well in combination. In Figure 16.5, each user interaction on the modal overlay refines the search results interactively. This dynamic interaction model works great because users can always see where they are and what filters they have applied, and they have easy access to further refinement options, all without ever leaving the context of the search results screen.

Note—Some touch phones—like the iPhone—do not provide an Application Programming Interface (API) for modal overlays but instead deliver content one screen at a time with transitions between screens. On such devices, you need to fake modal overlays. You can achieve this effect by rendering the same search results on a new screen—this time with a slightly darkened background—with a modal overlay over the results. When displaying this new screen, an application should minimize any transition to help to preserve the illusion of maintaining the search results context.

STATUS BAR DROP-DOWN MENU PATTERN

An important variation of the Four Corners with Modal Overlay pattern is the *Status Bar Drop-Down Menu* pattern, which also makes use of a thin, persistent status bar across the top of the screen. In this pattern, the status bar becomes the single menu button, which, when tapped, turns into a menu overlay containing search filters and navigation options. In this design pattern it is ideal if a smooth animation shows the menu coming down gradually, like a Roman shade being unrolled when pulled by a string.

The Status Bar Drop-Down Menu pattern draws inspiration from the recently updated Wells Fargo Mobile Web site that uses a novel approach to accessing apps' functions. Instead of the standard random-access navigation tab bar on the bottom of the screen, the Wells Fargo mobile Web site sports a Single Drop-Down Menu that houses all the apps functions, as shown in Figure 16.6.

FIGURE 16.6

Single Drop-Down Menu on the Wells Fargo Mobile Web site

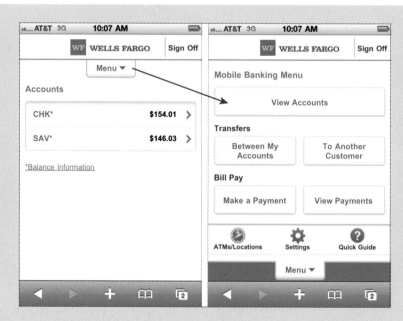

Much like in the Angry Birds app shown in Figure 16.7, the menu is unveiled like a Roman shade with a slick transition and covers up the current content without yanking the person out of the process flow. This design represents a conscious departure from the Web-based information architecture with random access to all the app's functions, instead optimizing the available real estate to show maximum content.

Unlike the Angry Birds app that devotes 100% of the screen to annihilating the egg-thieving pigs, the Wells Fargo mobile Web site is somewhat limited because it *is* a Web site, so it has to display the browser chrome and the app bar on the top of the browser. In contrast to the Wells Fargo mobile Web site, native mobile ecommerce apps have complete control of the screen. Thus, native apps can reclaim 100% of the screen real estate for showing search results by combining the semi-transparent status bar design pattern described in the previous section with the Single Drop-Down Menu. I dubbed the resulting powerful new pattern for immersive search Status Bar Drop-Down Menu, as shown it is shown in Figure 16.8.

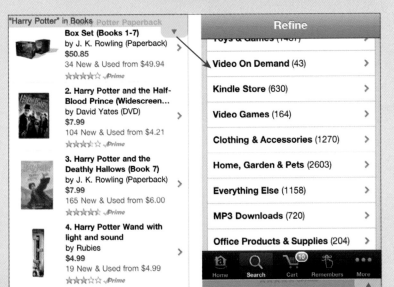

FIGURE 16.7

Action Screen and Menu of the Angry Birds iPhone App

FIGURE 16.8

Amazon.com app redesigned using the Status Bar Drop-Down Menu Design Pattern

In the case of Amazon.com, by using the Status Bar Drop-Down Menu pattern you can reclaim 24% of the real estate that was previously used for app chrome. Contrast the Status Bar Drop-Down Menu design with the original Amazon.com iPhone app, as shown in Figure 16.9.

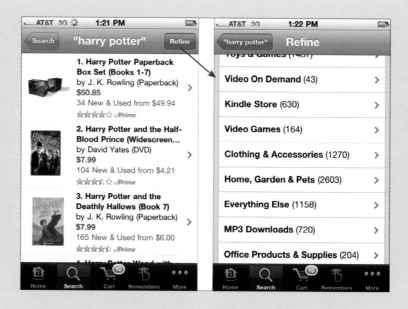

FIGURE 16.9

Original Amazon.com iPhone app and refinement menu

Some of the features of the novel Status Bar Drop-Down Menu pattern include the following:

:: **Unnecessary chrome is removed**—This novel pattern removes all the navigation and branding, utilizing 100% of the real estate for search results. If the signal is weak, or battery is critical, a warning can be shown on the semi-transparent status bar, removing the need to display the phone bar.

:: **Action screen is optimized for immersive experience**—Just as in the case of immersive games, on the search results screen, the customer's attention is exclusively devoted to search results, with the ability to access other functions via the menu.

:: **Menu is optimized for filtering**—If the menu is accessed while in search results, the menu also contains faceted search filters, as shown in Figure 16.8. In this case, the status bar disappears morphing into the actual filter values and keywords, creating an effective transition that fits the customer's mental model.

:: **Menu provides task-based access**—The menu contains the standard Apple Human Interface Guidelines' recommended tab bar. These tabs should be familiar to most mobile customers. The difference is that with this pattern, the tabs are out of the way until the customer asks for them, helping to create a more immersive search experience. In addition to the tabs, the rest of the menu could be contextual, presenting appropriate options and additional content on the shopping cart, home, and any other screens.

:: **Overlay menu maintains flow**—Just as in the Angry Birds app and Wells Fargo Web site, the menu overlay rolls down like a Roman shade on top of the search results, maintaining the illusion of keeping the customer "on the same page" and engaged in the current flow.

Note—Because of the small screen and the importance and variety of available transitions found on mobile devices, a small number of basic patterns can be extended to an almost infinite number of variations. For example, the Modal Overlay pattern in the previous section changed into the Roman Shade Overlay menu that works better with the Status Bar Drop-Down Menu pattern described in this section. However, despite the differences, both the Modal Overlay and the Roman Shade Overlay menu serve the same purpose: to keep the customer engaged in the current search flow.

This variation of the Four Corners with Modal Overlay pattern helps demonstrate that mobile search design is far from being a solved problem. Instead, it is a playground of novel applications and ideas, presenting unique challenges and unparalleled opportunities for exploration and experimentation.

WATERMARK PATTERN WITH THE FULL-PAGE REFINEMENT OPTIONS PATTERN

The latest generation of smartphones—including the Apple iPhone, Palm Pre, and Google Android—provides designers with a bevy of novel interaction models. Some of the ways in which people must interact with new smartphones may not be obvious to them because they may not match their existing mental models or the affordances of devices with which they're familiar. Nevertheless, after people discover these interactions, they seem surprisingly intuitive and fun, and people do not easily forget them.

As shown in Figure 16.10, in mobile computer games, it is common practice to teach players by enabling them to manipulate their mobile devices through various gestures, including tilting, turning, and shaking them—or even using a device's accelerometer to mimic the way you would use a magic wand: "Incendio!"

FIGURE 16.10

Fun ways of employing the iPhone's accelerometer in the Harry Potter game

In the Harry Potter game, the object of interacting with the mobile device's accelerometer is entertainment, so people will eagerly invest the time to learn the gestures required to defeat Professor Snape in a wizard's duel. On the other hand, in ecommerce search, the customers' object in interacting with a mobile device is efficient acquisition of goods, services, or information—which by necessity typically shortens the learning curve.

Note—If you want people to perform nonstandard actions to access essential system functionality, the required system interaction must be fairly obvious and easy to learn—and it must not require people to read instructions they would perceive as obnoxious or distracting.

This is where careful use of the *Watermark* design pattern can be especially powerful.

A *watermark* is a transparent outline that appears either over or behind the primary content on a screen. In some ways, a watermark is similar to a splash screen, but it is considerably less distracting because watermarks enable people to see the content on the screen at the same time. Figure 16.11 shows two variations of the Watermark pattern, plus a full-screen example of a *Refinement Options* pattern.

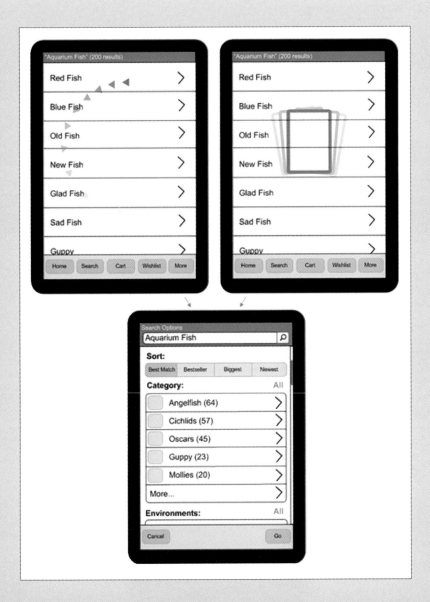

FIGURE 16.11

Two variations of the Watermark pattern and a Refinement Options pattern

The two examples of the Watermark pattern, shown in Figure 16.11, demonstrate a circular swiping gesture and a shaking gesture on a multitouch device. In both cases, after a user launches an application, each watermark appears just once or twice, gently dissolving to let the user view the screen's main content. Watermarks can also use animation—for example, to demonstrate the motion of the circular swipe by displaying one arrow at a time on the screen. However, animation greatly increases a watermark's visibility, so you should use it with care. Circular swiping emulates the motion of digging into a pile of puzzle pieces to find the right one, whereas shaking recalls the action of shaking up small, loose objects in a bag or a box.

In each case, the idea behind the watermark is to educate or remind people about the gesture or interaction necessary to view a screen containing additional search-refinement features. When people decide to dig in further or shake up their search results, the application displays a full screen of refinement options, as shown at the bottom of Figure 16.11. This screen provides an example of the Refinement Options pattern. Again, the thin, persistent status bar across the top of the screen shows the query. Together with the watermark, this helps maximize the real estate the screen can devote to search results, while making exploration intuitive.

With a full screen of refinement options, a customer can view four or five of the most popular values for each of the facets and select a facet value with a single tap. This is almost like having the entire array of refinement options on a typical faceted search results Web page. Having the search box integrated into the refinement options page also reinforces the idea of applying search query terms and facets together as a set, just as they are on a Web page. Together, these patterns enable you to duplicate the intuitive and efficient step-wise refinement and expansion flow your customers expect from a faceted search results page on an ecommerce site. Using a scrollable screen of facets rather than a modal overlay like that shown in Figure 16.5 enables you to devote the full screen width to the search results, sprucing them up with icons for popular refinement options and enabling customers to refine the results with fewer taps.

Does this mean presenting a full page of refinement options is better than a modal overlay? Not at all. A modal overlay displays its refinement options within the context of the search results, while displaying a separate results-refinement screen, along with its associated transition; yanks customers out of the search-results context; and presents what some people might think is an overwhelming variety of refinement options.

Note—When discussing design patterns, avoid getting caught up in judging one pattern to be better than another. Each pattern is useful in specific contexts and applications and for particular purposes and types of customers.

Design patterns are like a language you can use to communicate with your customers. It helps to have a vocabulary of patterns that is as complete and varied as possible, and to use each pattern appropriately to communicate your design message with clarity and precision.

TEASER MOBILE DESIGN PATTERN

Teasers are nothing new on mobile phones. Most mobile user interfaces implement this pattern in some manner or another. Consider, for example, the Yelp iPhone application, as shown in Figure 16.12.

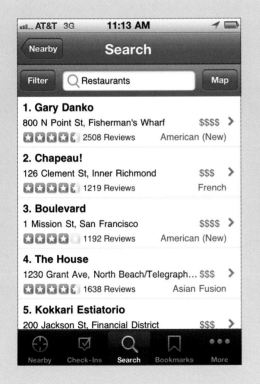

FIGURE 16.12

Teaser design pattern in Yelp's mobile app

Yelp displays four complete search results, plus a teaser at the bottom of the page that shows a partial view of the next result set. The Teaser design pattern is useful in showing that there are more search results below the fold. As mentioned in Chapter 3, "Choosing the Right Search Results Page Layout," usability testing has shown that Amazon.com is an absolute master of this pattern. Regardless of a screen's resolution, it always displays partial product descriptions and pictures just above the fold. Showing part of what is below the fold is an effective means of inviting visitors to scroll down and see more content.

Recently, when Microsoft came out with Windows 7 Mobile, it extended the Teaser pattern well beyond just showing the availability of search results below the fold. Figure 16.13 shows a Windows 7 Mobile Panorama control. Panorama consists of a surface larger than what can be seen in a single phone screen so that parts of the underlying page "poke through" reminding the user that more content is available on the left, right, above, and below what's currently visible on the screen. The phone's screen acts as a sort of viewfinder that displays only a small part of a much larger virtual space.

FIGURE 16.13

Teasers in Windows 7 Mobile Panorama control

Source: www.mobiletechworld.com/wordpress/wp-content/uploads/2010/08/Panorama.jpg

In its implementation of the Teaser pattern, Windows 7 Mobile uses lots of obvious cues, including screen titles that are cut off in midword, partially visible screen widgets, image fragments, and an abundant use of animated transitions.

Note—A teaser is a specific application of the more general design principle: *fixing imperfection*, in which a design immediately engages people by having them "fix" something that is intentionally not quite right with a user interface or object. In the process of fixing an imperfection, people learn the user interface's interaction model. Studies have shown that this process of fixing imperfection, or seeking symmetry, is natural to humans and quite immersive, even to the point of alleviating anxiety and pain in burn trauma.

The problem some may see with the Windows 7 Mobile design is that people cannot win at this particular game of fixing imperfection. There is absolutely no way to fix the user interface to simultaneously show *all* of a title, widget, or image that exceeds the size of the screen. It's kind of like a blanket that is intentionally made too small: If you cover your legs, your chest is exposed; pull the blanket up to your chin and your legs get cold.

Note—UX designers often seek a kind of minimalistic, authentic beauty and symmetry in their designs, so some designers might find this kind of user interface profoundly disturbing. However, you cannot argue against the effectiveness of this design approach.

The wireframe shown in Figure 16.14 takes advantage of the Teaser design pattern to show a partial view of some faceted search filters on the right and, thus, expand the available virtual screen real estate.

FIGURE 16.14

Teaser design pattern facilitates the discovery of faceted search filters

The search results are on the left in this wireframe; filters are on the right. Following a basic convention of mobile user interfaces, controls on the right side of the screen enable people to drill down deeper into the application's information architecture (IA) space, whereas controls on the left side move people "back" or closer to the top of the IA or to the home page.

The Teaser design pattern effectively facilitates discovery through its use of partially exposed screen elements—in the example, faceted search results filters. This pattern also enables people to make rapid transitions from looking at search results to narrowing down the search results, so it is highly suitable for applications in which it is advantageous for people to discover a set of filters quickly and use them often.

BASIC/ADVANCED PARALLEL ARCHITECTURE PATTERN

Another ideal design pattern for efficient discovery and use of filters is the *Basic/Advanced Parallel Architecture* design pattern, depicted in Figure 16.15. This design pattern is especially effective in applications that offer a fixed set of filters—for instance, booking air travel.

The idea behind the Basic/Advanced Parallel Architecture design pattern is that there are two modes of interacting with filters: basic and advanced. The *basic mode* enables customers to easily engage with your application and dramatically shortens their learning curve. However, people who want an *advanced mode* of filtering can easily obtain this functionality—by returning to the filter page and tapping the **Advanced Search** tab.

The *parallel architecture* part of this pattern comes in when a customer needs to adjust the filter values. For customers who started their query from the **Basic Search** tab, tapping **Back** returns them to that simple search tab. For customers who started from the **Advanced Search** tab, tapping **Back** returns them to that tab, where they can adjust the expanded set of filters. Although the relationships between these three contexts—Basic Search, Advanced Search, and Search Results—are a bit difficult to explain, they offer a natural interaction model that most people have found intuitive to use during testing.

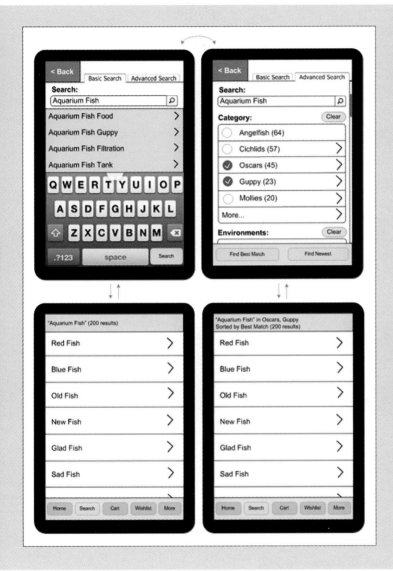

FIGURE 16.15

Basic/Advanced Parallel
Architecture design pattern

The Basic/Advanced Parallel Architecture design pattern offers the added
advantage of a flatter architecture. Instead of an advanced mode that requires
people to go deeper into an application's IA, the advanced flow sits in parallel
with the basic flow, so both are equally accessible with a single tap. It is important to note that, in both cases, the search results page has a persistent status
bar across the top of the screen, displaying an entire search query, plus any
applied filters.

One application that successfully implements the Basic/Advanced Parallel Architecture design pattern is the Thirsty Pocket iPhone app, shown in Figure 16.16.

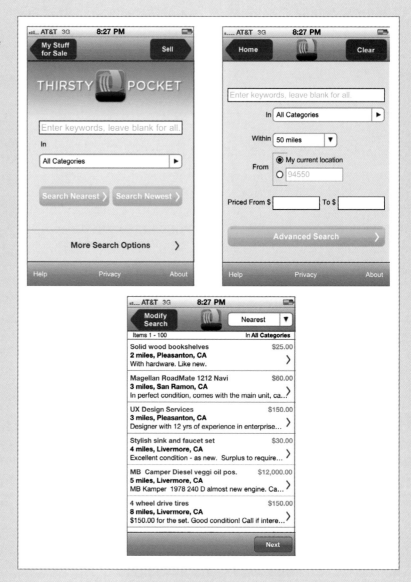

FIGURE 16.16

Basic/Advanced Parallel Architecture design pattern in Thirsty Pocket

In a slight variation on the Basic/Advanced Parallel Architecture design pattern, instead of **Basic Search** and **Advanced Search** tabs, Thirsty Pocket presents two buttons on its home page: a prominent **Search Nearest** for basic search and a de-emphasized **More Search Options** button for advanced search options. Tapping **More Search Options** enables you to set filters; then tap **Advanced Search** to see the filtered search results. Nevertheless, the Thirsty Pocket user interface still preserves the essential features of this pattern because tapping **Modify Search** on the search results page takes you back to the appropriate search page—basic or advanced—depending on how you initiated a search.

Interestingly, instead of labeling the price and distance filters page **Advanced**, Thirsty Pocket uses the label **More Search Options**. In Thirsty Pocket, the purpose of the advanced search page is to provide options for searching outside the device's current GPS location, and narrowing a search by price. Most people would not need to use the location filter, and the price filter might severely limit the effectiveness of search by frequently over-constraining a search to zero search results. The price filter is a great example of the "ejector seat lever" Alan Cooper et al. so eloquently describe in their book *About Face 3*. Therefore, this price filter is best "hidden" on a separate page. In the Thirsty Pocket app, the label **More Search Options** describes the purpose of the advanced search page perfectly and has the added bonus of being less intimidating than the label "Advanced Search".

REFERENCES

Bucolo, Sam et al. "The Design of a Tangible Interaction Device to Alleviate Anxiety and Pain in Pediatric Burns Patients." *CHI '06 Extended Abstracts on Human Factors in Computing Systems*, Montreal, Quebec, Canada, April 22–27, 2006.

Cooper, Alan, Robert Reimann, and David Cronin. *About Face 3: The Essentials of Interaction Design*. 3rd ed. Indianapolis, IN: John Wiley & Sons, Inc., 2007.

Nudelman, Greg. "Design Caffeine for Search and Browse UI." Information Architecture Summit 2010, Phoenix, Arizona, April 9–11, 2010. Retrieved April 30, 2010.

—"Design Patterns for Mobile Faceted Search." *UXmatters*, March 8, 2010. Retrieved April 30, 2010.

—"Experience Design for a Viral Mobile Community." Net Squared Conference, San Jose, CA, May 2009. Retrieved April 30, 2010.

—"Choosing the Right Search Results Page Layout: Make the Most of Your Width." *UXmatters*, March 9, 2009. Retrieved April 30, 2010.

—"Designing Immersive Search with Drop Down Menus." *UX Magazine*, February 2, 2011. Retrieved February 2, 2011.

Wroblewski, Luke. "Windows Phone: User Interface Teases & Transitions." LukeW Ideation + Design, February 17, 2010. Retrieved April 30, 2010.

CHAPTER 17

SEARCH ON TABLET DEVICES: THE FLIGHT OF DISCOVERY

In April of 2010, the original Apple iPad heralded the arrival of tablet devices. Tablets are bigger than typical smartphones, but with similar capabilities, so you might be tempted to assume that designing for tablets would be just like designing for smartphones—perhaps just on a bit larger scale. Do not let appearances fool you. Tablet devices with touchscreens operate under a different set of design and ergonomic constraints and support different goals and behaviors. Just as mobile ecommerce search requires you to think differently than when designing ecommerce search for the Web, designing for tablet devices such as the Apple iPad requires some novel approaches, as this chapter discusses.

TABLET BEHAVIORS AND ERGONOMICS

When designing for tablets such as Apple iPad, designers need to consider the mobility patterns and personalization issues that arise from the unique status of the tablet as a device shared between all family members. Other design considerations include two-handed ergonomics of the device and the unique paradigm of direct manipulation of on-screen content.

Mobility

Early Apple iPad TV advertisements show people browsing the Web while riding a bus or subway or while waiting at a doctor's office. Although, in principle, a tablet does support these activities, in practice, the mobility pattern for a typical consumer tablet device is found in the area between the refrigerator and the couch.

At least at the present moment, most people are not using their tablets as mobile devices outside their home (see Marijke Rijsberman's perspective, "A Fine Line: The iPad as a Portable Device.")

A FINE LINE: THE IPAD AS A PORTABLE DEVICE

When the iPad first hit the market, some people perceived it as another mobile device—an oversized iPod Touch; a big iPhone with suboptimal phone features. "We believe that Apple has successfully carved out a new category of mobile devices between the smartphone and the laptop," said a Piper Jaffray analyst a day or so after the iPad appeared in stores[1]. It's an easy mistake to make. Clearly Apple designed, built, and marketed the iPad as the big brother in the mobile device family. The fact that it runs on the Apple mobile OS seems to confirm its mobile identity.

However, if you look at user behavior, you can see only a few of the characteristic usage patterns for mobile devices among iPad users. In actual use, it turns out that the iPad, though highly portable, is different from mobile devices in essential ways, as shown in Table 17.1.

CHARACTERISTIC	MOBILE OR SMARTPHONE	IPAD
Wearable	Yes	No
Communications focus	Yes	No
Always on	Yes	No
Individually owned	Yes[2]	Sometimes
Long battery life	Yes	Yes
Easy to wake up	Yes	Yes

TABLE 17.1

How Mobile Phones and iPads Differ

My first indication that the iPad inclines toward sedentary habits came as a result of a lab study I conducted in August 2010—a few months after its introduction in the U.S. One of the very first participants walked into the lab with her iPad safely ensconced in its original box. The participant explained that she had not taken the device out of the house before. Although she was an extreme case, she was hardly unique. In all, half the participants in that lab study indicated that they used their iPads only at home.

Even more striking, in a different study of iPad users at a biotech company, it turned out that several participants did not usually bring their iPad to work with them, even though their company provided the device to them.

There are many different reasons for the iPad's limited mobility:

- **lack of wearability**—The iPad is too big to put in your pocket, so you need to carry it in your arms, a briefcase, or a purse.

- **shared ownership**—A significant proportion of our study participants bought their iPad "for the family." When that is the case, it cannot leave the house without negotiation with all "co-owners."

- **perceived fragility**—Many iPad owners worry that they might break or scratch their device if they treat it like a mobile device.

But perhaps the most significant influence on the way people use their iPads is the fact that the iPad doesn't replace their mobile phone[3]. Contemporary Americans have come to view phone access as a basic necessity, and not one out of 43 usability participants to date has evinced the slightest desire to try to use the iPad for phone communications—even if they do have 3G network access.

In other words, whenever a person has access to an iPad, he or she also has access to a mobile phone. This combination of phone and iPad means that people still associate many mobile behaviors—location-based services, on-the-go searching, and so on—with the phone, which is easier to handle while moving from place to place. The iPad, on the other hand, is likely to come into play when a person stops moving about and settles down somewhere.

These divergences suggest that it is important to maintain a distinction between mobile devices and portable devices, as users continue to discriminate between the two in their behaviors.

—Marijke Rijsberman

[1] Quoted in Phillip Elmer DeWitt, "Piper Jaffray Survey of iPad Buyers: 74% Owned Macs; 66% Had iPhones," at http://tech.fortune.cnn.com/2010/04/05/piper-jaffray-survey-of-ipad-buyers-74-owned-macs-66-had-iphones/ (Retrieved October 3, 2010).

[2] In the developing world, people sometimes share mobile phones, but in the U.S. market, a shared mobile phone is a rare occurrence.

[3] Piper Jaffray's survey of iPad buyers (http://tech.fortune.cnn.com/2010/04/05/piper-jaffray-survey-of-ipad-buyers-74-owned-macs-66-had-iphones/) suggests that the iPad does not replace any device except e-readers.

Although there may be a variety of reasons why people do not use their tablets outside their homes, this reality has profound implications for designing ecommerce search for the tablet device. Surprisingly, the closest familiar model for the tablet is the family TV—sometimes called the *alpha TV*. The tablet is first and foremost a consumption device. People use it primarily for playing games, browsing, and relaxing. This means the ecommerce search user interfaces you design for it need to support the primary goals of entertainment, consumption, and relaxation.

Consider the ecommerce search roles discussed in Chapter 2. On an iPhone, browsing can be particularly painful, so most ecommerce user interfaces tend to focus on supporting Targeted Shoppers, who already know what they want to buy. The mobile ecommerce application is just a quick and efficient means to convert a Targeted Shopper to a Committed Shopper. In contrast to iPhone usage, observation of iPad users reveals that they tend to use the iPad for longer periods of time, at a slower pace, when users are more relaxed or contemplative. Thus, an iPad ecommerce search interface needs to focus on supporting Browsers and Fun Seekers, who have more leisurely patterns of use. This is not to say that people won't use the iPad for quick information snacks—like checking a price or a package delivery date. However, it's not the primary use case for an iPad ecommerce user interface.

Note—On the tablet, your focus should be on making the *experience* of consumption into an art form by taking full advantage of visual browsing on a large, bright, high-resolution screen and direct manipulation of a user interface through multitouch gestures.

Personalization

It is essential to understand the personalization model for a tablet to design an optimal ecommerce application for that device. For an ecommerce application on a mobile phone, you can usually assume nearly total personalization because only one person typically uses the device. Thus, it makes a lot of sense to save a user's settings, browsing history, and the like—especially for a mobile context of use, in which users frequently get interrupted by incoming phone calls, or lose their connections, and often engage in multitasking.

The context of use for a tablet is different. Several factors in combination create less-than-ideal conditions for personalization: a lack of mobility; scarcity because, typically, there is only a single tablet device in a household; and the predominant use of the tablet as an entertainment device. The closest model you can follow for context of use is that of a family TV set in the early 1950s or a family computer in the early 1990s. Just as the entire family—sometimes including the neighbors' kids—gathered in front of the TV set to watch everyone's favorite shows, so is shared use of a tablet common. At the very least, it's likely that more than one person would use a tablet during the course of a day. Just as in the early 1990s, a single computer supported all members of a family in their different tasks, so does a typical tablet support the needs of a variety of family members, who take turns using it to play a game, read a newspaper, shop, or browse the Web.

Unlike a personal computer that enables the creation of several different user profiles, most tablets, including the Apple iPad, are not designed with multiple users in mind. What does this mean for designers and product developers? Because the iPad does not support multiple user profiles the way computers do, designers must design ecommerce applications to support the creation of a separate profile for each of a device's users. Unlike a Web browser that saves the last user's account information, or a personal computer, which loads an entirely different computing environment for each user, the most appropriate multi-user model for tablet apps may be that of the Nintendo Wii. The Wii does not require a system-wide login like a personal computer. Instead, individual games on the Wii support user profiles, called *Miis*, displaying all of them in an open list on each game's welcome page.

One possible feature ecommerce applications on a tablet could support, would be the ability to quickly switch between several predefined profiles—or at least, the ability to sign out and then easily sign in again. After all, the last thing you'd want is for your significant other to discover what gift you've just purchased for him or her on Amazon.com, thereby ruining the surprise.

Ergonomics

Although tablets come in a variety of sizes, studying the most popular tablet device on the market, the Apple iPad, will give you some general clues about the ergonomics of this new device class. It is especially enlightening to compare the iPad with the iPhone, its mobile phone counterpart. A common mistake is assuming people hold and tap their iPad in the same way they do their iPhone or iPod Touch. But this is where some of the biggest differences between these devices come into play. The iPhone is a small, lightweight device that people like to hold in one hand, while with their other hand, they may be holding onto an overhead bar on a subway or doing some other type of multitasking. For this reason, many developers optimize their iPhone apps expecting users to hold the device with their right hand and operate controls with their right thumb. According to Josh Clark's Design4Mobile 2010 presentation, iPad Design Headaches, when holding an iPhone in this way, the most comfortable touch zone on the screen falls in the pattern shown in Figure 17.1.

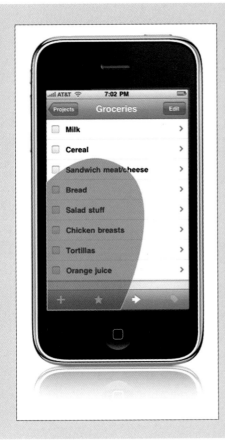

FIGURE 17.1

Most accessible one-handed touch zone on the iPhone

In sharp contrast to the iPhone, the iPad is quite heavy. Other than for a brief period of time, it is uncomfortable to hold an iPad in one hand. It is also quite impossible to hold the iPad in one hand, while manipulating on-screen controls with the same hand. Although I've observed little consistency in the way people hold the iPad, a wide, two-handed grip seems most common. As a result, the most accessible touch zones lie near the top half of the edges of the device, as shown in Figure 17.2.

Apple iPhone is much smaller than the iPad, so even the controls that lie completely outside the most comfortable touch zone are still readily accessible in a one-handed grip—even for adults with small hands. However, in comparison to an iPhone screen, the iPad screen is huge. The size of the touchscreen makes it impractical, if not impossible, for most people to tap targets that lie outside the most accessible touch zone without lifting a hand from the device. The problem of accessing portions of the screen is made worse because most people do not have a preferred orientation—depending on the task, people flip the device from portrait to landscape and back again. Landscape orientation tends to widen the area between device edges, further shrinking the area of the screen accessible without lifting ones hand from the device.

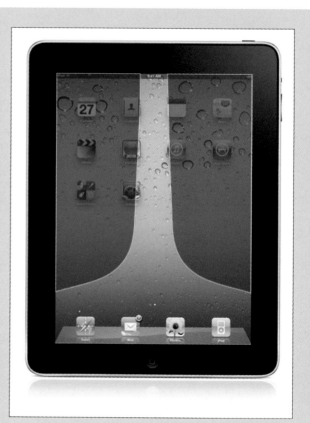

FIGURE 17.2

Most accessible touch zone with a two-handed iPad grip in portrait orientation

Of course, the usability of any target or button follows Fitts's law, which states that a person's ability to hit a target is directly proportional to the size of the target and inversely proportional to the distance from the pointer to the control.

Note—Although tapping a touchscreen may sound like a small effort for a person to make, *repeatedly* lifting a hand to tap a small button on a bar at the top or bottom of a screen is an awkward interaction Josh Clark has dubbed the *iPad Elbow* (see Josh Clark's perspective, *Buttons Are a Hack*).

BUTTONS ARE A HACK

To tap any button on a phone screen requires only the flick of a finger; on the desktop, a twitch of the mouse moves the cursor into place. But the work is harder on a tablet. The size of the iPad screen means that taps often require moving the entire arm. The risk is a bad case of "iPad elbow," a condition marked by the physical and mental fatigue of hauling your arm across the screen and concentrating to tap a tiny button.

Apple unfortunately builds lots of these tiny buttons into the standard toolkit. The tiny arrows for navigating the Calendar app are especially trying: miniscule tap targets at the bottom of the screen, where fingers rarely rest naturally. Likewise, the standard Back button at the top left of the screen in apps like Mail means dragging your arm, an unwieldy pointer, to move among email accounts and folders.

The ergonomics of buttons, or any small tap target, are naturally unfriendly on the iPad. But we need buttons, right? Not necessarily. A big screen invites big gestures. Ebook and newspaper apps let you swipe anywhere on the screen to flip the page, an effortless feature that Apple's Calendar app (Figure 17.3) sorely lacks, with its tiny navigation buttons.

FIGURE 17.3

Apple's Calendar app

Likewise, it would be a welcome convention to allow users to conjure the Mail app's list of email folders simply by touching the screen with five fingers, for example. These examples let you use the entire screen as a control, not just a small button.

Buttons are a hack. They're inelegant design solutions because they work from a distance. Flipping a switch over here to turn a light; on over there isn't a direct interaction with the object, the light, and that means it's not immediately intuitive. It's a behavior we have to learn. Over the last 25 years of visual computer culture, we've used buttons and other interface gizmos as a needed crutch to make software go. But we've had to learn it; it doesn't come naturally.

The touchscreen makes that crutch unnecessary in many cases. We can actually touch content and work with it directly: flipping through photos, enlarging maps, turning the pages of a book. The illusion of manipulating content directly is a powerful one, and it tickles the brain in new ways. It creates an intimate experience with the content, with the software.

The Twitter for iPad app, for example, eliminated buttons to navigate tweets (Figure 17.4). Twitter lets you browse content by tapping it directly [and] then move back and forth by swiping at big, easy-to-tap content panels.

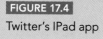

Twitter's IPad app

There's less arm work and less brain work, too; you don't have to think about what buttons do and where they might sit on the screen. Just manipulate the content directly: swipe through your history, or even peek into conversations by pulling down a tweet with two fingers, like a window shade. The Pinball HD app too, is a nice example of a screen without any buttons at all (Figure 17.5). Just tap the screen itself to make the flippers go.

FIGURE 17.5

The Pinball HD app

Designers should strive to embrace similarly direct interactions. We instinctively know how to flip through a book or move objects around a table. And sure, we know how to push a button, too, but pushing a button isn't really a direct interaction with anything except the button. We should think instead about designing touchscreen interfaces that mimic the exploration of a physical space.

I'm not suggesting that we should abandon buttons completely; they still have important roles, particularly for filling out forms, but designers should pause to ask, "Can I replace this control with a gesture or other direct interaction?"

Our brains evolved over millennia to navigate a physical environment. The alternate-universe exploration of computer interfaces is, by contrast, incredibly new. We might've grown accustomed to windows, buttons, and sliders over the last few decades, but that doesn't mean it's the best way to explore software. Designers should instead think how we can allow people to nudge, poke, and slide content directly.

—JOSH CLARK

Despite what superficially may seem to be form-factor similarities between the iPhone and iPad, the ergonomics of the iPad create a different set of user interface constraints.

Note—Perhaps the least accessible location for controls on an iPad is at the bottom of the screen—the location of the standard tab bar on the iPhone.

Because the iPad is fairly heavy, users typically position it at a slight angle, with its bottom edge resting on some solid surface. Most often—for example, when relaxing on a couch—the surface on which the iPad rests is a person's lap, making it all but impossible to tap a tab at the bottom edge of the screen without either lifting a hand or awkwardly juggling the device—and incidentally, yanking the person using the device right out of the relaxed, contemplative mood the iPad is supposed to induce.

I often hear clients who have already developed an iPhone app say they don't think they'll need to develop a separate iPad application, because people can use their iPhone app on their iPad as well. Unfortunately, the ergonomic differences between the iPhone and iPad mean this is simply not the case for most apps.

Note—Not only does a typical iPhone app look unattractive running on the larger iPad screen, it is also awkward to use because the key controls are either at the bottom of the screen or in the middle of the bar at the top of the screen, making it necessary to lift one's hand from the device to tap any of the controls.

Direct Manipulation of Content

In contrast to the problems just described, developing applications specifically for the tablet devices like the iPad lets you take full advantage of its unique ergonomics. Pek Pongpaet's BizTome iPad app, shown in Figure 17.6, provides an excellent example of ergonomic optimization.

The design of this application has carefully placed commonly used buttons near the top edge of the device in the hot zone that is accessible when using a wide, two-handed grip. Controls that people do not use as often, such as search, are slightly out of the way, to avoid accidental tapping.

FIGURE 17.6

BizTome app, optimized for the iPad

The design of the BizTome app brings another important iPad design principle to mind: Rather than recommending that an app should provide a separate set of controls for displaying content, the interface guidelines call for user interfaces in which users can directly manipulate the content. User interface elements look and behave like real-world objects. Users can open notebooks and turn pages. Coming from the Web world with its obvious buttons and standardized HTML controls, designing for the direct manipulation of content is not without its challenges and controversies.

Note—As the Nielsen Norman Group reports, overly visual user interfaces can create considerable discovery issues because people often miss the visual cues they're accustomed to seeing on the Web, which tell them where they can click.

Another issue with tablet apps seems to be a general lack of consistency in interactions in different apps, where the same action might result in many different and conflicting behaviors: "The first crop of iPad user apps revived memories of Web designs from 1993, when Mosaic first introduced the image map.... Graphic designers went wild: anything they could draw could be a UI, whether it made sense or not." (iPad Usability: First Findings From User Testing, Jakob Nielsen's *Alertbox*, May 10, 2010)

Although some confusion definitely exists, the antidote seems to be to follow real-world mental models of how objects should behave. Design guidelines that consistently produce the best user experiences include the following:

- Err on the side of tradition and simplicity.
- Use real-world metaphors whenever appropriate.
- Provide robust ways to undo an action or go back.
- Provide a home page accessible from everywhere in an app.
- Allow pages to scroll whenever appropriate.

Currently, the best metaphors seem to be those that are not exactly nostalgic but *classic*—familiar and comfortable. In his Design4Mobile 2010 presentation, Josh Clark cited the familiar newspaper metaphor *The New York Times* iPad app uses, as shown in Figure 17.7.

Now, explore in detail how you can apply some of these facts and guidelines to ecommerce search user interfaces.

FIGURE 17.7

The classy newspaper metaphor of *The New York Times* iPad app

TABLET ECOMMERCE SEARCH

Creating intuitive and usable ecommerce search on the tablet devices can take many different paths. Using iPad and iPhone apps as examples, the next section compares two popular real-estate search apps, Zillow and ZipRealty, to demonstrate how tablet search is different from the search on the mobile phone and explores the importance of maintaining task flow and direct manipulation of on-screen content in the design of the tablet search user interface.

eCommerce Search on the iPad versus the iPhone

To understand how to approach the design of ecommerce search on the iPad, it helps to first understand the differences between designing for the iPad and the iPhone. As an example, consider the differences between the Zillow apps for these two devices. Figure 17.8 shows Zillow search on the iPhone, which is both geographical and local and focuses, as you might expect, on maps.

FIGURE 17.8

Zillow iPhone app

In the upper-left corner—the most prominent place for a user interface control—is the GPS locator button. In the upper-right corner, there is a prominent **Filter** button, which takes customers to a separate page where they can narrow down a large inventory to a more manageable size. Because the iPhone screen is so small, the app presents the inventory in a variety of useful views: **Map**, **Hybrid**, and **List**, in a classic tab metaphor across the bottom of the screen. One of the views is **Favorites**, to which customers can add homes in which they're particularly interested. Phone integration makes it easy to call an agent with a single tap and schedule a property-viewing appointment. Google Maps integration makes it easy to get directions to a property while on the go. Overall, Zillow for iPhone is an excellent application that fits mobility and usage patterns perfectly.

Next, consider the Zillow iPad app, shown in Figure 17.9.

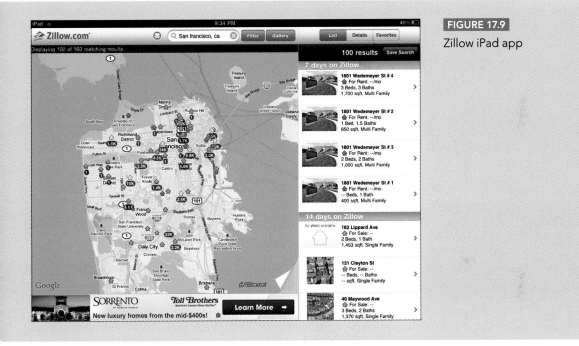

FIGURE 17.9

Zillow iPad app

You must consider the new context of use for the iPad—it's no longer necessarily mobile or local, as for the iPhone. Customers would likely use the Zillow iPad app while sitting comfortably on their couch beside their significant other to plan what homes to visit that day. If the application performs well, they may take the iPad along in the car and use the app while driving to and viewing the homes. Or more likely, they'll view the list of favorites they created using the iPad on the Zillow mobile site, using their smartphone, and the iPad will remain at home on the coffee table.

The Zillow iPad app follows this usage model quite well. The GPS locator button is highly visible—in case customers do take their iPad with them—yet its placement is quite well out of the way on the top bar, optimizing the user interface for at-home real estate searches. To take full advantage of the large screen and more leisurely, in-depth exploration the iPad supports best, Zillow has added a **Gallery** feature.

Gone is the Views tab bar at the bottom of the screen because the much larger screen of the iPad easily accommodates both the map view and the list view of properties, much like the Zillow Web site. Unfortunately, this is also where the iPhone app's elegantly simple information architecture fails somewhat when it is translated to the iPad. The user interface offers **List**, **Detail**, **Favorites**, and **Gallery**, but in two different control groups. **Gallery** is a button above the map pane because it ostensibly controls the view in that pane, whereas **Favorites** provides access to yet another view of the inventory. Splitting the screen into two panes and providing separate controls for each pane can be confusing to customers because it seems to fragment the on-screen inventory of items and doesn't offer a clear, consistent way of interacting with the app. A more effective information architecture would enable customers to think about the same inventory in different ways, with less need to consider the different user interfaces of specific devices.

What about the ergonomics? The most easily accessible controls are the properties list on the right and, unfortunately, the **Save Search** button, whereas the **Filter** button, which customers are likely to use more frequently, requires customers to let go of the device with one hand and lift their hand to tap it.

Another interesting thing to note is the "peel corner" interaction, which enables customers to view the search filters. This implementation of the Four Corners pattern discussed in Chapter 16, provides an elegant way of filtering content. Unfortunately, the peel corner control is at the lower-right corner of the map, so it is almost undiscoverable, both because few people look at the bottom edge of the iPad screen and because the control is not at the corner of the device, but at the corner of the *map*. Therefore, the designers had to add a *second* way to access the same features—the awkward **Filter** button previously mentioned. Peel corner can be a powerful and an effective call to action, but on the iPad, with its large, busy screen, you need to put the peel corner control at the corner—preferably one of the top corners to ensure reliable discoverability.

What about the filters themselves? On the larger iPad screen, customers would expect to spend more time, refine more thoroughly, and contemplate more deeply than they would ever do in the mobile context of use of the iPhone. Unfortunately, the filters on the iPad use the same highly abbreviated user interface as the iPhone app (Figure 17.10), leaving customers wondering whether this is all there is. Moreover, the property-type filters employ custom on/off buttons, which appear to represent exclusive choices because of their being grouped in a way usually reserved for tab selections. The nonstandard check box implementation makes it all but impossible to tell which filters are currently selected.

Used by permission from Chris Smith, TechSavvyAgent.com www.youtube.com/watch?v=NOdaSKX1s0)

FIGURE 17.10

Filtering on
Zillow—iPhone
app versus
iPad app

Many Different Designs

Although you might expect most Web sites to look similar, the current iPad app
landscape is extremely dynamic. It's the Wild West of user interface design.
Contrast the Zillow iPad app user interface with that of ZipRealty, its close competitor, which is shown in Figure 17.11.

FIGURE 17.11

ZipRealty iPad app

In comparing these two realty apps, it's easy to see quite a few differences—the most glaring of which is the lack of a combined map and list view. Instead, the map and list are separate views accessible from an iPhone-style tab bar. Recall that tabs at the bottom of an iPad screen are not discoverable and are fairly awkward to use. Interestingly, the **Location** button in ZipRealty is also the most prominent control on the screen.

These drawbacks *seem,* at first glance, to make the ZipRealty app less usable than Zillow. However, this is not the case because of the pure interaction model and superior filtering controls ZipRealty offers. Rather than splitting the customer's focus between the map and list views, as on Zillow, the ZipRealty user interface focuses much more on manipulating the map directly and getting information about various properties by zooming into a specific area and interacting directly with the content. Another important difference is the prominent filtering user interface, which employs an iPad popover control that occupies a much smaller area than the Peel Corner control shown in Figure 17.8, so it obscures less of the map and enables customers to remain completely within the context of the finding flow. Together, the map-only view, plus the smaller popover filters combine to create a seamless, natural finding interaction that is much more in keeping with the spirit of the guidelines for interacting with information on the iPad.

An added bonus of the ZipRealty filtering mechanism is a set of standard on/off switches that unequivocally indicate independent property-type selections. In contrast with the funky tab control that accomplishes the same selections on Zillow, anyone using the ZipRealty app would have little confusion about which filters are on.

One unfortunate thing is that both applications conspicuously lack any data display for their numeric filters. Neither of the applications enable customers to see how many properties are in a particular price range—for example, the $150K–$350K range—or shows the real minimum or maximum values in the price-range filter.

Note—As discussed in Chapter 8, when customers operate sliders to set ranges without knowing anything about the underlying inventory, it's too easy to over-constrain a search, leading to frequent frustrations when they receive no results.

Unfortunately, the sliders and dual-range numeric pickers that dominate both the Zillow and ZipRealty iPad apps suffer from similar risks of over-constraining searches.

By far the most important difference between these two apps is the way each maintains the sense of finding flow and direct interaction with content. ZipRealty does a better job of this, both through its map-only display and pop-over filters that use standard buttons.

Note—The moral of this story is to avoid designing gimmicky user interface elements that replace standard controls. Instead, follow this primary design guideline: Focus on creating and maintaining clear interaction flows for the finding experience. Remove, or at least strongly downplay, whatever does not directly serve the finding flow in a tablet app's user interface.

Tablet devices such as Apple iPad could bring a future in which you feel as though you're flying through information ever closer to reality. As Richard Saul Wurman said in his IA Summit 2010 keynote:

"You're going to be able to have a journey. You're going to have experiences of going to the thing.... It's going to be a movie...an infinite...personal flight... through information of your choosing."

Have a great flight!

WHAT'S NEXT?

The Apple iPad launched what is perhaps the most interesting design platform to come along in years—and tablet app design is still in its infancy. This new platform offers designers and product developers some unique opportunities to experiment with ecommerce search user interfaces. So, rather than offering more case studies and suggestions for redesigns that are likely to be premature, following are three near-future tablet app design scenarios in the spirit of Peter Morville's *Tangible Futures* search scenarios from his brilliant book, *Search Patterns* (O'Reilly Media, 2010). These scenarios, which hopefully demonstrate some interesting uses for this new class of tablet devices, cannot predict the future but can inspire and provoke new ideas.

Scenario: Mad About Shoes

Sarah looked out the window into the cold, wet street and frowned. A late November rain had turned to sleet, putting an end to her much anticipated trip to the mall. Oh, well. She'd just have to do some shopping from home. She lit up her fireplace and cuddled up on the couch with a steaming cup of cocoa and her tablet. Sarah's love affair with shoes has been a lifetime passion, and she loves to shop. Her favorite tablet app, Mad About Shoes (MAS), seems to be made just for people like her.

Sarah taps the MAS icon on the home screen to display the shoe map, her favorite starting point for searches, which represents the entire inventory of shoes available on MAS, showing clusters of shoes gathered around popular styles such as sandals, heels, boots, flats, and more. A few interesting cross-over styles are scattered between these clusters. Sarah immediately goes to work, stretching the screen to zoom into the map and then swiping to move between clusters. She isn't sure what she is looking for—it is fun to be simply browsing the enormous inventory on MAS to see what catches her eye.

A few shoes do catch Sarah's eye, but she has seen most of them before, so she changes a filter to **New Arrivals** using a popover menu. Immediately, the map morphs into a rendition of a 3D matrix, with subtle light variations that add depth. New arrivals are lit up near the front, whereas older models recede, darkening slightly. Sarah adjusts the slider to change the depth of the newness scale, homing in on the shoes that arrived during the current week. Displaying the popover menu again, she turns on the ecofriendly filter, causing more models to disappear, until only a handful of shoes remain. A pair of new Patagonia Mahas catch her eye, so she taps a picture of the shoes to zoom in. Tilting her tablet causes the perspective of the picture to shift, showing her the Maha's sleek curves and beautiful workmanship. She tilts the tablet forward to see the shoes' soles. It is close to what she is looking for, but a bit more sporty than she wants, so she circles a part of the heel she did not like with her finger and then chooses **Show variations of highlighted portion** from the menu that appears, displaying a new gallery of shoes, with each image showing the top and sole of a shoe. Success! It is going to be a fun day for shoe shopping after all.

Although this tale is still fictional, you are close to achieving a similar user experience on the tablet—at least in terms of the technology's capabilities. The central theme of this scenario is the easy flow through the information; the way the application encourages Sarah to explore a product space that is both complex and difficult to quantify. Clustering is an old technique for introducing patterns in data. When a computer can employ a powerful similarity algorithm along with people's tagging and folksonomies, users stand the best chance to make sense of large collections of products.

In this scenario, applying different filters is almost effortless, with intelligent defaults and smart settings keeping Sarah engaged in the flow, even as her role transforms from a Casual Shopper, browsing a large collection of shoes, to a Targeted Shopper when she discovers some shoes that are similar to Mahas, but with a more attractive sole. Because the tablet app's user interface takes full advantage of the high-resolution screen and supports multitouch gestures that enable Sarah to interact directly with on-screen content, it can deliver a more engaging user experience than a traditional desktop user interface can. In the near future, tablet apps will employ novel user interface metaphors to aggregate products from various companies in search results and offer the most comprehensive product selection at the best prices possible.

Scenario: Home Décor Pro

Paul is excited. His client's magnificent mansion and large decorating budget offers excellent potential for creating a décor that will be welcoming, classic, and posh—everything his client wants. Paul had been an interior designer for 10 years and had built up quite a reputation in the field. He considers himself a veteran designer, yet a new tool, the Home Décor Pro (HDP) app on his tablet, has truly transformed both the way he does his work and the way he communicates with his clients. Paul used to drag along a bunch of equipment—including a computer and a digital camera—take lots of pictures, and draw a lot of sketches to help him explain what he wanted to do for his clients. Now, with Home Décor Pro, all he does is bring his tablet to the client meeting.

Standing in the middle of a room for which he is going to create an interior design, Paul turns on his tablet and activates its on-board camera. Then, turning slowly in place, Paul takes a panoramic shot of the entire room. After Paul has completed his scan of the room, the HDP app's rendering engine goes to work, measuring and cutting and creating a wireframe of the room. Then, the tablet cleverly orients itself using the on-board GPS locator, adding it to a plan of the entire house. After the application finishes, a replica of the room in which Paul is standing pops up on the screen—empty and ready to be painted and then filled with furniture, plants, and objects of art that enable Paul to create the desired atmosphere.

Paul shows the screen to his client, points the tablet at the opposite wall and taps the screen with three fingers—an **Overlay** multitouch gesture. The screen displays an overlay showing the existing room and the new structure Paul is putting in place. "I think we can put the loveseat I was talking about here," Paul said, tapping the screen. A menu pops up, filled with various options for furniture and other elements of a décor. Paul taps the **Loveseat** icon, and the tablet promptly displays a carousel control, showing outlines of various styles of loveseats. "I think a Mission Style piece would be the best fit," Paul says, tapping the corresponding silhouette in the carousel.

"Now let's take a stab at the color." Paul displays a menu showing fabric and color options he preselected before his client meeting. I think this honey-yellow might go well with the paint color we discussed and infuse the room with a feeling of warmth." "Maybe not quite so bright?" his client asks. "Sure, let me bring the saturation down a bit," Paul says, displaying a color menu and adjusting the color through another multitouch gesture. This is Paul's favorite part of his work. The HDP app enables him do much more than merely select colors and hues. He can *play* the color as one would an instrument. Paul placed all the fingers of his hand on the screen and squeezed them together slightly, while in the same motion sliding his hand to the right and up to darken the color. "What do you think?" Paul asks. "We can run through some color variations together right now, and then I can create several 3D walkthroughs tonight when I get back to my office. They'll be ready for you to look at tomorrow."

Attentive readers of Chapter 14 can readily recognize an application of augmented reality. On the larger tablet screen, augmented reality can come into its own, offering both professionals and amateurs a great segue into context-rich search and exploration.

Note—Note that until recently, one important feature that's missing from the current Apple iPad was the on-board camera. However, with the release of the iPad 2 with its dual cameras, powerful augmented reality apps that enable users to touch and interact directly with augmented-reality objects—in the same way Paul puts a loveseat directly into an augmented projection of the room—will be only a matter of time.

One more point: Mixing color by using multitouch gestures might seem like a complex or even unattainable feat—one that would be difficult to learn and even harder to master. However, tablet applications such as Uzu (http://uzumotion.com/), as shown in Figure 17.12, already exist, demonstrating that—given the right controls and a slick, responsive user interface—a multi-touch color picker may well be possible.

Used by permission from Chris Pirillo, http://chris.pirillo.com/

FIGURE 17.12

Uzu iPad app

Tablet multitouch user interfaces that enable direct interaction with content will likely make possible many user interfaces that enable people to explore or play with color, motion, sound, or the shape of an object through direct manipulation, similarly to playing a musical instrument. Eventually, such user interfaces will probably become fairly widespread, but initial experimentation will likely occur in games or target applications for professional use. In these cases, users would have strong motivation to master complex gestures.

Scenario: Dear Diary

Alexa was nervous. Prom night was just around the corner, and she wanted everything to be perfect. She used Dear Diary, her personal stylist app on her tablet, to help her choose a dress from among the latest styles, and she felt she'd chosen the style that best reflected her personality. Still, she wanted to choose some jewelry to complete the look to make the right impression, so she opened the Dear Diary app again. "Good afternoon," the app said in a familiar, pleasant woman's voice. "Shall we continue where we left off yesterday, planning for your big prom night? Or is there something else I can help you with?"

Alexa answered, "I'd like to look at some jewelry to go with my new prom dress I ordered yesterday. I saw one of the girls at school wearing a kind of chunky necklace with blue stones that had funky shapes, kind of natural. I thought something like that might be just the thing to go with my dress."

"Let me see. Do they look anything like any of these?" the app replies, displaying several different types of colored stones in a gallery on the tablet screen. Alexa looks at the stones and then scrolls down as more samples appeared on the screen. "I'm not sure," she muses, continuing to look at samples. Then, tapping a blue-green stone, she says, "I think it was *close* to this one, but more rough looking." "Ah," the app responded, "Those stones may be turquoise. They come in various colors and many different sizes and shapes. Let me show you...." The tablet screen refreshes, displaying many varieties of turquoise stone. "Yes, that's it, exactly!" says Alexa, excited. "Can I get a turquoise necklace to wear with my prom dress?"

"Yes, of course," the app replies, transforming the tablet screen into a reflection of Alexa's head and shoulders, which appear to be clothed in her new prom dress—not the gym clothes she was actually wearing at that moment. In this virtual image of Alexa, an elegant necklace of blue and green stones hangs around her neck—and in a neat border around her image, there are photos of several other necklaces, ready for her to try on by tapping a photo. "Turquoise stones are typically part of a more casual look," the app's stylist observes contemplatively. "Also, for some of these stones, there are environmental justice implications in using land that belongs to native populations to mine stones in Latin America. Perhaps I can interest you in a style of necklace that has less environmental impact and is a bit more appropriate for the occasion?"

"What was it you said about environmental justice issues?" asks Alexa—"Can you show me more about that?" "Of course," Dear Diary responds, replacing the image of Alexa in her prom dress with a collage of images of mining towns, videos of clear-cut forests, and links to investigative documents. "The history of turquoise-jewelry production goes back many centuries...."

In *The Diamond Age: Or, a Young Lady's Illustrated Primer,* Neil Stephenson describes a future high-tech learning appliance that has the shape of a book, yet carries the technology of an entire generation, and the soul of a human being who creates a personal connection to its user and provides so much more than information. Throughout the book, this device educates, advises, and helps a special young woman to grow and achieve her full potential in the complex modern world.

In this third scenario, by combining a skilled and knowledgeable human operator with a computer's artificial intelligence (AI), the Dear Diary tablet app can converse, give fashion advice, and bring up relevant, interesting topics a customer might not be aware of—such as the environmental impact of the customer's shopping choices.

Although this scenario of a Dear Diary app is, of course, speculative fiction, something similar might soon be possible. Currently, highly trained shopping assistants in India, China, and Russia are happy to do instant chats with shoppers and answer their questions. It is only a short leap from the current ecommerce reality to an AI application in the guise of a personal stylist who is capable of learning about your wants and needs. What better way to grow a brand than to build personal relationships with young, affluent people *before* they realize their full earning—and spending—potential. The Amazon Remembers feature discussed in Chapter 15 is already moving toward creating a high-touch experience in which human operators can augment an image-based search user interface. For the ultimate in service, these specially trained salespeople would be ready to chat the moment a customer opens an ecommerce application. Through speech recognition and speech synthesis technology, people could communicate with their virtual personal assistant, who's a great multitasker and is always ready to chat, whether they need help shopping or tutoring on various life matters.

REFERENCES

Clark, Josh. "iPad Design Headaches." Design4Mobile, September 20–24, 2010.

Morville, Peter. Callender, Jeffery. *Search Patterns: Design for Discovery.* O'Reilly Media, 2010.

Nielsen, Jakob. "iPad Usability: First Findings From User Testing." *Alertbox,* May 10, 2010.

Parks, Jeff. "IA Summit 10: Richard Saul Wurman Keynote: A Podcast from the IA Summit 2010 in Phoenix, AZ." *Boxes and Arrows,* April 11, 2010. Retrieved November 16, 2010.

Pongpaet, Pek. "Design of BizTome iPad App." Design4Mobile, September 20–24, 2010.

Stephenson, Neil. *The Diamond Age: Or a Young Lady's Illustrated Primer.* New York: Spectra, 1996.

CONCLUSION

The three scenarios explored in this chapter are just conversation starters as you consider what might be the ecommerce search user interfaces in the near future. Some of these possibilities might be strange by today's standards; yet as advances in technology march relentlessly onward it can be useful to consider what possibilities lie just around the corner.

Ever since man began bartering with one another—perhaps trading a stone ax for the skin of a woolly mammoth—the engine of commerce has driven technology, communication, and an exploration of the world. There is no reason to suppose the next evolution in commerce—possibly augmented-reality ecommerce on the tablet devices—will have a less transformative effect on society. The next incarnation of ecommerce can have lasting impact on the way you think about consumption—raising your awareness of the worldwide consequences of everything you buy and sell. To perform this role, ecommerce must strive to educate, inform, and encourage positive change needed to improve social conditions and stewardship of environmental resources, while still turning a hefty profit, creating millions of interesting jobs, and providing new opportunities for self-expression. The need to halt global climate change and cope with the pressures of the world's increasing population means our very survival might depend on what the ecommerce search interfaces of the future will be.

Perhaps, as society turns away from excessive consumption and ostentation and returns to the more restrained, human-centered commercial interactions of the past, people might again enjoy the pastime of window-shopping rather than purchasing everything that catches their eye. As ecommerce designers and product developers, you can be the force behind this transformation. People shape their tools, but in the end the tools also shape the people who use them. Whatever the future holds, as point and click user interfaces recede and augmented reality enables people to interact directly with the products and services that provide their livelihood and self-expression, ecommerce search will lead the way.

So get to work!

Index